U. S. Martial and Semi-Martial
Single-Shot Pistols

Other gun books by the same author

THE ART OF SHOOTING

FIELD, SKEET AND TRAP SHOOTING

FORENSIC BALLISTICS

GUN CARE AND REPAIR—
A Manual of Gunsmithing

GUN COLLECTING

GUNS OF THE OLD WEST

THE COMPLETE BOOK OF GUN COLLECTING

THE GUN COLLECTOR'S HANDBOOK OF VALUES

SIMPLIFIED PISTOL AND REVOLVER SHOOTING

SIMPLIFIED RIFLE SHOOTING

U. S. Martial and

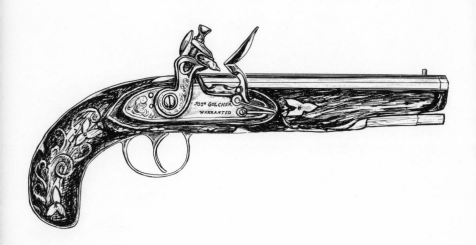

NEW YORK

Semi-Martial Single-Shot Pistols

CHARLES EDWARD CHAPEL

First Lieutenant, U. S. Marine Corps, Retired

FIRST EDITION

Coward-McCann, Inc.

Contents

DEDICATED TO MY WIFE,

Dorothy M. Chapel

Introduction

A S far back in history as the invention of rockets and the development of the hand cannon, even before the use of movable type in China in A.D. 1051, there existed illustrated manuscripts and books dealing with firearms, including rude forms of what we call today single-shot pistols.

Hundreds of books were published on firearms and warfare in Europe during medieval times. Today there is still a stream of foreign publications devoted to hand and shoulder firearms. None, however, deals exclusively with single-shot pistols.

What is probably the first book in the English language on U. S. Martial Single-Shot Pistols was written by Charles Winthrop Sawyer of Boston, Massachusetts. Published in 1913 in a small, paper-bound, illustrated edition, the book was entitled *United States Single-Shot Martial Pistols*. It consists of one hundred pages with line drawings by the author. Ostensibly issued by The Arms Company, Boston, the book was actually published privately by Sawyer himself. It was printed at the Press of G. R. Willis & Co., 11 Franklin Street, Boston. In addition to the text, there is a full-page advertisement by Charles Noé Daly, who wanted to buy old weapons at 998 Madison Avenue, New York. On the back of this notice

Sawyer advertised the two other gun books he had written. Charles Winthrop Sawyer also wrote and published *Firearms in American History, 1600–1800* (1910), *Firearms in American History, Vol. II, The Revolver, 1800–1911* (1911), and *Firearms in American History, Our Rifles* (1920). These books were supposed to form a series, but the only volume carrying a number was *The Revolver. United States Single-Shot Martial Pistols* was published between the so-called Volume II and the final book of the series.

In 1913 a great polio epidemic swept the United States. I was nine that year and one of the victims. I was supposed to be attending the fourth grade of grammar school in Manchester, Iowa, but I had to stay out of school because I could not walk well. It was during that year that I read Charles Winthrop Sawyer and became interested in collecting obsolete firearms, particularly United States Martial and United States Secondary Martial hand and shoulder arms, especially U. S. Martial and U. S. Secondary Martial Single-Shot Pistols.

I taught myself to shoot a rifle in the basement of our home despite the fact that there were no books for boys on marksmanship. I decided that one day I would write a book on that subject especially for boys, and, in time, I did.

During that same year, my relatives took me all over Iowa, Illinois, Wisconsin, and southern Minnesota. We attended auctions at farms and homes where people were selling old firearms. That is how I acquired my first collection of U. S. Martial Single-Shot Pistols.

Years passed. I served as a Trooper (Private) in Troop A, 113th Cavalry Regiment, Iowa National Guard; in the R.O.T.C. at the State University of Iowa and also at Missouri University; as a Midshipman, U. S. Naval Academy, Annapolis, Maryland; for a short period as a Second Lieutenant, Infantry, U. S. Army Reserve, at Fort Des Moines, Iowa; and then for eleven years as a regular officer of the United States Marine Corps. During all this time, I collected antique firearms—especially U. S. Martial and U. S. Secondary Martial Single-Shot Pistols, which were difficult to find even then.

After many years of writing magazine articles on firearms, I wrote *Gun Collecting,* which was published by Coward-McCann, Inc., in 1939. This book went through many editions and revisions, all of which were prepared with the help of many gun collectors and dealers. Today, in a revised form, it is known as *The Complete Book of Gun Collecting.*

In 1940, I privately published *The Gun Collector's Handbook of Values,* which sold out an edition of three thousand copies within a few months. Later issued by Coward-McCann, Inc., the book has now gone through many editions, always with the generous advice of hundreds of collectors and dealers.

Meanwhile, I was corresponding with Charles Winthrop Sawyer, who offered many suggestions for writing my own book on *U. S. Martial and Semi-Martial Single-Shot Pistols.* Sawyer regarded his pioneer work on this subject as an incentive for further research by others.

At the suggestion of hundreds of collectors and dealers who own my other gun books, I completed the present text. My principal source of help was Samuel E. Smith, of Markesan, Wisconsin, who owns or has owned almost all the pistols described here. My second source of assistance was Dr. J. H. Mathews, Firearms Consultant at the University of Wisconsin in Madison. Dr. Mathews provided photographs of pistols not in my own collection, offered advice, and gave guidance to Nancy Beale Gantert of Redondo Beach, California, who drew most of the pictures of the pistols made or used in America.

The illustrations by Nancy Gantert are not engineering drawings but an artist's conception of how the pistols look. Such pictures give the reader a better idea of the form of each pistol than the cold lines of an engineering drawing.

Several drawings were prepared by Herschel C. Logan of Salina, Kansas, and used here by permission of the copyright owners, Herman P. Dean, President, Standard Printing & Publishing Co., Huntington, West Virginia; and Edward J. Stackpole, Lieutenant General, U. S. Army, Retired, President, The Stackpole Co., Harrisburg, Pennsylvania.

Most of the drawings demonstrating the early development

of firearms were prepared from ancient documents and books by Dick Spencer. All of the Spencer drawings were originally copyrighted by the author of this text.

Others who have helped through the many years spent in preparing this book are listed in the Acknowledgments.

Finally, the author realizes that in the years to come we may uncover more records of early American arms. This book is not presented as the final and complete text on these "Guns of Glory," these side arms which helped make and preserve the United States as a free and independent republic. In future revisions, the author hopes to present facts now unknown about the single-shot pistols used in our wars and campaigns.

CHAPTER 1

The Development of the Flintlock Pistol

DEFINITION OF PISTOL

THE word "pistol" has several definitions. First, it refers generally to all handguns, which are weapons usually held in one hand when fired, such as single-shot pistols, revolvers, and semiautomatic pistols (ordinarily called "automatic pistols," although they are not actually automatic in the technical sense).

A *single-shot pistol* is designed and made to be fired with only one load, that is, one charge, at one time. This means that there is only one bullet, one charge of powder propelling the bullet toward the target, and one method of firing, igniting, or setting afire that one charge of powder.

A *revolver* has one barrel, behind which is a cylinder containing several chambers, usually five or six, although sometimes more. The *chamber* is merely a compartment or cutout portion of the cylinder. In early revolvers it contained merely the powder charge and the bullet, loaded from the front. In later revolvers and especially in modern and semimodern revolvers, it is an entire cartridge, including the powder charge, bullet, and primer.

In firing a *single-action revolver,* the hammer must be cocked (pulled back) by the thumb, and the trigger must be squeezed for each shot. A *double-action revolver* is made so that the revolver is first cocked, and thereafter it is cocked by pressing (squeezing) the trigger, releasing the trigger, and squeezing the trigger again, continuing this process until the desired number of shots is fired, or until all the loads in the cylinders are fired.

Some of the early revolvers were called "hand-turning" revolvers because the shooter had to turn the cylinder by hand to line up each load with the barrel.

Automatic and Semiautomatic Handguns

Automatic and semiautomatic weapons are operated either by the recoil (kick) of the gun, or by the pressure developed by the gas generated by the combustion of the powder. In either system, the breech (rear of the barrel) is opened after each shot is fired. The empty cartridge case (shell) is extracted from the chamber and ejected (thrown out of the weapon); a new cartridge is loaded into the chamber, the chamber is closed by a spring, and the weapon is ready to fire when the trigger is squeezed again.

When a weapon of this type is made so that it will fire continually as long as the trigger is held back and until the ammunition supply is exhausted, it is *fully automatic* and can be described technically as an *automatic* weapon.

When a new squeeze of the trigger is required for each shot, the weapon is actually only *semiautomatic,* although it may be described by the manufacturer as automatic, autoloading, or self-loading, or otherwise. Modern pistols generally described by the manufacturers as automatic are almost always semiautomatic.

Definition by Elimination

This analysis of the definitions of the word "pistol" makes it possible to proceed with an examination of the development of single-shot flintlock pistols, the first handguns which can be regarded as either U. S. Martial or Semi-Martial Single-

Shot Pistols. We have eliminated from consideration in this book all pistols except single-shot pistols. A few exceptions occur, but they are limited in number and included for the sake of historical background.

Martial and Semi-Martial Single-Shot Pistols

Almost all the pistols described or illustrated in this book are either U. S. Martial or U. S. Secondary Martial Pistols, which are fully defined and explained in each chapter. However, there are Confederate pistols, dueling pistols, Kentucky (Pennsylvania) pistols, and other pistols which in the strict sense of the terms we use are neither U. S. Martial nor U. S. Secondary Martial Pistols. Hence the title of this text is *U. S. Martial and Semi-Martial Single-Shot Pistols.*

Origin of the Word "Pistol" According to Encyclopaedia Britannica

The *Encyclopaedia Britannica,* edited with the advice and consent of the University of Chicago and Oxford, Cambridge and London Universities and published in Chicago, London, and Toronto, is universally accepted as the authoritative reference work. The author of this text works on sections of the *Britannica* dealing with firearms—and this presents a problem. The author must work in harmony with men and women from all over the world in preparing the *Britannica,* and yet he reserves the American right in his own books to be an individualist.

According to the *Britannica,* a pistol is "a small firearm designed for one-hand use, dating from the early 15th century. Tradition ascribes the derivation of the word to two distinct sources, viz., (1) *Pistoia,* a city in Italy where some claim the weapon originated; and (2) *Pistole,* an ancient coin to the diameter of which it is said the earliest handguns were bored. (Yet another explanation of its origin is that it derives from 'pistallo'—meaning *pommel* [of the saddle]—the common location of the weapon for mounted troops over centuries of use.) "

*Origin of the Word "Pistol" According to the
Author of This Text*

Gun collectors respect a tradition that about the year 1540, a short, lightweight, wheel-lock handgun was developed by Camillo Vitelli in Pistoia, Italy. This weapon was comparatively small and handy enough to be carried by mounted soldiers on the saddle. At the Battle of Renty in 1544, German cavalry used a pistol successfully for the first time in the history of warfare when they charged French soldiers in squadrons fifteen to twenty ranks deep.

The Germans halted as soon as they came close enough to fire their pistols effectively, each rank of German cavalry turning (wheeling) to the left or right, and then going to the rear of the line of battle, where they reloaded and came back again to fire at the French soldiers. The records are not accurate, but it is assumed that the German cavalrymen carried two single-shot pistols in holsters on their saddles.

The French, after their defeat, adopted pistols to replace the lances they had used until the Battle of Renty. In addition, the French soldiers copied the German method of having one rank of mounted soldiers fire at a time, retire, reload, and come back to fire again.

Historians also report that in 1678, Louis de Gaya, a French arms historian, wrote a treatise titled *Arms and Engines of War,* in which he mentioned the pistol and its use.

Nevertheless, handguns were used by both infantry and mounted soldiers long before the fifteenth century. These were small hand cannon of crude construction, used in battle as early as 1322 and possibly even before. Therefore, dating the first use of a pistol in warfare from the early fifteenth century is nothing more than a classical legend.

Gunpowder in Flintlock Days

Gunpowder, sometimes called black powder in flintlock days and before, was a black or brown explosive substance consisting of an intimate mechanical mixture of potassium nitrate (commonly known as saltpeter), charcoal, and sulphur. It was the only explosive used in gunnery, blasting, and firing salutes from its discovery until the invention of guncotton in 1846. It is still used in many parts of the world for gunnery, it is a common explosive for blasting even now, and all saluting batteries use it in firing ceremonial volleys from ships of war or land batteries. Historically, it has always consisted of from 70 to 80 percent potassium nitrate, and from 10 to 15 percent of each of its other ingredients, although the usual formula today is 75 parts potassium nitrate by weight, 10 parts sulphur, and 15 parts charcoal.

We do not know where or when gunpowder was invented. Roger Bacon mentioned it in his early writings sometime before 1267, probably as early as 1249. Ancient manuscripts indicate that it was in use as early as A.D. 846. Its invention has been attributed to the Chinese, the Arabs, and others, but historians agree that it was used in European warfare about 1300, and that around A.D. 1350 it was the propellant for pistols and other firearms in Europe and many other parts of the world.

HAND CANNON

The earliest firearms were probably rockets, which were fired from a bamboo tube or a hollowed log to give them direction and elevation. Anyone who has lived in China and traveled throughout what was the original Chinese Empire has had an opportunity to examine primitive firearms in the museums and look at illustrated books in the libraries, all of which tend to indicate that the Chinese may have been the originators of the first firearms. However, some authorities give the credit to the Arabs and others to India.

The next step was the construction of wooden cannon bound with iron hoops, and from these very early and extremely primitive fieldpieces it was a short transition to the cannon made of iron or bronze. It may be argued that the first portable firearms were nothing more than small cannon which could be moved by hand. On the other hand, some historians believe that the *hand cannon*, which we all recognize as the early ancestor of the true pistol, was developed later than the primitive fieldpieces. Here we are confronted with an academic argument which is no more important than the debate about whether the chicken came first or the egg.

Figure 1 is a drawing of a wooden cannon bound with metal hoops, made in Cochin China (also known as French Indochina and in modern terms the region including Laos and Vietnam). The exact date of its manufacture is unknown, but it was probably before the fourteenth century.

FIGURE 1. Wooden cannon bound with metal hoops, made in Cochin China, before fourteenth century

Figure 2 is a fourteenth-century Italian cannon made entirely of metal. It is mounted on a semiportable carriage and probably was used as a fieldpiece during the siege of a castle or other fortified place.

Figure 3 shows the cannon that can be seen today at Edinburgh Castle in Scotland. For centuries it has been known to the Scots as "Mons Meg." It was made of metal about the middle of the fifteenth century, has a bore diameter of 20 inches, and originally fired stone balls weighing about 300 pounds apiece.

Figure 4 is a German breech-loading cannon of the sixteenth century. The soldier is loading the cannon from the breech. Near his feet is the breech plug which was screwed into the breech after loading.

FIGURE 2. Italian cannon made entirely of metal in Italy during fourteenth century

FIGURE 3. "Mons Meg," an all-metal cannon made in Scotland about 1450

FIGURE 4. German breech-loading cannon of sixteenth century

Figure 5 shows a soldier firing a mortar containing a bomb. With his right hand he is holding a taper to light the fuse to the charge inside the bombshell. In his left hand he holds a flaming torch for lighting the fuse leading into the powder charge in the mortar. If everything went well, the gunpowder in the mortar exploded first, throwing the bombshell into the air toward the target. The bombshell then exploded and scattered pieces of iron over the enemy. If the bombshell fired before it was projected out of the mortar, it destroyed the mortar—and the soldier. Incidentally, although this picture is reproduced from an ancient manuscript, the author doubts that the men who fired such mortars in battle wore these artistic dress uniforms.

Figure 6 is a semiportable cannon on a forked rest. Some historians believe that the large cannon shown in Figures 1 through 5 came first, but others say that the type shown in Figure 6 antedated the more elaborate fieldpieces.

FIGURE 5. A soldier firing a mortar containing a bomb

FIGURE 6. A semiportable cannon on a forked rest

During the centuries that firearms were being improved, soldiers and hunters continued to use spears, bows and arrows, and the crossbow, the latter being used to fire either arrows or darts. Although the crossbow was not a firearm, it had a wooden stock which fitted against the shoulder. The shape of this stock probably was the basis for the design of the wooden stock of the fifteenth-century hand cannon (shown in Figure 7 being fired from the shoulder).

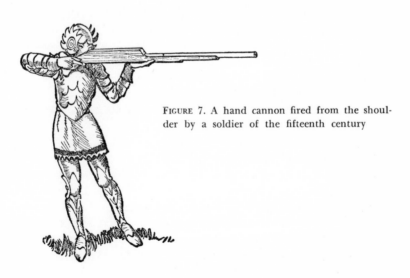

FIGURE 7. A hand cannon fired from the shoulder by a soldier of the fifteenth century

FIGURE 8. A mounted knight about to fire a
small hand cannon called a petronel

Figure 8 is an ancient drawing of a mounted knight about
to fire a *petronel,* a small hand cannon. It was aimed and
rested through a forked device steadied at its lower end by
a metal or leather support in front of the lower portion of
the knight's body and also fitted to the partial armor on the
horse. A heavy cord ran through a ring at the rear of the
petronel during battle. The picture shows the knight holding
in his right hand a lighted fuse, which was merely a burning
cord used to fire the powder charge.

Figure 9, from a manuscript prepared about 1400, shows
a German peasant holding in his left hand a short iron tube
fastened to a wooden handle. The iron tube was loaded with
gunpowder and a lead or iron ball was dropped down the
tube or pushed down with a primitive ramrod. The German
holds in his right hand what may have been the ramrod.
When ready to fire, a flaming torch, or a burning fuse on the
end of a stick, was applied to the muzzle. When the fire

reached the powder in the iron tube, the powder burned and the gases of combustion threw the lead or iron ball toward the enemy. The drawing shows that the end of the stick in the man's right hand may have been notched to receive a burning fuse (also called a wick and eventually known as a match). It is difficult to determine from the drawing whether the stick in the man's right hand was a ramrod or a holder for the burning wick or match.

Figure 10 shows a soldier with a flaming torch about to ignite the powder charge of a semiportable cannon at the muzzle. His facial expression and posture clearly show that he was afraid that the explosion might do him more harm than the enemy.

FIGURE 9. A German peasant holding hand cannon in his left hand

FIGURE 10. A semiportable cannon

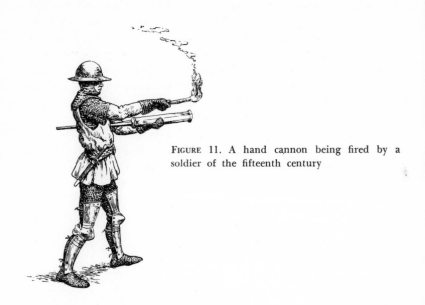

FIGURE 11. A hand cannon being fired by a soldier of the fifteenth century

Figure 11 shows a hand cannon about to be fired by an armored foot soldier of the fifteenth century. Notice that the hand cannon is a metal tube with a wooden rod at the rear which is steadied under the soldier's left arm, and that he holds a flaming torch in his right hand. Both hands are protected by gauntlets.

Development of the Vent or Touchhole

Figure 12 shows an armored knight or cavalryman about to fire a petronel while the horse is standing. It is similar to Figure 8 except that possibly there is a hole at the rear of the metal tube where the soldier can apply the lighted cord instead of igniting the powder charge at the muzzle. This hole was called a vent and sometimes a touchhole. Obviously, its use decreased the danger to the soldier.

Figure 13 is a reproduction from a German manuscript (circa 1400) showing a partially armored foot soldier with his left hand on the wooden portion of a hand cannon supported by a tripod. The drawing shows the projectile in flight and flames coming out of the muzzle, but the important feature is that the soldier is still holding a lighted torch to a vent or touchhole at the rear of the metal barrel.

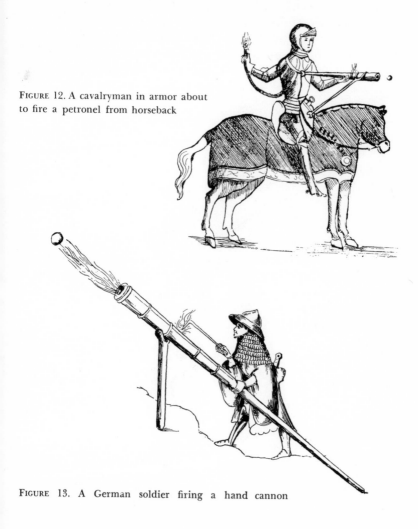

FIGURE 12. A cavalryman in armor about to fire a petronel from horseback

FIGURE 13. A German soldier firing a hand cannon

Figure 14 shows a French armored soldier about to ignite his hand cannon at the vent with a burning match or wick (about 1450).

Some reliable historians have said that these early hand cannon were fired by inserting a red-hot wire in the touchhole. This may be true, but in battle it was much simpler to use a torch for the larger weapons, or a match, than it would be to run to a fire to get a red-hot rod or wire.

The touchhole was originally on the top of the barrel. Eventually it was moved to the right side, and later some genius thought of providing a small pan in which the soldier could place powder, thus increasing the probability that the fire would reach the main powder charge in the barrel.

FIGURE 14. A French soldier firing a hand cannon

In the centuries to follow, the pan was called the priming pan and the powder placed in the pan was known as priming powder. Actually, the author has never seen a hand cannon *made* with a priming pan and he has never seen an illustration of one. Hence we cannot assume that any hand cannon had priming pans, although the possibility exists.

Pistols of the Hand-Cannon Type

The firearms previously described could not be fired with one hand. Hence they were not pistols, but they provided steps in the development of the single-shot pistol. However, Figure 15 is a small hand cannon called a *hand culverin*. The word "culverin" itself refers to a crude firearm with a shoulder stock. Later, during the sixteenth and seventeenth centuries, culverin meant a long cannon with a serpent-shaped rear, but the weapon illustrated in Figure 15 is definitely a pistol of the hand-cannon type. The barrel is held to the wooden stock by means of metal bands and a metal Y-shaped device which the soldier could hold with his left hand while aiming and holding the pistol principally with his right hand. It *could* be fired with one hand, thus placing it in the pistol class, but the left-hand support was normally used.

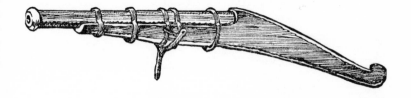

FIGURE 15. A small hand cannon called a hand culverin

FIGURE 16. The two-hand kneeling position with a revolver

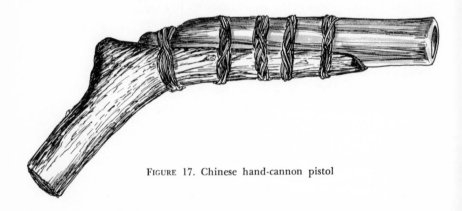

FIGURE 17. Chinese hand-cannon pistol

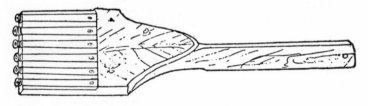

FIGURE 18. A multishot hand cannon with its barrels side by side

Although a pistol is usually considered a firearm fired with one hand, the fact that it can be fired better with two hands does not take it out of the pistol classification. This is shown in Figure 16, a drawing of the two-hand kneeling position with a modern revolver, a position taught to many law-enforcement organizations.

Figure 17 is a Chinese pistol of the hand-cannon type, made in the fourteenth century. It consists of a metal tube held to a wooden stock by means of iron wire woven into bands. This pistol was originally on display in the museum of the Imperial Summer Palace in Peking.

Multishot Hand Cannon

Figure 18 is a drawing of a multishot hand cannon with its six barrels mounted side by side. Figure 19 is a hand cannon with two barrels side by side and a third barrel on top. These were probably designed and made about the year 1500. It is difficult to believe that they were practical as handguns, and even as shoulder arms they would not be safe. If all barrels were fired at the same time, the recoil would severely hurt the shooter. If he tried to fire one at a time, the discharge of one barrel might set off the others, with unfortunate results. Although we cannot classify them as pistols, they do illustrate an early effort to produce a weapon that would fire more than one shot without requiring time to reload.

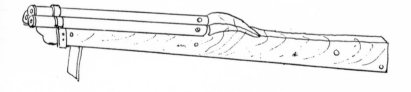

FIGURE 19. A hand cannon with two barrels side by side and a third on top

THE MATCH

After the invention of the vent or touchhole at or near the rear of the barrel, the flaming torch and the red-hot rod or wire were abandoned. Men began to use the *match*. This was usually a hemp cord or rope soaked in saltpeter, alcohol, strong wine, or some other substance which would burn steadily at a reasonably fixed rate. Fundamentally, the idea was similar to the use of burning punk to light firecrackers.

THE TRIGGER

Sometime early in the fifteenth century, a curved piece of metal was mounted on firearms. This primitive trigger was shaped something like the letter S and called a *serpentine* because it resembled a snake. It was pivoted at its center. A small pair of jaws were formed on the upper, forward end, to serve as a clamp to hold the burning end of the match. The lower, rear end of the serpentine was pulled to lower the burning end of the match into the vent of the early firearms, and into the pan containing the priming powder of the later weapons. The burning end of the match set fire to the priming powder; the flame passed through the vent into the rear of the barrel, where it set fire to the main powder charge. The powder in the barrel burned, generated gases, and the pressure of the gases sent the lead or iron ball through the barrel, out the muzzle, and on its way to the target.

This was an important improvement because the shooter could pull the trigger with one finger while the remainder of his right hand held the gun. If it was a shoulder weapon, he could use his left hand to give additional support. Furthermore, he could concentrate on aiming at the target instead of worrying whether the burning match would fire the gun.

THE MATCHLOCK

The Firing Mechanism of an Early Matchlock

The *matchlock* is a firearm with a slow-burning match (wick, cord, or rope) lowered by the serpentine to ignite the priming powder and thus fire the main charge in the barrel. This form of ignition was used for both pistols and shoulder arms.

Figure 20 illustrates the firing mechanism of an early matchlock. The burning match, with its burning end marked A, is carried in a pair of small jaws or tiny clamp, marked C, which is the upper, forward portion of the serpentine (trigger), marked B. When the serpentine is pulled to the rear, the burning end of the match is lowered into the priming pan, marked D, where it sets fire to the priming powder. The fire from the priming powder then enters the barrel through the vent (touchhole or powder hole), marked E, and ignites the main powder charge in the barrel. In the drawing, the letter F represents the barrel, although only a small portion of the barrel is shown.

To insure that the slow-burning match would ignite the priming powder, the shooter often had to blow on the match. We have mentioned various substances in which the match was soaked to permit a slow, steady, reliable burning, but

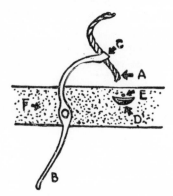

FIGURE 20. Firing mechanism of an early matchlock

potassium nitrate (saltpeter) was generally regarded as the most reliable. The match was soaked in a saltpeter solution, dried, and then cut into lengths of four or five feet, the exact length depending upon the tactical situation of soldiers going into battle. The burning end was attached to the clamp at the forward, upper end of the serpentine and the remainder of the match was left dangling or wrapped around the stock of a shoulder arm, or wrapped around a portion of the saddle when the soldier was mounted. This was true whether the mounted soldier was armed with a pistol or shoulder arm.

Unfortunately, when the soldier pulled the serpentine, he not only had to lift the lighted end of the match, but he had to lift at least a portion of the remainder of the match.

Crude as this mechanism was, it was an ancestor of the U. S. Martial and Semi-Martial Single-Shot Pistols. It probably came into existence in Europe sometime before 1450, and it is possible that it existed in other parts of the world before 1400.

Figure 21 is a highly ornamented matchlock shoulder weapon. Figure 22 is a Chinese matchlock pistol. The barrel is made of brass and bears the Chinese characters meaning "The Doctrine of the Mean," the title of one of the famous "Four Books" by Confucius. (Up to 1935, the pistol was exhibited in the museum of the Imperial Summer Palace in Peking.) Notice that the vent is on top of the barrel, there is a front sight, and the mechanism is a great improvement over the original matchlock trigger design.

Figure 23 is another Chinese matchlock pistol with a front sight, but most of the mechanism is inside.

FIGURE 21. A matchlock shoulder weapon

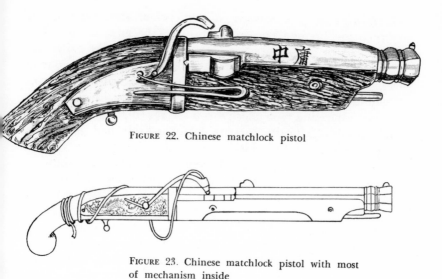

FIGURE 22. Chinese matchlock pistol

FIGURE 23. Chinese matchlock pistol with most
of mechanism inside

The Snapping Matchlock

The problems of the serpentine with the dragging match were eventually solved, probably after 1450, by the adoption of the *snapping matchlock*. This had a spring and lever arrangement so that the serpentine would be held back by what engineers call a link mechanism.

The pull of the leverlike trigger on the snapping-type matchlock lowered the upper, forward end of the serpentine so that the burning end of the match ignited the priming powder. When the soldier released his pressure on the trigger, a spring pulled back the forward, upper portion of the serpentine, thus taking the burning end of the match away from the priming pan. Also, the ashes were knocked off the burning end of the match after it ignited the priming powder.

The mechanism of the snapping-type matchlock was usually built inside an external metal plate (now called the *lock plate*) which protected the ignition system from weather and damage.

In Europe, the forward, upper end of the snapping-type serpentine became known as the *cock* because it resembled the head of a rooster. Years later, the cock was called the *hammer.* When we come to U. S. Martial and Semi-Martial Single-Shot Pistols, we shall see that the words "cock" and "hammer" mean the same thing unless otherwise stated.

The snapping-type mechanism of the matchlock was not developed specifically for the matchlock. It had been used years before the matchlock emerged as a distinct type of firearm. Originally, it was developed for the crossbow in order to discharge arrows and darts more efficiently. Throughout the history of firearms, men have sincerely believed that they were inventing a new device when they were actually designing something that had been used many years before.

The explanation is simple. Before the development of mass communication, men of the same nation often worked on the solution of the same problem.

Disadvantages of the Matchlock

Even after the development of the snapping-type matchlock, rain, snow, wind, and rough handling by the soldiers often extinguished the glowing end of the match. It could be smelled at a distance and the glowing end could be seen at night even farther than it could be smelled. It was slow to prepare for firing and it often failed to fire at all.

Advantages of the Matchlock

However, it was inexpensive to make and soldiers could learn to fire it easily. And even though there were many accidental explosions of reserve-supply gunpowder touched off by the burning matches, the matchlock (often called a firelock in early history books) was the fundamental martial firearm in European armed forces from about 1450 until about 1700. It was used in the American colonies for many years while they were under the British Empire. Therefore, the matchlock is part of American colonial history, even though matchlock pistols cannot be classified as U. S. Martial or

Semi-Martial Single-Shot Pistols because they were not used as either primary or secondary martial weapons after the Declaration of Independence. A few were used by Indians fighting for the United States against the British in the Revolutionary War, but this does not place them in our category.

THE WHEEL LOCK

Nobody knows exactly where or when the *wheel lock* was invented or developed. Traditionally, most authors say it probably was invented in Germany about 1515. A few have the historical courage to say that it was invented by Johann Kiefuss in Nürnberg about 1517.

The ignition system was based on the principle of making sparks by striking steel against flint. The system consisted of a rough-edged, notched or serrated revolving wheel which entered the priming pan where the priming powder was poured around it. After the main charge was placed in the barrel and the priming powder placed in the pan, the wheel was wound up against the tension of a spring, something like a clock spring, using a specially designed wrench called a spanner. The cover of the priming pan was then closed, and the pair of jaws, which formed the cock or hammer (sometimes called a doghead), was lowered against the lid of the priming pan, where a spring held it under tension. When the trigger was pulled, the pan cover opened and the wheel revolved rapidly against a piece of iron pyrites held in the jaws of the cock. This produced sparks, something like a modern cigarette lighter. The priming powder in the pan was ignited, the flame went through the touchhole at the rear of the barrel, set fire to the main powder charge, generated gas, and fired the bullet.

Wheel-Lock Firing Mechanism

Figure 24 shows two views of the wheel-lock firing mechanism. The upper view is the exterior appearance. The lower

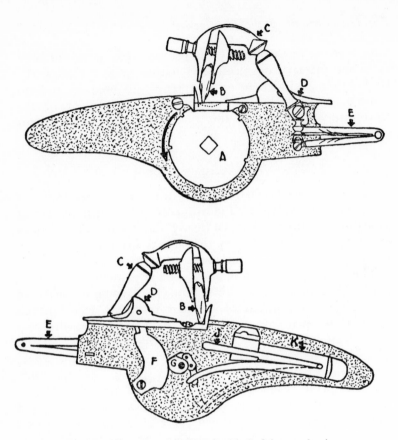

FIGURE 24. Two views of the wheel-lock firing mechanism

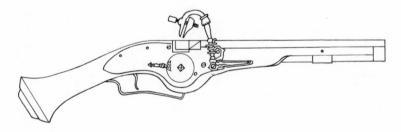

FIGURE 25. Simplified drawing of martial wheel-lock pistol without iron pyrites in jaw

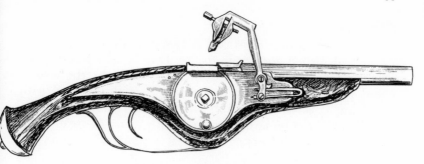

FIGURE 26. Detailed drawing of martial wheel-
lock pistol with iron pyrites in the jaw

view shows what it looks like from the inside when removed
from the weapon. The notched wheel marked A rotates in
a counterclockwise direction. It strikes sparks as its notched
perimeter hits the piece of iron pyrites (often loosely referred
to as flint), which is held against the rotating wheel by the
clamp (C), and the spring (E).

When the lock is cocked, the cam (G) presses against the
arm (F). This holds the cover (D) away from priming pan.
Pulling the trigger releases the catch (J) which holds the
wheel in the locked position, and also the spring (K) which
rotates the wheel when it returns to the normal position
shown in the drawing by dotted lines.

Typical Martial Wheel-Lock Pistols

Figure 25 is a simplified drawing of a typical martial wheel-
lock pistol, but it does not show the piece of iron pyrites held
in jaw.

Figure 26 is an artist's conception of another martial wheel-
lock pistol. It shows the piece of iron pyrites in the jaw, the
trigger guard has a different design, and there are other
structural differences from the one in Figure 25. This particular specimen has a 6-inch barrel, and a total length of
nearly 12 inches. Both of these martial wheel-lock pistols
lack the elaborate ornamentation found on specimens made
for private use by wealthy civilians or high-ranking officers.

Advantages of the Wheel Lock

Wheel-lock ignition was generally fast and certain. It could be carried loaded and ready to fire. Only a very severe wind or snowstorm or extremely careless handling by the soldier could render it ineffective in combat. It could be fired with one hand if it were a pistol, although it is obvious that a wheel-lock shoulder arm required both arms to steady and aim it. All these advantages made it a practical weapon for both infantry and cavalry.

Disadvantages of the Wheel Lock

The wheel lock was a very expensive weapon to manufacture, even in the days when labor was a small item in gunmaking. It required extremely skilled men to make and repair it. For example, a man had to have the skill and experience of an expert clockmaker to produce or maintain a wheel lock. If the soldier lost the special wrench, called the spanner, he could not operate the gun. Furthermore, it was more difficult to train soldiers in its use than it was to drill them in the loading and firing of the matchlock.

For all of these reasons, the wheel lock was primarily the personal weapon of wealthy men, emperors, kings, and princes, who had it made for both martial and sporting use. They also acquired it for their personal bodyguards and for elite military organizations. It was not issued to the rank and file of soldiers.

Evidence of this is found in an examination of existing specimens. Almost all are engraved, inlaid with precious or semiprecious metals and stones, and exhibit a high degree of craftsmanship.

Since the wheel lock was highly suitable for elite cavalry units, it became popular in the northern European countries and led to changes in battle tactics. It was used in southern Europe to a smaller extent and was even employed by a few of the rulers of the Near East and Asia. In the United States, during colonial days before the United States came into existence, it was a comparative rarity.

ARQUEBUS

Stories of colonial days in America often mention the arquebus. Early publications showed a colonial soldier resting a shoulder arm called an arquebus on a forked stick to steady his aim and absorb some of the recoil. Illustrations of that era, when drawn in detail, often show that the arquebus was merely a variation of the matchlock shoulder arm, except that the butt of the stock was lower than the barrel so that the shooter could sight better along the barrel.

In addition, such pictures show the cock (serpentine) falling to the rear into the priming pan, instead of dropping forward. Other illustrations portray it as a shoulder arm, sometimes with a deeply curved butt, smaller than the so-called musket and fired without any tripod or rest. In the same texts, very similar shoulder arms are described and illustrated as *calivers*. Modern gun experts insist that a caliver was a martial shoulder arm of a size and weight that could be fired without a tripod or any other type of rest.

Figure 27 shows a Spanish soldier of the sixteenth century firing an arquebus.

FIGURE 27. Spanish soldier of sixteenth century firing an arquebus

From about 1600 to about 1650, some old books and manuscripts describe and illustrate wheel locks as arquebuses, usually as shoulder arms, and rarely as pistols. Therefore, it is difficult to say that there was such a thing as an arquebus pistol as a distinct type.

No Hacquebut Pistols

There is no such thing as a hacquebut, hagbut, or hakbuchse pistol. These words all mean a shoulder arm with a hook attached to the bottom of the barrel to lay over the edge of a tripod, forked stick, rampart wall, or some other rest or support to steady the aim and absorb part of the recoil. These were usually comparatively small and lightweight shoulder arms, judging by the martial standards of their era, but some of them were what we now call "rampart guns," weighing as much as forty or fifty pounds.

THE SNAPHANCE, ALSO SPELLED SNAPHAUNCE

The snaphance, also spelled snaphaunce, was the first of the weapons in the flintlock family. The name is of Dutch or German origin and comes from the word *snaphaan*, meaning a snapping cock, because the cock (hammer), connected to a spring, falls forward with a snap, sending sparks into a pan containing priming powder and connected through a touchhole (vent) with the main powder charge in the barrel. The jaws (clamp) holding the flint were called the *cock,* and the piece of steel against which the flint strikes to make fire was called the *hen*. The pan cover and the *battery,* also called the *frizzen,* which is the steel part against which the flint strikes, are separate parts. This is a distinguishing feature of the true snaphance as contrasted with a flintlock weapon having the pan cover and battery (frizzen) in one piece. Always remember that frizzen and battery mean the same thing.

Somewhere along the line in the history of firearm development, someone decided that the priming pan needed a movable cover to keep the priming powder from getting wet, blowing away, or falling out of the pan. This led to the use of the movable pan cover.

Figure 28 is a snaphance pistol made in northern Italy sometime before 1600, but it is generally believed that the snaphance was developed about 1550, probably in Holland, Germany, or one of the Scandinavian countries, although Scotland and Spain have been credited by some authorities as countries of origin.

Unfortunately, from about 1550 to about 1700, the words snaphance, snaphaunce and firelock were frequently used interchangeably in referring to the same weapon. Hence it is extremely difficult in searching original sources to know whether a snaphance is really a snaphance or not. This is especially confusing because matchlocks were called firelocks for centuries.

Figure 29 is an illustration from *Deanes' Manual of the History and Science of Fire-Arms,* published in London in

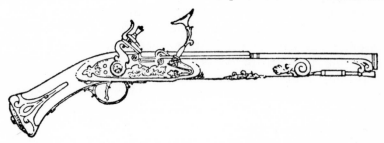

FIGURE 28. An Italian snaphance pistol

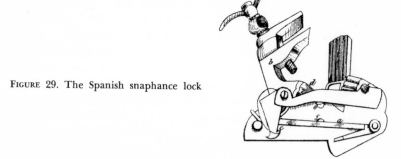

FIGURE 29. The Spanish snaphance lock

1858 by Longman, Brown, Green, Longmans & Roberts. The title of the drawing is: "The Spanish or Snaphame Lock, almost Contemporary with German Wheel-Lock."

The spelling of the title of the book and the title of the illustration follows the original. Whether or not a Spanish snaphance lock was in the author's mind when he called it "The Spanish or Snaphame Lock" is one of the many questions in the history of arms literature.

The Miquelet Pistol

The word "miquelet" comes from a body of armed men known as Miquelites, probably more correctly as Miqueletos, who performed duty as escorts for wealthy and distinguished persons and guards for the shipments of valuable merchandise in Spain. They are supposed to have acquired their name from one of their leaders, Miquel de Prats, an armed ruffian on the payroll of the notorious Cesare Borgia, who lived from 1476 to 1507.

The miquelet lock has a strong mainspring on the outside of the lock plate and a short straight battery (frizzen) made in one piece with the pan cover so that the pan is uncovered when the flint hits the battery (frizzen).

Because these important parts are mounted outside the lock plate, the miquelet was more subject to damage than the snaphance which normally had its lock mechanism inside the lock plate. Another feature of the miquelet is a safety catch, necessitated by a defect in the design which would allow the cock to slip when in the half-cock position. This safety catch consists of a bolt at right angles to the lock plate, and a nose on the front of the cock that rests on the bolt at the half-cock position. The first part of the pull of the trigger releases the bolt and leaves the cock free to strike the battery (frizzen). Another feature is that the miquelet always has a straight hammer and not one that is S-shaped, or, to use other terminology, it does not have a gooseneck shape.

Figure 30 is a drawing of an Arabian miquelet pistol. Although the word "miquelet" is of Spanish origin, it is im-

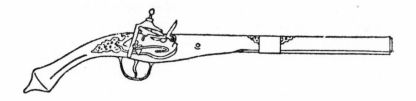

FIGURE 30. An Arabian miquelet pistol

possible to say exactly when or where the miquelet was developed or invented. Both pistols and shoulder arms with miquelet locks were used for centuries in many different countries. It is definitely known that this type of lock was used in southern Europe, especially in Spain, Portugal, and Italy, from about 1600 to about 1800. Many specimens of excellent workmanship and beautiful ornamentation were made during the same period in the Near East and northern Africa and are on exhibition in many museums. Those made by the Arabs are outstanding examples of craftsmanship and decoration.

The miquelet, like the other types of arms we have discussed before, is definitely one of the important steps in the transition leading to the true flintlock, and hence to the design and development of U. S. Martial and Semi-Martial Single-Shot Pistols.

WARNING REGARDING FAKES

For centuries, in all parts of the world, there has been a thriving business in the reproduction of works of art and antiques of all types, including firearms. Generally, the works of art and antiques which have been faked have been those which would bring high prices when the buyers thought they were acquiring genuine articles, but faking has been accomplished even in the low-price range, especially when tourists were the suckers.

An example is that of a man who bought in Tangier,

Morocco, in 1923, what he believed to be a genuine Arabian miquelet pistol. When he brought it to me for examination, my first impression was that it was a beautiful specimen made about 1700. The stock was made of what appeared to be Circassian walnut. The· barrel and other metal parts were elaborately ornamented with what seemed to be engraving.

The owner urgently requested that I give him a written appraisal because he had paid $150 for it and wanted the written appraisal for insurance purposes. In his presence, I took it apart and found it was of recent manufacture and that it definitely was a fake. Since the owner was dissatisfied with my comments, I sent him to a metallurgist who reported that the metal ornamentation was not engraving but etching produced by an acid process, and the barrel was not made of steel or even good iron, but simply *pot metal,* which is a low grade of cast iron used for making pots and other objects not expected to be subjected to stress.

Still unhappy, the owner of the fake miquelet pistol went to an ethical antique gun dealer who confirmed all that the metallurgist and I had said, but also discovered that the wood was not Circassian walnut or any other kind of walnut, but a comparatively soft wood cleverly finished to superficially resemble Circassian walnut.

A vast amount of labor had been spent in making the fake, but labor was cheap and both good metal and good wood were expensive according to the economic standards of the fakers, hence they had saved money on material and devoted many hours to the creation of a beautiful forgery.

I do not know what eventually happened to the pistol, but I do know that the victim of the swindle became extremely angry with the metallurgist, the antique gun dealer, and me, simply because it hurt his ego to discover he was a chump.

Faking continues today. There are many men in the United States who are producing excellent reproductions of ancient and even semimodern firearms. They advertise in magazines and newspapers, and through the mail, that they make and sell almost perfect reproductions at comparatively low prices.

Those who buy them know they are acquiring reproductions and even when the manufacturer engraves, etches or stamps REPRODUCTION or other words of warning on the gun, such warning can be removed by any person skilled in metalwork, and then we have another fake which can be sold on the antique market at a price many times the amount charged by the manufacturer of the forgery.

This warning regarding fake arms is placed in this chapter because it logically belongs with the comments on the transition firearms leading to the true flintlock, but it applies to all items of interest to gun collectors. In later chapters the warning will not be repeated in detail, but certain pistols which are frequently faked will carry a brief warning in their descriptions.

How to Avoid Buying Fakes

In order to avoid buying fakes, investigate the reputation of the person offering collectors' specimens for sale. Before you invest heavily, get an examination and appraisal from a reliable expert. The fee he charges will be well worth the money you spend. If you exercise the same caution in buying expensive firearms that you would use in buying real estate, you will reduce the hazard of loss. Finally, the author of this text refuses to identify or appraise firearms through the mail even when detailed descriptions and photographs are sent to him. Furthermore, the author does not solicit or accept assignments for the appraisal of individual firearms even when he can personally inspect them. If you want an appraisal, write to the National Rifle Association of America, 1600 Rhode Island Avenue, N. W., Washington 6, D. C., and ask for the names and addresses of ethical, expert appraisers in your own area.

THE SCANDINAVIAN SNAPLOCK

During approximately the same period that the miquelet was being developed in southern Europe and in the countries south of the Mediterranean Sea, a somewhat similar firearm was developed in the Scandinavian countries. This is known to some historians, collectors and dealers as the *Scandinavian Snaplock*.

One point of similarity to the miquelet is the location of the mainspring outside the lock plate. Another point of similarity is that the battery (frizzen) is made in one piece with the priming-powder pan so that the pan is uncovered when the flint hits the battery.

Every expert agrees that the mainspring on a typical miquelet or typical Scandinavian snaplock must be outside the lock plate; that is, it must not be located inside where it is not visible unless the weapon is taken apart. However, experts are not in full agreement that a true Scandinavian snaplock must have the battery made in one piece with the pan, because some specimens which have been classified by collectors and dealers as Scandinavian snaplocks do not have the battery and pan made as one part. Therefore, the author of this text does not present an illustration of the Scandinavian snaplock and offers these comments merely because it is recognized that the Scandinavians did develop a snaplock, which is one of the many transition types leading to the true flintlock.

THE ENGLISH DOG-LOCK FLINTLOCK PISTOL

Figure 31 is a drawing of an *English dog-lock flintlock pistol*. The distinctive feature is a safety device which is a pivoted catch, sometimes called a "dog," and also referred to loosely as a "hook," on the outside of the lock plate. This catch engages a notch in the lower, rear portion of the cock (hammer) when the latter is in the half-cock position. When thus engaged, the catch must be drawn to the rear with the shooter's thumb before the pistol can be fired.

This safety device was called a "dog catch" by the English who developed it. Hence locks with this feature were called "dog locks."

Major H. B. C. Pollard, in his 1931 book *A History of Firearms* (published in London by Geoffrey Bles and in Boston and New York by Houghton Mifflin Co.), said:

> Dog locks occur not only on muskets, but on cavalry pistols of rare and early type and occasionally on smaller holster pistols of crude type. They are, however, not simply ordinary flint locks with a dog catch, but represent a definite mechanism and a specific type of lock. The dog lock is really an early idea of a half cock notch and is found on the early Moorish locks. Its importation from Scotland is probably from Spanish and Moorish sources and dates from the earliest years of the 17th century.

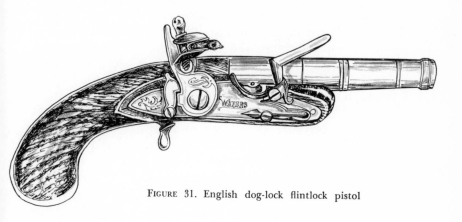

FIGURE 31. English dog-lock flintlock pistol

Major H. B. C. Pollard made several other references to the English dog lock in the above-mentioned book. J. N. George, another English authority on English firearms, made many references to the English dog lock in his book *English Pistols and Revolvers,* published in 1938 by the Small-Arms Technical Publishing Co., Onslow County, North Carolina, and in *English Guns and Rifles,* published in 1947 by the

Small-Arms Technical Publishing Co., Plantersville, South Carolina. These books by J. N. George are now published by The Stackpole Co., Harrisburg, Pennsylvania.

The conclusion which anyone must draw who has carefully studied the above-mentioned texts by eminent English authorities is that the English dog-lock flintlock pistol was not what we now regard as the true flintlock but one of the many transitionary steps leading to the presently accepted definition of a true flintlock.

The English dog lock came into existence in England either shortly before or shortly after 1600. The firearms on which the dog lock was used were usually closely patterned after the snaphance (snaphaunce). In addition to the adoption of the dog lock, the principal improvement was the combination of the battery (frizzen) and the priming-pan cover in one piece. The internal mechanism was almost identical with that of the snaphance, but there was no provision within the internal mechanism for a safety or half-cock position simply because the snaphance, having its battery separate from the priming-pan cover, did not need an internal safety device because the snaphance was safe when the battery was simply moved out of position to receive the blow from the flint that made the sparks and ignited the charge. Therefore, those who were attempting to improve the snaphance found that when they combined the battery and pan cover in one piece they had to provide some external safety device. This led to the use of the dog catch.

The dog lock was used by the English and others until about 1659, when the French or true flintlock began to come into general use in Europe and other parts of the world. Nevertheless, dog-lock firearms, both pistols and shoulder arms, were manufactured and used as late as 1725, even though the necessity for the dog catch as a safety device no longer existed.

In spite of strong evidence to the contrary, some authorities deny that the English dog lock was a distinct type. The reason they take this position is that the dog latch was used on many firearms long after the production of the true English dog-lock firearms ceased.

The English dog-lock flintlock pistol in Figure 31 has what collectors call a "cannon-shaped barrel." In the drawing, the pistol is in the half-cock position and the catch (dog) engages the notch in the lower, rear portion of the cock (hammer). The battery (frizzen) and priming-pan cover are made as a single part, which is thrown forward in the drawing, just as it would be if the shooter were about to place priming powder in the pan.

The lock plate is marked "WATERS". The lower side of the wooden stock of the specimen from which the drawing was made is marked "1725". The trigger is of a design known to collectors as either "ball-shaped" or "lemon-shaped." The total length is eight inches. Apparently, this was one of the last of the true English dog-lock pistols.

In the next chapter we shall examine the working mechanism of the true flintlock in order that we may have a basic understanding of the U. S. Martial and U. S. Secondary Martial Flintlock Pistols which played vital roles in the creation of what is now the United States of America.

CHAPTER 2

The Firing Mechansm of a Flintlock

THE TRUE FLINTLOCK

IN the previous chapter we discussed the long period of development which prepared the way, step by step, for the design of the true flintlock which began to come into general use in Europe and other parts of the world about 1650. In this chapter we shall examine the firing mechanism of the flintlock in order to understand more easily the technical terms used in describing U. S. Martial Flintlock Pistols and U. S. Secondary Martial Flintlock Pistols, discussed in the next two chapters This is necessary not only for the beginner but also for the advanced collector because the same part of a firing mechanism of a flintlock often has two or more names.

The true flintlock pistol, like the true flintlock shoulder arm, was not invented at any one time or place by one man. Instead, it was the result of many men working to improve firearms in various countries. However, the *Encyclopaedia Britannica* states: "The true flintlock was invented in France probably by Marin Le Bourgeoys about 1610–1615."

Notice the word "probably" and the phrase "about 1610–1615." Marin Le Bourgeoys was a gun manufacturer for King Louis XIII of France, who was born in 1601 and died in 1643. On the death of his father in 1610, he became king when he was only about nine years old, but throughout his lifetime many of his powers were exercised for him, first by his mother and later by Cardinal Richelieu and others. Therefore, it is not to be assumed that he exercised any control over the design and manufacture of the true flintlock.

The true flintlock included features of both the snaphance and the miquelet, but it was more reliable, safer, and simpler to make and use than the transitional types which preceded it. The battery (frizzen) and the cover for the priming pan were "made integral," to use a phrase adopted by some gun authors; that is, they were combined into one piece or part so that the blow of the piece of flint against the steel of the battery automatically uncovered the priming pan, thus enabling the sparks to ignite the priming powder.

The internal mechanism of the true flintlock was designed so that there was a half cock or safety device inside the lock plate. This was accomplished by having the sear, a part operating between the trigger and the hammer, function vertically instead of horizontally as it had in the transitional types leading to the true flintlock. This made it possible to hold the weapon more securely and safely at both the half-cock and the full-cock positions.

The design of the true flintlock was copied for pistols and shoulder arms by many European countries. As we have said before, it came into general use not only in Europe but in other parts of the world about 1650, although this does not mean that the miquelet and other types of lock preceding the true flintlock were all junked in 1650. In the American colonies, the matchlock was replaced by the flintlock before 1677. After 1700, the flintlock completely replaced the matchlock and other predecessors of the flintlock for military and naval use throughout almost all of Europe and in many other areas of the world.

Advantages of the Flintlock

The true flintlock was simple in design, could be manufactured at a low price, could be maintained and repaired by workmen with limited skill, was safe and reliable in comparison with the preceding types, and did not need special tools in the field, excepting, of course, a ramrod, which was usually mounted under the barrel. If the ramrod—used for both ramming the bullet down the barrel and for cleaning the barrel —were lost, it was a simple matter to cut a small branch from a tree and make a new ramrod with only a knife for a tool.

Obviously, the disadvantages of the matchlock—the burning match—and the wheel lock which required a spanner or wrench to wind the spring were eliminated.

THE MECHANISM OF THE TRUE FLINTLOCK

Figure 1 is a simplified drawing of the lock mechanism of a true flintlock. (The drawing was prepared by the National Rifle Association of America.) When the trigger, which is not shown in this drawing, is pulled, the cock (hammer), marked B, flies forward, carrying with it a piece of flint (A) which strikes against the steel battery (frizzen), marked C. In some old texts the battery (frizzen) is called an anvil. When the flint hits the steel, a shower of sparks is produced and at the same time the battery (frizzen or anvil) flies forward, uncovering the priming pan. The sparks fall into the priming powder in the pan (D), where the sparks set fire to the priming powder. The fire enters the rear of the barrel of the gun through a vent (touchhole) and ignites the main charge of powder, which burns and creates gases. The pressure from the gases drives the bullet out of the barrel. The frizzen spring in this drawing is marked E.

A TYPICAL LOCK USED ON U. S. MARTIAL AND SEMI-MARTIAL FLINTLOCK PISTOLS

Figure 2 is the exterior view of a typical lock used on U. S. Martial and Semi-Martial Flintlock Pistols. The more important parts are numbered in the drawing and explained below:

1. The lock plate is the external metal plate (usually iron, but sometimes brass, bronze and even steel) on which the

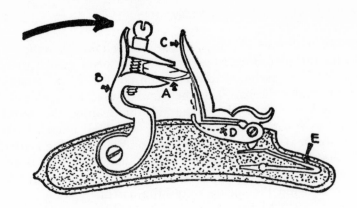

FIGURE 1. The mechanism of a typical flintlock

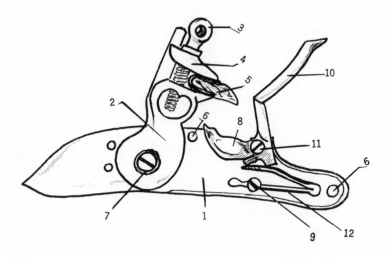

FIGURE 2. The exterior view of a typical lock used
on U. S. Martial and Semi-Martial Flintlock Pistols

1. lock plate
2. hammer
3. hammer screw
4. cap
5. flint
6. side screw holes (2)

7. tumbler screw
8. pan
9. frizzen spring screw
10. frizzen
11. frizzen screw
12. frizzen spring

lock mechanism is mounted. This definition of lock plate also applies to percussion arms.

2. The hammer is the external movable part of the lock mechanism, also called the cock, which holds in its clamplike jaws the flint which hits the battery (frizzen) to produce sparks for igniting the priming powder in the pan.

3. The hammer screw, also called the cock screw, is a screw which can be tightened to hold the piece of flint firmly between the jaws, or loosened when the position of the flint must be adjusted or the flint removed.

4. The cap is the upper jaw which is movable and holds the flint against the lower jaw. The cap is movable to permit the adjustment of the hammer screw. The lower jaw is a fixed portion of the hammer.

5. The flint is a piece of hard stone of the quartz family. It is used to produce sparks when it hits the battery (frizzen). A more detailed discussion of flint is given later in this chapter.

6. Side screw holes. There are two in this drawing. They are holes through which screws are driven to hold the lock plate to the stock.

7. The tumbler screw superficially appears to be nothing more than a screw which holds the lower portion of the hammer (cock) to the lock plate, but actually it has a much more important function. Assuming the hammer is cocked (pulled all the way back for firing), when the trigger is pulled, the sear releases the tumbler which revolves forward through the action of the mainspring. When we come to an analysis of the interior view of the lock, this will be explained further.

8. The pan is the receptacle for holding the priming powder. When the priming powder, which usually was a powder with a finer grain than the powder in the barrel, was ignited, the flame from the burning priming powder entered the barrel through the vent (touchhole).

9. The frizzen spring screw fastens the frizzen spring to the lock plate.

10. The frizzen (battery) is the upright, pivoted portion of the lock mechanism against which the piece of flint strikes to make sparks. It was usually made of iron with a steel face, although some were entirely iron and others were made entirely of steel.

11. The frizzen screw is simply a fastener for the frizzen.

12. The frizzen spring is a U-shaped spring which either keeps the frizzen (battery) upright in a vertical position over the pan when the pan is covered before firing, or tilted forward after the flint has struck the frizzen and uncovered the pan.

Figure 3 is the interior view of the same lock. The numbers in the drawing refer to the following parts:

1. Lock plate
2. Hammer (cock)
3. Hammer screw
4. Cap
5. Flint
6. Side screw holes (2)
7. Sear, which we have previously explained is a part operating between the trigger and the hammer. When the hammer is cocked, that is, pulled all the way back, pulling the trigger causes the sear to release the tumbler which revolves forward by the force of the mainspring. The hammer then flies forward and the flint strikes the frizzen (battery). In other words, the sear is a connecting link between the hammer and the tumbler.
8. Pan
9. Pan screw holds the pan to the lock plate.
10. Frizzen
11. Frizzen screw
12. Sear spring keeps the sear from operating until the trigger is pulled and then causes the sear to release the tumbler.
13. The sear-spring screw holds the sear spring in place.
14. The mainspring is the principal spring in the lock mechanism. When the pistol is cocked, the mainspring

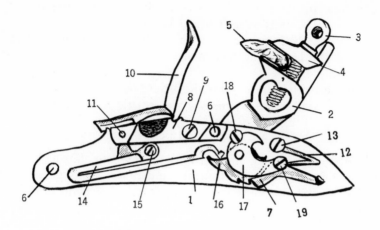

FIGURE 3. The interior view of a typical lock used
on U. S. Martial and Semi-Martial Flintlock Pistols

1. lock plate
2. hammer
3. hammer screw
4. cap
5. flint
6. side screw holes (2)
7. sear
8. pan
9. pan screw
10. frizzen

11. frizzen screw
12. sear spring
13. sear-spring screw
14. mainspring
15 mainspring screw
16. tumbler
17. bridle
18. bridle screw
19. sear screw

is put under tension. When the trigger is pulled, the
sear releases the tumbler, which revolves forward by
the force of the mainspring and the hammer flies forward, causing the flint to hit the frizzen. It is necessary
to repeat much of the explanation of the sear in order
to explain the action of the mainspring.

15. The mainspring screw holds the mainspring to the lock
plate.

16. The tumbler is that part of the lock mechanism which
provides an operating link between the sear and the
mainspring.

17. The bridle is an iron part serving as a bearing for the tumbler. It is a mechanical feature of the true flintlock which distinguishes it from all the transitionary types. In the latter, the lock plate served as a bearing for the tumbler.
18. The bridle screw holds the bridle on the lock plate.
19. The sear screw fastens the sear spring to the sear.

Variations in Lock Design

Although all lock mechanisms of the true flintlock conform generally to the definitions and descriptions previously given, one of the most interesting features of collecting firearms made prior to the development of assembly-line, machine-produced weapons, manufactured so that all parts were interchangeable, is the infinite variety of designs and mechanical details found in these "handmade" single-shot flintlock and percussion pistols.

Although Figure 2 shows the exterior features and Figure 3 the interior parts of a typical lock for a U. S. Martial or U. S. Secondary Martial Flintlock Pistol, a variation of lock design is portrayed in Figure 4. Figure 4 gives an exterior view and Figure 5 an interior view of a lock mechanism which is not essentially typical of martial specimens but includes features found in several flintlock pistols of the martial and semi-martial classification during the later period of their development.

Figures 4 and 5 also present variations in nomenclature. Hence it is useful to compare Figure 2 with Figure 4, and Figure 3 with Figure 5, in order to understand technical terms of the flintlock era. Those features already explained will be mentioned without definition.

The lock plate of Figure 4, marked 1, varies slightly in shape from the lock plate of Figure 2. The tumbler screw (2), is the same for both lock designs. The hammer of Figure 4, marked 3, is S-shaped, and is sometimes called a "gooseneck" hammer, whereas the hammer of Figure 2 is sometimes called a "straight" hammer. The comb, marked 4 in

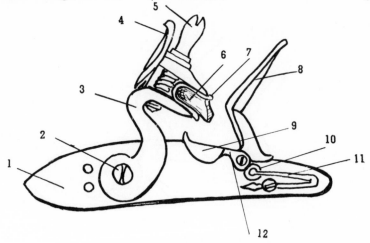

FIGURE 4. The exterior view of a lock showing features of the improved lock of a later period of the flintlock era

1. lock plate
2. tumbler screw
3. hammer
4. comb
5. hammer screw
6. flint
7. leather
8. frizzen
9. pan
10. roller
11. frizzen spring
12. frizzen bridle

Figure 4, is that part of the hammer which is behind the hammer screw. In Figure 4 it is slightly curved, whereas in Figure 2 the comb (not numbered in that drawing) is straight. The hammer screw, marked 5 in Figure 4, has a slot at the top for adjustment instead of the hole (3), in Figure 2. The flint, marked 6 in Figure 4, is essentially the same as the flint in Figure 2.

The flint, marked 6 in Figure 4 and 5 in Figure 2, was placed between the jaws of the hammer with a beveled upper surface, in a folded piece of leather, although sometimes a folded piece of thin sheet lead was used. The purpose of using either leather or lead was to give the jaws of the hammer a better grip on the flint. The lower surface of the flint was flat. However, some locks were designed in such a manner that the shooter could get better results by placing the flint

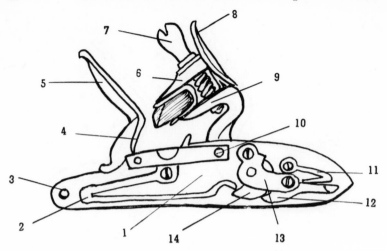

FIGURE 5. The interior view of a lock showing features of
the improved lock of a later period of the flintlock era

1. lock plate
2. mainspring
3. screw hole
4. pan cover
5. frizzen
6. top jaw
7. hammer screw

8. comb
9. bottom jaw
10. screw hole
11. sear spring
12. sear
13. bridle
14. tumbler

in the jaws of the hammer with the flat side uppermost and
the beveled surface below. These comments apply especially
to U. S. Martial and U. S. Secondary Martial Single-Shot
Pistols, although they have general application to all flintlock
arms, including both pistols and shoulder arms, martial or
nonmartial.

With this explanation we come to the "leather," marked 7
in Figure 4. Although the leather is shown in Figures 2 and
3, it is not labeled.

The frizzen is essentially identical in Figures 2, 3, 4, and 5;
and the pan, marked 9 in Figure 4, is almost identical with
the pan shown in Figures 2, 3, and 5.

The roller, marked 10 in Figure 4, is a separate, round
piece of steel fastened on the end of the frizzen spring by a

pin. The roller relieves the friction on the end of the pan cover so that the pan cover can fly forward when the pistol is fired. This device is not part of the locks shown in Figures 1, 2, and 3, because it was an improvement which was adopted by some lock manufacturers several years after the true flintlock came into existence as a distinct type.

The frizzen spring of Figures 4 and 5 is slightly different in design than the frizzen springs of Figures 2 and 3, but mechanically it is not different. It is marked 11 in Figure 4.

The frizzen bridle, marked 12 in Figure 4, is merely the name used by some collectors for that portion of the frizzen indicated in the drawing.

Figure 5, the interior view of the lock mechanism of Figure 4, shows that the frizzen and pan cover have been thrown forward after the firing of the pistol. The parts are essentially the same as those of Figure 3, the interior view of the lock in Figure 2, but there are a few differences. The top jaw, marked 6 in Figure 5, is the same as the cap, marked 4 in Figure 3. The bottom jaw, marked 9 in Figure 5, is not indicated by name or number in Figures 2 and 3, but is the same part. With these exceptions, the interior views of the two different lock mechanisms are functionally the same; hence it is not necessary to call out the parts by numbers and define them again.

LOADING THE FLINTLOCK

In order to tie the functioning of the lock to the pistol itself, the loading and firing processes should be understood.

The flintlock pistol was loaded from the muzzle. A cylindrical paper cartridge, containing the desired amount of black powder and a round ball of soft lead, was usually issued to the soldiers. Both ends of this cylindrical paper cartridge were sealed by twisting the paper or using paste. When the cartridges were not available, it was necessary simply to pour black powder into the muzzle and then ram the round lead ball down the muzzle with a short ramrod.

The hammer (cock) was placed at the half-cock position. The pan was uncovered by pushing the frizzen (battery) forward manually. One end of the prepared cylindrical paper cartridge was bitten off by the soldier and a very small portion of the powder was poured out of the cartridge into the priming pan. The frizzen was then pulled all the way back, thus covering the priming pan.

The soldier then poured the remainder of the powder into the barrel and rammed the lead ball down the muzzzle until it rested against the powder. He wadded up the remainder of the paper cartridge and rammed it down the muzzle to prevent the lead ball from falling out.

When a pistol barrel was rifled (grooves cut into the bore to give the bullet a rotary motion), paper wadding was not satisfactory. Instead, a small piece of greased leather or linen, called a patch, was wrapped around the bullet so that it would not lose its shape by being forced down the muzzle against the resistance of the lands. The lands are the uncut portions of the original barrel bore that remain after the grooves have been cut out to form the rifling. Figure 6 is a cross section of a rifled barrel with one land, one groove, and the caliber dimension indicated.

When prepared paper cartridges were not available, the powder was carried either in a powder horn (made from the horn of a cow) or in a metal flask. Under ordinary military circumstances the same grade of powder was used for both the main charge and priming, but when the shooter desired increased efficiency, he used powder with a finer grain for priming. This made it necessary for him to carry one container for the main charge and another for priming. Obviously, this was unpopular with most soldiers because soldiers of all armies, of all nations, in all centuries, hate to carry any more equipment than absolutely necessary. It was usually the officers, who bought their own pistols and were proud of their pistol marksmanship, who used two grades of powder.

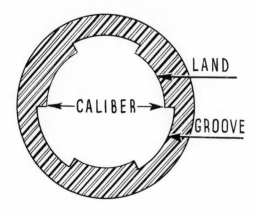

FIGURE 6. A cross-sectional view of a rifled barrel, showing a
land, a groove, and the measurement of caliber between lands

FIRING THE FLINTLOCK PISTOL

The hammer (cock) was cocked by pulling it all the way
back. The trigger was pulled. The sear released the tumbler
which was caused to revolve forward by the mainspring. The
hammer struck forward and the flint held between its jaws
hit the steel face of the frizzen (battery), knocked the
frizzen forward, thus uncovering the priming pan and throwing a shower of sparks into the priming powder, which ignited.
The fire from the priming powder entered the vent (touchhole), ignited the main charge, and the gases of combustion
generated pressure that drove the bullet out of the barrel
toward the target.

SIGHTS ON FLINTLOCK PISTOLS

When anyone fires a flintlock pistol for the first time, the
above steps between pulling the trigger and the discharge of
the pistol seem to occur simultaneously because the shooter
is amazed by the loud noise, the smoke, and the recoil. But
actually the time between pulling the trigger and the dis-

charge of the pistol is relatively great enough to make it impossible to accurately aim the earlier models of the U. S. Martial and U. S. Secondary Martial Pistols. For this reason, many of them did not have sights. Later models had a front sight but this was intended to allow the shooter at least to point the barrel in the general direction of the target. Usually the soldier or sailor was not expected to achieve any great degree of accuracy and he was not expected to hit anything with a pistol at any great distance.

WHY SOLDIERS AND SAILORS CARRIED TWO PISTOLS

Since the pistol might fail to fire at all when the trigger was pulled, or it might fire and miss the target, martial flintlock pistols were normally issued in pairs. The mounted soldiers carried their pistols in leather holsters attached on each side of the pommel of the saddle. This is why large single-shot pistols often were called horse pistols.

Men of the U. S. Navy also carried pistols in pairs, sometimes in leather holsters and often simply thrust into their trouser bands or into a sash worn around the waist. Since weight and bulk were important factors, the Navy favored smaller pistols when it could get them, and this also applied to foot troops of the Army. The U. S. Marine Corps relied primarily upon shoulder arms because the Marines have always emphasized aimed, accurate fire. But when armed with pistols they normally used leather holsters.

The term "dragoon pistol" is often found in gun books. A dragoon was originally a mounted infantryman armed with a shoulder weapon having a barrel shorter than shoulder weapons used by infantry of the same period. That is, he carried a musketoon when the infantry carried muskets, or he carried a carbine when the infantry carried rifles. The dragoon got his name from the fact that some of the very early, short-barreled shoulder arms issued to mounted infantry were called dragoons. Regardless of whether a soldier was called a mounted infantryman, a dragoon, or a cavalryman, his large horse pistol is sometimes called a **dragoon** pistol, although this is grossly inaccurate unless the pistol actually was issued to and used by cavalrymen officially designated as dragoons.

These details are relevant in discussing the lock mechanism of the true flintlock because the size of the lock mechanism depended upon the size of the weapon. Obviously, the lock mechanism for a comparatively small pistol was smaller than one for a very large one, and the lock mechanism for shoulder arms was normally much larger than it was for a pistol.

CALIBER DESIGNATION

The size of the lock mechanism of the flintlock depended upon the size of the weapon on which it was mounted, but this in turn was fundamentally related to the powder charge and the bullet. Early martial and semi-martial arms of the flintlock period were not designated by calibers. Instead, the word "gauge" was used. For example, it was usually possible to cast sixteen one-ounce lead balls from one pound of lead. Hence the one-ounce lead ball was described as "16 gauge," and the weapon from which it was fired was described in the same manner in designating what we now call caliber. A smoothbore pistol firing a one-ounce, round lead ball was a "16-gauge pistol," and it would have a bore diameter of 0.69 inch. Therefore we would say it was caliber .69. The one-ounce, round lead ball of 16 gauge was normally 0.675 inch in diameter, but it was necessary to provide a clearance for loading of 0.015 inch. Therefore, the pistol would be designated 16 gauge during the flintlock era and today we describe it as caliber .69, although the diameter of the lead ball, which also was called 16 gauge in flintlock days, was only 0.675 inch.

The lead balls were cast from molds, and all flintlock arms were handmade; hence it was common for a bullet or a pistol to be either 0.05 inch larger or smaller than the dimensions given above and still have the designations we have listed.

Furthermore, a collector may find that a specimen in his

collection has a bore diameter greater than the one we give for a pistol which otherwise conforms to the specifications of the one in his possession. The reason may be either that the manufacturer made it that way or that repeated loading, firing, and cleaning wore down the bore, thus giving it a larger caliber measurement than that stated in this text.

Engraved and Stamped Inscriptions on Lock Plates

The gun manufacturers in the flintlock and percussion eras frequently marked the lock plate and other parts of the firearm with their name and sometimes the city and state where they made guns. Such marking was engraved on the better-quality arms, but the engraving was frequently "light engraving"; that is, shallow engraving.

Firearms of lower quality usually had the name of the maker and other information stamped on the lock plate, barrel, and other parts. This was done by holding a steel die over the metal part to be stamped and then hitting the die with a hammer or mallet. When the stamped inscription was shallow, rusting or too much polishing through the years has destroyed the inscription or made it difficult to read, just as such treatment has affected engraved inscriptions.

The inscription on the lock plate does not necessarily coincide with that on the barrel. This is because the man who assembled the firearm was not always the man who made either the barrel or the lock. Frequently, the lock mechanism was imported from Europe, removed from other firearms, or made by a man who specialized in lock mechanisms. Likewise, the barrel may have been imported, taken from another weapon, or made by someone who specialized in barrel making. Furthermore, some men specialized in making stocks. Therefore, the barrel may have been made by one man, the lock mechanism by a second person, the stock by a third, and the whole pistol or shoulder arm assembled and sold by a fourth man.

Adding to the confusion of modern collectors and historians, the man who assembled and sold the firearm may have had his name stamped on the barrel, lock plate and other parts if the specialists he bought the various gun assemblies from had not already done their own marking. Fortunately, many flintlock and percussion arms were made entirely in the same shop, either by a single gun manufacturer or by a master gunsmith who supervised the work of his apprentices and journeymen.

THE FLINT

The flint used in U. S. Martial and U. S. Secondary Martial Single-Shot Flintlock Pistols was usually imported from either England or France. When pure, it is translucent, and the flint preferred for use in the flintlock pistols described in this book was not only translucent but prepared with one surface beveled and the other flat for mounting between the jaws of the cock. The armed forces using flintlock weapons in the United States preferred flint of a very light yellow color and uniform shade throughout, but when this quality was not available, flint which was opaque and colored light brown (because of impurities) was used. Flint which was dark brown or black because of a greater degree of impurities was rejected for martial use except in emergencies.

When flint was not obtainable from England or France, native American flint was obtained from the same regions where our American Indians found flint for their arrowheads. The preference for flint from England or France was not due so much to the lack of pure flint in the United States as it was the lack of skilled "knappers." The knapper's trade consisted of cutting, shaping and dressing flint.

LOCK TIME

The phrase "lock time" can mean the time elapsed between pulling the trigger and the forward travel of the bullet. Another meaning is the time elapsed between the disengagement of the sear in the lock mechanism and the beginning of the forward motion of the bullet through the barrel.

Using this second definition, the lock time of a well-made flintlock pistol—of the type U. S. officers or wealthy civilians bought at their own expense—was sometimes as short as 0.0454 second (1/22 second) but more often 0.714 second (1/14 second). These were lock times for the flintlock pistols of the very finest craftsmanship.

Still using the second definition, the lock time of flintlock pistols of medium-quality workmanship varied from 0.050 second (1/20 second) down to 0.100 second (1/10 second).

The lock time of low-priced civilian and almost all U. S. Martial and U. S. Secondary Martial Single-Shot Pistols usually was much slower. It generally ranged from 0.100 second (1/10 second) down to 0.500 second (1/2 second). However, when skilled gunsmiths were enlisted in the armed forces of the United States, or attached to them as civilian employees, the lock time of martial and semi-martial flintlock pistols could be increased by either adjusting the existing locks or substituting new and better lock parts.

RELIABILITY OF U. S. FLINTLOCK PISTOLS

The archives of the United States show that it was customary in many units of the armed forces to issue one flint to a soldier for each twenty shots that he was expected to fire, although a flint of good quality could be used successfully at least fifty and sometimes sixty times before it required replacement.

The archives also show that many unit commanders complained that their flintlock pistols failed to fire (had misfires) at least one time out of ten attempts to fire, and sometimes one time out of seven.

When flintlock pistols were not adequately covered by a holster or the clothing of the soldier or sailor, they became useless in a heavy rainstorm or snowstorm after one minute of exposure to the weather, and frequently in half that time.

The above are general statements applying to the early-type flintlock pistols issued to the armed forces of the United States when such pistols were not properly adjusted by gunsmiths after they were received by the men, and when they were not properly cared for or protected against the elements.

Flintlock pistols of high-quality workmanship—especially those made with various improvements late in the flintlock period and correctly adjusted by gunsmiths and properly cared for and protected by the shooters—could be fired hundreds of times without a single misfire, assuming that the flint was replaced after each twenty shots, and preferably after each fifteen shots.

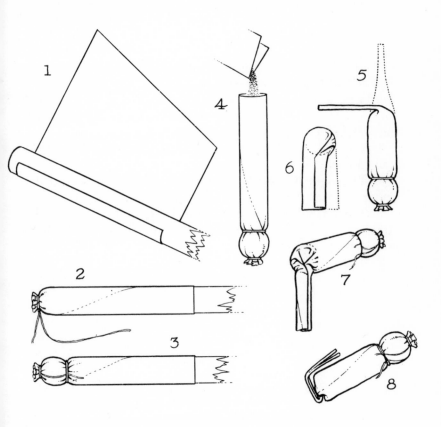

FIGURE 7. The manufacture of a paper cartridge

The Manufacture of Paper Cartridges

Figure 7 shows one method of manufacturing paper cartridges. The steps illustrated are as follows:

1. Cartridge paper of the appropriate length and width, depending upon the caliber and the powder charge, is wrapped around a cartridge stick having a diameter less than the caliber of the completed cartridge.

2. The cartridge stick is pulled out of the paper far enough to permit the end to be pasted or tied.

3. The cartridge stick is removed and the round lead ball is inserted. Then, the stick is inserted to hold the paper case in shape while the ball is held in place by tying, usually with two "half hitches," to use the terminology of knot tying.

4. Black powder of sufficient quantity to provide the force required in firing is poured into the case. The black powder should be weighed on a scale reading in grains, or measured with a device which has been tested so that it holds exactly the weight desired.

5. The end of the paper case is pinched and bent at a right angle.

6. The right side of the paper case is folded in toward the center.

7. The left side is folded in toward the center and then the "tail," which is the end opposite the end containing the ball, is folded up and over.

8. The cartridge is now complete.

Figure 7 was drawn by Herschel Logan.

CHAPTER 3

U. S. Martial Flintlock Pistols

DEFINITION

UNITED STATES flintlock pistols are those flintlock pistols made in the United States armories at Harpers Ferry, Virginia, and at Springfield, Massachusetts; and the flintlock pistols made by private contractors who manufactured and delivered pistols for the United States armed forces, or for state forces called into the service of the United States. This is a strict definition.

Historically and practically, the definition can be broadened to include those pistols made for the Committees of Safety, the Continental Congress, and for privateers who fought for the United States. In other words, we can include pistols used during the Revolutionary War and later campaigns and wars, even though they were made, delivered and used before the United States of America came into formal and legal existence as a nation.

The Congress of the United States passed a resolution in 1777 that all arms belonging to the United States be stamped or otherwise marked with the words "United States". This resolution was obeyed in general, but there were many arms not marked at all, some were marked "U.States", and others were merely marked "U S".

The absence of the "U S" mark, or some other mark made in obedience to the resolution of Congress, may raise a doubt about the federal status of the weapon, but this can be overcome by other evidence. Also, the presence of the "U S" mark, or similar mark conforming to the resolution of Congress, does not, in itself, clearly determine that the pistol belongs in the federal classification because it is easy for anyone to use a die, stamp, etching, or engraving, or some other process to give a pistol the appearance of federal use, thereby raising its value.

ORDER OF PRESENTATION OF PISTOLS

Throughout this book, arms are generally presented in the chronological order of their model years. The *model year* is the year in which the pistol became recognized for the first time by U. S. officials. It is usually the year in which the contract, or the official order for manufacture, was signed, but in some cases it is the year in which the pistol was made for the first time. When a model year is given and another year appears in parentheses after it, the year in parentheses is the one long used by authors, collectors, and dealers, but the first year given is the one the author believes to be the correct model year.

Some of the pistols classified by the author as U. S. Secondary Martial Pistols in *The Gun Collector's Handbook of Values,* Fifth Revised Edition, copyrighted in 1960, have been advanced to the U. S. Martial Flintlock classification because of research conducted since 1960.

THE PERIOD FROM THE REVOLUTIONARY WAR TO THE WAR OF 1812

From the end of the Revolutionary War to the beginning of the War of 1812, the United States of America had both domestic and foreign problems. Within the United States, there were campaigns with the Indian tribes and with the people who were not yet ready to accept federal authority.

Abroad there was the naval war with France, and the war with the so-called Barbary States, or nations of Morocco, Algiers, Tunis, and Tripoli, the four Barbary States in North Africa. In 1786, a treaty was signed with Morocco and this remained effective, with a few exceptions, because of the campaigns of our Navy and the U. S. Marine Corps. Since Morocco was the farthest west of the Barbary States and commanded the Strait of Gibraltar, the treaty with Morocco was important.

In 1794, the Congress of the United States prohibited the export of arms and ammunition, and authorized the importation, duty free, of foreign arms and ammunition.

The United States Armory, at Springfield, Massachusetts, was established by the United States in 1794. Although it delivered only 245 muskets during its first year, in 1799 it produced 4,595 acceptable muskets. Obviously, the Springfield Armory was unable to produce enough arms for all the armed forces. Therefore, Congress appropriated $800,000 in 1798 for arms and ammunition to be produced by private contractors.

Contracts were executed between the United States and gunsmiths, armorers, and companies formed to handle this type of business. Muskets, pistols, swords, and other martial equipment were made and delivered to the United States and to state troops called into federal service, as well as the U. S. Navy and privateers, which were merchant ships armed and authorized to fight as battleships.

Pistols in this privateer classification used during the Revolutionary War were mostly English and French pistols. These had been acquired by the American colonies in the early colonial days, during the French and Indian Wars when Americans fought under the British flag, and included those French pistols captured during the wars and campaigns. In addition, there were French pistols delivered to the Revolutionary forces by Lafayette and those bought one way or another from the French.

The British were well aware of the attitude of the American colonies before the Revolution, hence the export of arms and ammunition to the unhappy colonies was prohibited by the British. Despite the royal embargo the American colonies took no affirmative action to produce arms and ammunition for the American Revolution until the fighting began at Lexington in 1775.

When war was declared in 1776, the colonies began to contract for the manufacture of arms, ammunition and military equipment. In order to keep men who were already engaged in such manufacture from entering the armed forces, military exemptions, bonuses, and other inducements were offered.

Committees of Safety were formed in each of the colonies, and in addition to other duties they provided for the organization, equipment, and armament of armed forces for both the sea and land organizations.

Officers, mounted orderlies, naval forces, cavalrymen, dragoons, and to some extent artillerymen were provided with pistols, but handguns were regarded as weapons of limited usefulness; hence they were given a lower priority than rifles and muskets.

It is probable that English and French martial pistols were acquired during the Revolution, but unless they are positively marked to show United States use, they cannot be regarded as U. S. Martial Pistols.

In addition to Committee of Safety arms, the Continental Congress bought and issued weapons, but these, too, cannot be accepted unless properly marked and found described in the archives.

After the Revolutionary War ended, there was an inventory of weapons in United States warehouses which showed that there were on hand 251 serviceable pistols at Philadelphia, 495 at Springfield, and 59 at West Point, New York, making a total of 805. In addition, there were 420 unserviceable pistols altogether, of which 407 were in Philadelphia, but there is no record of the make, type, model, or other means of identification.

Typical Specimens

It is extremely difficult to state definitely that some flintlock pistols are U. S. martial flintlock pistols and others are not. Furthermore, when anyone attempts to classify a martial flintlock pistol as a U. S. Martial Flintlock Pistol, he immediately runs into a controversy. For example, in writing books on antique guns in the past the author has attempted to describe and classify two or more Rappahannock Forge pistols, but now we find that there are only three of these pistols in the possession of collectors and for all practical purposes they are almost identical.

One of the three pistols has "J. HUNTER" stamped on the barrel and the other two do not have this mark. All three have 9-inch barrels, and all three do not vary in barrel caliber, as measured now, although allowance must be made for wear and erosion; hence the present bore diameters vary from caliber .67 to caliber .69.

The total length of these three specimens also varies from 14.5 to 15 inches, depending upon how straight or how curved the stock happens to be at the butt.

None of the Rappahannock Forge pistols in their original flintlock condition were marked "C P".

These are only a few of the conditions and specifications which control the designation and classification of U. S. Martial Flintlock Pistols. Similar argumentative details can be found in examining all single-shot pistols.

RAPPAHANNOCK FORGE PISTOL, cal. .67 to cal. .69, as measured today. Barrel is 9 inches long, smoothbore, pin-fastened, and marked "J. HUNTER" on some specimens, but not all. Total length about 15 inches, but some specimens are listed as having a total length of 14.5 inches. Brass trigger guard. Full-length stock. No sights. Gooseneck, flat, beveled hammer. Iron pan with flat, beveled edges and fence to rear. Hickory ramrod held by brass thimbles. Brass mountings. Lock plate marked "RAPᴬ FORGE", with the capital "A" in "RAPᴬ" raised above the horizontal line. The

"RAP^A" is in one line and the word "FORGE" is a parallel line underneath. Figure 1.

Marked on side plate with organization designation, such as "A.L.D." for Albemarle Light Dragoons, followed by the serial number assigned to that particular pistol by the organization. The butt plate may have an organization mark, such as "3 Rgt", meaning the Third Regiment.

Although listed in *The Gun Collector's Handbook of Values* as a U. S. Secondary Martial Flintlock Pistol, this weapon is now regarded as a U. S. martial pistol by experts, because it was the very first of the U. S. martial pistols adopted and used by the United States during the Revolutionary War.

The Rappahannock Forge also was known as James Hunter's Iron Works. It was located at Falmouth, Virginia, on the Rappahannock River, north of Fredericksburg. Before the Revolutionary War, Hunter made hardware for housewives and farmers, but at the outbreak of the Revolutionary War he began to manufacture pistols, muskets, carbines, wall rifles (sometimes called rampart rifles), and sabers primarily for the troops raised in Virginia, but he also made arms for the United States. His weapons show a resemblance to the British arms owned and used by the Virginia militia before the Revolution. According to tradition, he stopped making arms, or at least he stopped marking arms with his own name or company symbol, when the British troops approached his arms works in 1781.

The single-shot flintlock pistols were made for cavalry, dragoons, and mounted infantry, including organizations led by Baylor, Lee, and Moylan, all famous names in Revolutionary War history.

According to tradition, after the threat of the raid by British troops proved unfounded about May 30, 1781, James Hunter attempted to obtain financial help from the State of Virginia, but this failed and the United States also rejected his pleas for help. He discharged his employees and permanently closed his factory on December 1, 1781.

Some collectors and historians believe that Hunter bought

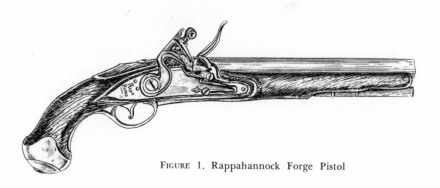

FIGURE 1. Rappahannock Forge Pistol

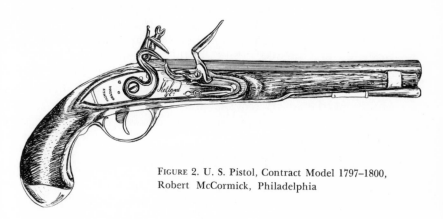

FIGURE 2. U. S. Pistol, Contract Model 1797–1800, Robert McCormick, Philadelphia

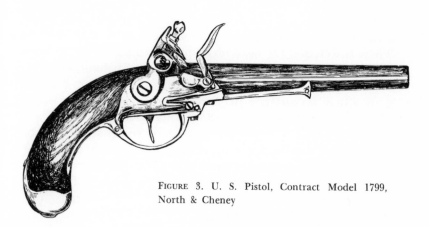

FIGURE 3. U. S. Pistol, Contract Model 1799, North & Cheney

79

pistols in Europe, probably from Prussia, between 1777 and 1778, through the help of William Lee, state agent for Virginia, and that these pistols were marked like those he made himself, but there is no evidence for this statement.

U. S. PISTOL, CONTRACT MODEL 1797–1800, ROBERT McCORMICK, PHILADELPHIA, cal. .64, smoothbore; 10.25-inch, round barrel, proofmarked with eagle head over P, within an oval, and also stamped "U.S." Engraved "KET-LAND & CO." on lock plate under pan and stamped at rear of lock plate "UNITED STATES" in two curving lines. Left side of stock stamped "U.S." Brass-mounted. Total weight 2 lbs., 7 oz. Although not so marked, this pistol is probably one of 100 "ships' pistols" assembled by Robert McCormick in Philadelphia between 1797 and 1800. This extremely rare pistol is from the collection of Samuel E. Smith, Markesan, Wisconsin, and is shown in Figure 2. It has a brass trigger guard, butt cap and side plate. There is one brass thimble.

Robert McCormick was principally known as a musket manufacturer and contractor with the U. S. Government, although he also had a contract with the State of Virginia for the manufacture of muskets. He failed financially, closed his business in July, 1801, and was imprisoned for debt.

The phrase "Ketland & Co." on the lock plate may refer either to John and Thomas Ketland of Philadelphia, Pennsylvania, who were in the arms business, or it may refer to Thomas Ketland, the head of an arms manufacturing business with branches in London and Birmingham, England. Whether the lock plate was made in the United States or in England is of minor importance in view of evidence that the pistol, when examined as a whole and compared with records in official archives, is regarded as one of those assembled by Robert McCormick for federal use. There is a full-length walnut stock with a brass band extending partly around the barrel. The iron pan has a fence. The hammer is of the flat, S-shaped or "gooseneck" type. The stock is marked "US" and "McCORMICK" on the left.

U. S. PISTOL, CONTRACT MODEL 1799, NORTH & CHENEY,

cal. .69, smoothbore, illustrated in Figure 3, has an 8.5-inch barrel which was originally marked "U S", "P", and "V". Stock 5.75 inches long. Total length 14.5 inches. Weight 3 lbs., 4 oz. Lock plate 3.313 inches long. Brass trigger guard 4.85 inches long with round ends. Brass frame may be marked either "NORTH & CHENEY BERLIN" or "S. NORTH & E. CHENEY BERLIN". Brass pan made as part of frame. Brass butt cap. Steel ramrod. Double-neck hammer. Resembles Model 1777 French Army Pistol but has longer barrel and other variations. Manufactured by Simeon North and Elisha Cheney at Berlin, Connecticut, from 1799 to 1802. The original contract of 1799 for 500 pistols was not yet fulfilled when the United States executed another contract, this time for 1,500 pistols. It was executed and all pistols were delivered during 1802. The contract date for delivery was February 6, 1802.

Simeon North was born at Berlin, Connecticut, July 13, 1765, the son of a long-established farm family. When he was about thirty years old, he bought a sawmill, operated by water power, near the family farm. At the mill, he began making scythes for farmers in 1795. About four years later, on March 9, 1799, he obtained a government contract to make cavalry pistols. The "Cheney" of North & Cheney was Elisha Cheney, a brother-in-law of Simeon North. Cheney manufactured clocks and is known to have made screws and pins for the pistols made by North, but despite the fact that from 1799 to 1802 the pistols bear the Cheney name, there is no record of a formal, legal partnership and it is believed that Simeon North was the man primarily responsible for these pistols.

U. S. PISTOL, MODEL 1805 (1806), HARPERS FERRY,

cal. .54, smoothbore, 10.0625-inch, round barrel, key-fastened, with projecting rib, illustrated in Figure 4. Lock plate 4.875 inches long and 1 inch wide, marked with spread eagle, and "US" under the pan; and marked behind the hammer "HARPERS FERRY", with the year, in three lines. The date may be 1806, 1807, or 1808. Walnut half stock, 11.75 inches long. Total length 16 inches. Trigger guard 5.75 inches long with round rear end. Weight 2 lbs., 9 oz. Flat, double-neck hammer.

Steel ramrod on some specimens but original ramrods were made of hickory. Originally made without sights. Brass-mounted. The manufacture of pistols of this type and model may have been started sooner, but the official authorization was dated November 13, 1805. Most specimens were made and dated 1807. Some collectors list this pistol as having a 10-inch barrel, but the author has found that most authentic specimens have a barrel 10.0625 inches long.

The original ramrods were made of hickory, with a brass tip at one end for loading the ball, and with a slotted steel tip at the other end for a cleaning patch. Originally, the pistol had no sights, but today specimens are sometimes found with a front sight and less commonly with both front and rear sights, evidently added after the original manufacture. Furthermore, if a person measures the barrel carelessly, he finds that it is 10 inches long, but if he is extremely careful, he will find that it is 10.0625 inches long, as stated above. The spread eagle is clearly visible on the lock plate, behind the hammer, of the specimen illustrated in Figure 4, but the "US" was apparently either lightly stamped originally or worn down by polishing because the artist was unable to reproduce it accurately in the drawing.

This was the first United States single-shot, flintlock, martial pistol manufactured at the United States Armory, Harpers Ferry, Virginia. There were 4,096 of these pistols made there according to records going back as far as 1840.

The year of manufacture does not appear on the barrel. The barrel marking is a serial number, a sunken United States eagle head, and the letter "P", in that order, from muzzle back to the breech. Since mounted troops, including cavalry, dragoons, and artillery, normally carried flintlock pistols in pairs, the same serial number was usually stamped on the barrel of each pistol of a pair.

As explained above, the barrel is key-fastened with a projecting rib. This means that the barrel is fastened to the stock with a key and has a rib extension underneath, extending from the end of the half stock to the muzzle.

This pistol was originally made without sights, as explained above, but many specimens available today have either a brass bead or a low, knife-blade-type front sight, dovetailed into the barrel. A few specimens reported to have been used by troops had a V-notch, steel, rear, open sight on the tang, but this was probably exceptional. Experts believe that any sights, front or rear, were added in the field or at arsenals.

The butt has what collectors call a modified fishtail shape where the butt cap is fastened. The butt cap has an extension on each side, sometimes called spurs, about three inches long, set into the wood, flush with the surface of the wood, and extending upward and forward to provide reinforcement.

The flat, beveled lock plate is sometimes described as being 4.75 inches long and 0.875 inch wide, but like other measurements of early flintlock pistols, the difference found in various specimens may be due to variations in manufacture, or caused by failure to take the measurements accurately. When the lock plate is removed, it may or may not have the marks of an inspector.

The Chief of Ordnance, U. S. Army, reported in 1822 that 8 pattern pistols of this Model 1805 (1806) were made in 1806; that 2,880 pistols were manufactured in 1807; and that in 1808, there were manufactured 1,208 pistols of this model. This adds up to 4,096 pistols, as stated above.

Although the records available today indicate that only 8 pattern pistols were made in 1806, it is possible that a far greater number of lock plates were made, marked with the year 1806, and assembled into pistols bearing a later date in the records or in markings on the pistols.

U. S. PISTOL, MODEL 1807, SPRINGFIELD, cal. .69, illustrated in Figure 5, has an 11.0625-inch, round, smoothbore barrel marked over the breech plug "1818"; a total length of 17.75 inches; and a weight of 3 lbs., 3 ozs. The barrel is held to the stock by means of a double-strap iron band. There is a low, brass, blade-type front sight on the band which is barely visible even in a full-scale drawing or photograph. The double-strap iron band is spring-fastened by means of a stud between the straps, but this feature also is not noticeable in an illustration.

There is an iron trigger guard; an iron back strap which, like all back straps on pistols and revolvers, is merely a strip of metal along the back of the grip for reinforcement; and an iron butt cap, the latter being merely a cap to cover and protect the bottom surface of the butt. The trigger guard is 6.188 inches long with round ends.

The beveled-edge lock plate is 5.125 inches long and 1.0625 inches wide. There is an eagle over "U S" forward of the hammer. Behind the hammer, the lock plate is marked in three lines "SPRINGFIELD 1818", but "SPRING" is on the top line, "FIELD" on the middle line, and "1818" on the bottom line. These lines are approximately horizontal when the barrel is pointed vertically upward. The rear of the lock plate is described by collectors as "teat-shaped."

There is a horizontal iron pan forged with the lock plate so that together they constitute one part. Technically, "the pan is forged integral with the lock plate."

The hammer has an S-shape, which is often called the goose-neck type; it is flat, and it has beveled edges. The hammer screw, used to adjust the jaws of the hammer to hold the flint, has a slot at the top instead of the hole found in many hammer screws. In Figure 5, the jaw is shown without a flint.

The frizzen resembles that of the French Charleville musket with its turned-up toe. It is 1.5 inches high and 0.75 inch wide. The frizzen spring has a diamond-shaped point. In the illustration this is easily found by looking to the right of the eagle over the "US" on the lock plate. The diamond-shaped point appears to be pointing toward the "US".

The pistol has a hickory ramrod with an enlarged forward

tip, called by some collectors a "swell tip." The small end, not visible in the drawing because the ramrod is in place, has a slotted iron ferrule which is threaded internally to receive either a "wiper head" to hold a cleaning patch or to hold a screw to remove a ball stuck in the bore.

The barrel on some specimens is marked "P" inside an oval, which means "Proved," and "V", meaning "Viewed." There is an eagle head between the "P" and the "V". These marks are on top of the barrel and not visible in a side-view illustration. The "P" is over the eagle head and the "V" is under the eagle head, all in a vertical column when the barrel is pointed vertically upward. These marks on the barrel indicate inspection and acceptance by a United States inspector.

The stock is made of black walnut, is oil-finished, has a rounded butt and carries the initials of inspectors.

Both the turned-up toe of the frizzen and the teat-shaped rear of the lock plate resemble the French Charleville musket so much that these two characteristics alone have evoked the curiosity of collectors and historians for many years.

A few very reliable experts on U. S. Martial Flintlock Pistols maintain that this pistol was actually authorized in 1807. Many experts report the existence of authentic specimens with lock plates dated 1815. This tends to indicate that the design of the pistol was approved by the United States War Department before 1815 and reinforces the contention of those experts who believe that this pistol was actually authorized in 1807.

The designation U. S. Pistol, Model 1807, Springfield is probably correct because even those who have previously called it "U. S. Flintlock Pistol, Model 1818, Springfield," or by other names including 1818 as the model year, have admitted that their choice of 1818 was only a tentative one. Probably the experts will eventually agree that it was authorized in 1807 but not assembled until a later date.

When a specimen which superficially resembles this pistol is dated 1818, has an ordinary frizzen, a lock plate with a

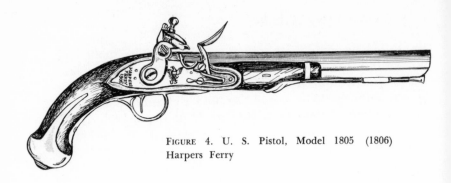

FIGURE 4. U. S. Pistol, Model 1805 (1806) Harpers Ferry

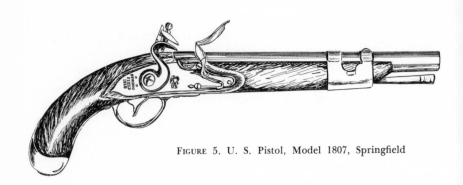

FIGURE 5. U. S. Pistol, Model 1807, Springfield

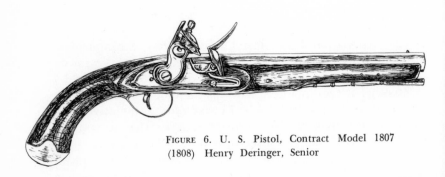

FIGURE 6. U. S. Pistol, Contract Model 1807 (1808) Henry Deringer, Senior

86

blunt rear end, and a double-neck hammer, it is not a U. S. Pistol, Model 1807, Springfield, but can be described as a U. S. Pistol, Model 1817, Springfield, or as a U. S. Pistol, Model 1818, Springfield. The latter two designations refer to the same pistol. Selecting either 1817 or 1818 as a model year is merely an arbitrary designation made by some collectors and historians.

For all of these reasons, the so-called U. S. Model 1818, Springfield Pistol has been described in the 1960 edition of *The Gun Collector's Handbook of Values,* and in previous editions of the same book, as a "debatable model."

THE TWO NATIONAL ARMORIES

The Congress of the United States in 1792 authorized the establishment of two national arsenals. An *arsenal* is a place where arms and all types of military and naval equipment are manufactured, repaired, stored, or issued. An *armory,* spelled *armoury* by the British, is a place where the principal function is the deposit and storage of arms and military equipment, but the same word has been used in the past to designate a building or group of buildings where weapons are manufactured, thus giving armory and arsenal an overlapping meaning. Today, most civilians think of an armory as nothing more than a large building used by the National Guard as a drill hall and a convenient place to hold large civic functions having nothing to do with national defense.

Nevertheless, the Congress of the United States in April, 1794, authorized the construction and operation of two national armories. President George Washington did not quibble over dictionary definitions, but combined the functions of arsenals and armories and chose two locations, one at Springfield, Massachusetts; and another at Harpers Ferry, Virginia. Both of these have been called National Armories since their establishment, and both have combined manufacturing and storage functions.

The manufacture of firearms started at the Springfield Armory in 1795, in which year 245 muskets were made by hand. The Springfield Armory has continued operations throughout all our wars and is still a vital part of our national defense. The National Armory at Harpers Ferry, Virginia, although authorized to be built in 1794, was not started until the construction of a few shops and buildings began in 1796. The first production record was that of 1801 when 293 muskets were made.

The history of the National Armory at Harpers Ferry is a fascinating one, but beyond the scope of this text. During the night of April 18, 1861, when Virginia State Militia were advancing on Harpers Ferry, Lieutenant Roger Jones, U. S. Army, who commanded a small caretaking establishment of 45 enlisted men, had his men set fire to the building where finished weapons were stored and attempted unsuccessfully to set fire to the remainder of the armory, but had to retreat.

The Virginia State Militia arrived, put out the fires, and eventually turned over to the Confederate States of America the major portion of the machinery, tools, gun parts, and equipment, all of which was taken South and utilized to make weapons used against the United States. This ended the United States Armory at Harpers Ferry.

The Necessity for Hiring Private Contractors

During their existence, neither of the two National Armories was able to manufacture all the firearms and equipment needed by the armed forces of the United States in emergencies. That is why the United States had to turn to private contractors to obtain arms, ammunition, and other military and naval equipment in all of the wars we have fought. This was true during the days of the National Armory at Harpers Ferry and it has been the same for the National Armory at Springfield from its establishment until today. Free enterprise, and not government, has been the major source of our weapons of war throughout our recorded history as a republic.

During the Civil War, an effort was made by the Confederacy to make arms and ammunition in government plants, but the Confederates turned early to private contractors and relied upon them until the end of the unfortunate War Between the States.

U. S. PISTOLS, MODEL 1807, MANUFACTURED BY CONTRACTORS

Pistols in this group are sometimes called officers' pistols, militia pistols, or privateers' pistols. Some of them were used by regular enlisted men of the federal forces, some by militia or volunteer enlisted men called into the federal service, but all were used for the United States of America, one way or another.

There were many contractors who probably made pistols which belong in this group. It is difficult to name all of them, but among them were A. & J. Ansted (also called Adam Angstadt and Jacob Angstadt) ; William Calderwood; Jacob Cook, also called Jacob Cooke; De Huff, Gonter & Dickert, which consisted of De Huff, whose name was also spelled Dehuff and Dehulf, together with Jacob Dickert and Peter Gonter; Henry Deringer, Senior, and his son, Henry Deringer, Jr., for whom the derringer pistol was named; O. & E. Evans; Thomas French; Martin Frey, also known as Martin Frye and M. Fry; John Guest, also known as I. Guest because the letters "I" and "J" were aften interchanged in those days; Abraham Henry; Joseph Henry, who may or may not have been the same man known to gun collectors as I. HENRY; Adam Leitner; John Miles; Joseph Perkin, also known as Joseph Perkins, and either I. Perkin, I. Perkins, J. Perkin, or J. Perkins; Henry Pickel, also known as Henry Pickell; William Shannon, also known as William and Hugh Shannon; John Shuler, also known as John Schuler; Daniel Swietzer & Co.; Winner, Nippes & Co.; others.

Since this text is illustrated entirely with drawings, only those specimens to which the author had access at the time of writing this book are illustrated.

In the listing of these U. S. Martial Flintlock Pistols, we have used the word "Contract" to show that they were made by contractors, and not at the U. S. National Armory at

Springfield, Massachusetts, or the National Armory at Harpers Ferry, Virginia. Unless otherwise stated each of these pistols is primarily an army pistol, and only secondarily a navy or privateer pistol.

Obviously, those who own these pistols want to upgrade them from U. S. Secondary Martial to U. S. Martial Pistols, because this increases the value, and those who want to buy such pistols want to downgrade them, but we have presented the facts according to the best available information.

There will be a continuing dispute about these pistols because the records have been lost, mislaid, destroyed, or misinterpreted. In case of doubt, we can classify them as U. S. Secondary Martial Flintlock Pistols, but even in that group they are rare, valuable, and difficult to obtain in their original, unaltered, flintlock condition. Collectors, historians, and dealers are reminded again and again that it is an unfortunately common practice to alter percussion pistols back to flintlock, to place false marks on pistols, and even make pistols which are entire reproductions of the original models.

One of the contract-made pistols of this period deserves special attention. This is the one made by O. & E. Evans under one of the later contracts. It resembles the French Model Year IX (1800–1801) Cavalry Pistol, cal. .689, with a 7.87-inch barrel, and a total length of 14.564 inches. The barrel is dated 1814 on the under side and the lock plate is marked "EVANS". Obviously, this is a distinct departure from the other pistols of this contract period.

A. & J. ANSTED CONTRACT PISTOL, MODEL 1807, cal. .54, with 8.625-inch, round-octagon, pin-fastened, smooth-bore barrel marked "ANSTED", usually in engraved block letters. Total length 13.5 inches. Brass-mounted. Brass trigger guard and brass front sight. No rear sight. No back strap. Iron pan with fence. Flat gooseneck hammer. Hickory ramrod. Full-length, curly maple stock extending to muzzle.

A. & J. Ansted had a contract with Tench Coxe, U. S. Purveyor of Public Supplies, on April 22, 1808, to make 50 pairs of pistols of this description. The makers were probably

Adam Angstadt and Jacob Angstadt who anglicized the spelling of their names, but there were several men with similar names. Furthermore, many men of the flintlock period did not always spell their own names in the same manner in marking pistols. For example, the barrel of one of the specimens identical with the above description is marked "ANSTAT" (not illustrated in this text).

CALDERWOOD CONTRACT PISTOL, MODEL 1807, cal. .54, with 10-inch, round, smoothbore, pin-fastened barrel with an eagle head and the proofmark "P" Total length 16 inches. Brass butt cap, trigger guard, front sight, pan, and mountings. No rear sight. Flat, beveled-edge lock plate marked "CALDERWOOD PHILA" between the hammer and the frizzen spring, and also marked "U S" with the year, usually "1808", vertically behind the hammer. William Calderwood was a Philadelphia gun manufacturer from 1807 to 1819. He had a contract with Tench Coxe, U. S. Purveyor of Public Supplies, to make 60 pairs of pistols of this description in 1808. It is believed that it was issued to state troops called into the service of the United States. Although this specimen is not illustrated in this chapter, a Calderwood flintlock dueling pistol is illustrated in the chapter on dueling pistols and shows typical Calderwood details.

COOK CONTRACT PISTOL, MODEL 1807, also called COOKE CONTRACT PISTOL, MODEL 1807, was made by Jacob Cooke, who also signed his name Jacob Cook. He had an 1807 contract with Tench Coxe, U. S. Purveyor of Public Supplies, for 25 pairs of pistols of the Model 1807 specifications, and in 1808 he obtained another contract, or an extension on the first contract, for 50 more pairs of pistols. The author has never seen a specimen of the Cook pistol and presents this information in case some collector acquires one and wants to classify it.

De HUFF, GONTER & DICKERT CONTRACT PISTOL, MODEL 1807, was supposedly made by an organization consisting of De Huff, who also spelled his name Dehuff and Dehulf; together with Jacob Dickert and Peter Gonter. Records indicate that these men had a contract to make the Model 1807 pistol. If they carried out the contract, it should conform to the specifications given for other contract pistols of this model, but the author has never seen a specimen.

U. S. PISTOL, CONTRACT MODEL 1807 (1808) HENRY DERINGER, SENIOR, cal. .52, with 10-inch, round, smooth-bore, pin-fastened barrel, proofmarked "P" within a circle, on which is mounted a small, rounded front sight, sometimes described as pyramidal in shape. There is no rear sight. Total length 16.5 inches. Weight 2 lbs., 10 oz., although some specimens weigh 2 lbs., 9.5 oz. The full-length walnut stock extends to within 0.25 inch from muzzle. Brass-mounted. Brass trigger guard, butt cap and thimbles. Not only the barrel, but also the trigger guard and the two thimbles are fastened by means of pins. Horizontal iron pan with fence. Flat, beveled, double-necked hammer. Hickory ramrod with enlarged front tip, commonly called a "swell-tipped ramrod."

The rounded butt has a brass butt cap for protection and reinforcement. The butt cap has short, rounded extensions, sometimes called spurs, extending into and flush with the stock on each side of the stock.

The trigger guard forks at the rear of the trigger-guard loop to extend along the under side of the stock, but the fork is so small that it is barely visible in an illustration.

The flat, beveled-edge lock plate comes to a small point at the rear which collectors describe as "teat-shaped." The lock plate is marked "H. DERINGER PHILA" between the hammer and the frizzen.

This pistol was made by Henry Deringer, Senior, in Philadelphia, the father of Henry Deringer, Jr., for whom the famous deringer (also spelled "derringer") pistol is named. It closely resembles the U. S. Pistol, Model 1808, S. North, Navy, described later in this chapter, hence it is assumed that it was made as a result of a contract signed in either 1807 or 1808.

In the past, historians and collectors have assumed that this pistol was made for the use of state militia. If they were called into the federal service, the pistol qualifies as a United States Martial Pistol. Some experts believe that it was used by federal forces in the War of 1812. On that basis, it is classified as a U. S. Martial Pistol.

Figure 6 is a drawing of a typical specimen, showing the position of the hammer and frizzen after the pistol has been fired.

This pistol, like all other firearms made by the Deringer family, is of great interest to all Americans and to many collectors and historians in foreign countries. Deringer is one of the very few family names in gun history which has become an accepted word in our language. Usually it is spelled "derringer" in dictionaries, and curiously enough the Deringer family actually used two "r's" in signing many of its letters.

Henry Deringer, Senior, who made the Deringer Contract Pistol, came from Germany to Pennsylvania, moved to Richmond, Virginia, and there made Kentucky rifles, Kentucky pistols, martial pistols, civilian pistols, dueling pistols, and other firearms. Working with him was his son, Henry Junior, who was born October 26, 1786, at Easton, Pennsylvania. In 1806, the Deringers moved from Richmond back to Pennsylvania, where they made all types of firearms. Further details about the Deringer family, especially Henry Deringer, Jr., are given in *Guns of the Old West,* published by Coward-McCann, Inc.

U. S. PISTOL, EVANS CONTRACT; also known as O. & E. EVANS CONTRACT PISTOL, MODEL 1807–1808; also known as EVANS FLINTLOCK PISTOL, FRENCH MODEL 1805 TYPE; and further known as O. & E. EVANS, FRENCH MODEL IX (1800–1801), CAVALRY AND DRAGOON PISTOL; cal. .689, with 7.87-inch barrel, and a total length of 14.564 inches. Brass butt cap, band, side plate, and separate trigger bow. Lock plate may or may not be marked "EVANS", and it has a rounded rear.

Although the total length is 14.564 inches, it is commonly described as 15 inches. Weight 2 lbs., 13 oz. Brass-mounted. Brass butt cap, band, and separate trigger bow are conventional, but variations are found. The flat, beveled-edge lock plate may or may not be marked "EVANS" between the hammer and the frizzen spring, and in any case the lock plate must have a rounded end, as stated above.

The barrel is usually marked with the proofmark "P" on the left side of the barrel, and the lower side of the barrel is normally marked "P M", with the year, which is often 1814.

The curved butt is reinforced with an iron back strap having extensions (spurs) from the tang to the unornamented, plain, brass butt cap. The trigger guard has the usual oval shape of the period and is made of brass. The hammer is of the double-neck type. The brass pan does not have a fence. The steel ramrod has a button-type head.

A typical specimen is illustrated by the drawing in Figure 7, which shows the hammer and frizzen in the post-firing position.

Many experts believe that this pistol was patterned after the French Army Pistol made in France in 1805. It was manufactured by Owen and Edward Evans, known in business as O. & E. Evans, in Evansburg, Pennsylvania, a village a few miles from Valley Forge, possibly under a contract dated October 25, 1808, and with a possible extension to the contract dated August 14, 1815.

Owen Evans died in 1812. His son, William L. Evans, made muskets and pistols for the United States, and his name appears frequently in any accurate account of firearms history. Throughout the whole story of American firearms, authors, historians, museum curators, and dealers often mistake the father for the son, and vice versa. Although gun collectors do not seem to appreciate humor, the Evans confusion reminds the author of a song from the French musical comedy *Moulin Rouge (The Red Mill)*, in which the young leading lady does a skirt dance and sings:

> "Oh, oh, what have I done?
> I've married the father,
> Instead of the son!"

Regardless of the usual date assigned the Evans pistol, the year 1814 marked on the underside of the barrel of most specimens places it in a much later period than that usually accepted.

After the death of Owen Evans, his brother, Edward Evans, operating under the name of O. & E. Evans, obtained a contract with the United States on August 14, 1815. This raises a question, because it is believed that the contract of August 14, 1815, did not provide for the manufacture and delivery of the same arms as the previous contract.

In other words, the Evans Contract Pistol may have been made under the contract of 1808, in spite of being marked 1814, because the 1808 contract was for a five-year period, and it is known that the manufacturers of flintlock arms did not always complete their contracts within the period specified. Also, it is possible that the Evans Contract Pistol was made and sold to state troops called into federal service, even though the contract with the federal government did not provide for such arms.

T. FRENCH CONTRACT PISTOL, MODEL 1807–1808, made by Thomas French, Canton, Massachusetts, for use by militia under a contract dated October 20, 1808, resembles the other contract pistols with Model years of 1807 or 1808, but in no way resembles the Evans Contract Pistol described above. Since it follows closely the specifications of the other 1807–1808 Contract Pistols, it is not illustrated in this text. It is cal. .64, with a 10.625-inch, round, smoothbore, pin-fastened barrel without sights and marked "P.M." and "P.C." inside a rectangle, together with the year, usually 1814. The total length is 16.75 inches.

It has a full walnut stock extending to 0.375 inch from the muzzle. The pistol is brass-mounted, and it has a brass trigger guard; a flat, beveled-edge gooseneck type hammer; and an iron pan with fence (although some specimens have an iron pan without a fence). A long iron tang serves as a back strap to reinforce the rounded butt which has a brass cap. The lock plate is marked with an eagle, "U S", and "T. FRENCH", between the hammer and the frizzen spring. The lock plate also is marked vertically behind the hammer with the word "CANTON".

The "U S" mark raises a strong presumption that this pistol was made for and used by troops in the federal service. It is believed that it was used during and after the War of 1812.

FRY CONTRACT PISTOL; also known as the MARTIN FRYE CONTRACT PISTOL, MODEL 1807–1808; and sometimes called the M. FRYE or the M. FRY PISTOL. Martin Fry, also spelled Martin Frye, of Pennsylvania, was related to John Fry and Joseph Fry, both of Westmoreland County, Pennsylvania, who were gunsmiths specializing in the manufacture of rifles, and known as Fry as well as Frye. There are records showing that Martin Fry obtained a contract with Tench Coxe, U. S. Purveyor of Public Supplies, to make 54 cavalry-type pistols in 1809.

The Fry or Frye pistols resemble the U. S. Pistol, Model 1805 (1806), Harpers Ferry, except that the Fry or Frye pistols are usually pin-fastened and full-stocked, somewhat resembling the Kentucky pistols of that period. Since the Fry or Frye Pistol follows the principal features of the Model 1805 (1806) Harpers Ferry, it is not illustrated in this text. For many years it was believed that the Fry pistols were for state troops, hence they were classified as U. S. Secondary Martial Pistols, but the tendency now is to group them as U. S. Martial Flintlock Pistols because of the contract of 1809.

The variation of spelling between Fry and Frye does not mean anything, because in flintlock days gunsmiths often spelled their names in different ways. Sometimes it was merely a matter of phonetic spelling, sometimes it was an abbreviation, and often the gunmaker simply did not care.

U. S. PISTOL, CONTRACT MODEL 1807–1808, I. GUEST, cal. .54, with 10.25-inch, round, smoothbore barrel, with brass, blade-type front sight and no rear sight, marked with an eagle head and the proofmark "P" within an oval, and "I. GUEST" in script, which probably means "J. GUEST" because during the flintlock period the letters "I" and "J" were commonly interchanged. Total length 16 inches. Figure 8.

Brass-mounted. Barrel and two thimbles are pin-fastened. Full-length walnut stock extends to within 0.0625 inch from muzzle. No back strap. Flat, beveled-edge, double-neck hammer. Iron pan with fence. Hickory ramrod with flare or bell at tip. Brass butt cap has extensions, sometimes called spurs, one inch long on each side of butt. Brass trigger guard forks at rear to complete the conventional oval for the trigger guard itself.

Flat, beveled lock plate is marked "DREPERT" between the hammer and the frizzen spring and "U S" behind the hammer.

John Guest, often listed as I. Guest, contracted with Tench Coxe, U. S. Purveyor of Public Supplies, to manufacture both rifles and pistols, during the period of manufacture of the Model 1807–1808 Pistol. There is no doubt about this being a U. S. martial flintlock pistol, although it may have been used by organizations and individuals which justified the previous classification of this pistol as a U. S. Secondary Martial Flintlock Pistol. It was probably used during and after the War of 1812.

HENRY (ABRAHAM) CONTRACT MODEL 1807–1808 PISTOL. Abraham Henry was among those who signed a contract with the United States for the production of the Model 1807–1808 Pistol. He is listed among gunmakers who signed contracts with Tench Coxe, U. S. Purveyor of Public Supplies, acting for the War Department, on December 9, 1807. Abraham Henry agreed to deliver 200 pairs of pistols and 200 rifles. We have not examined a pistol of this model and type which could be attributed to Abraham Henry; hence it is not illustrated here.

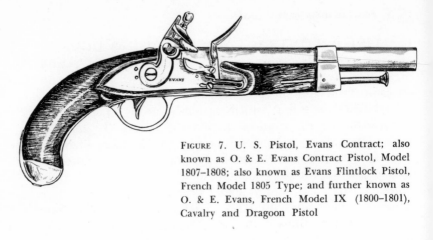

Figure 7. U. S. Pistol, Evans Contract; also known as O. & E. Evans Contract Pistol, Model 1807–1808; also known as Evans Flintlock Pistol, French Model 1805 Type; and further known as O. & E. Evans, French Model IX (1800–1801), Cavalry and Dragoon Pistol

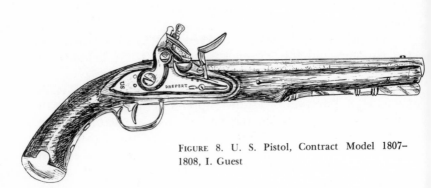

Figure 8. U. S. Pistol, Contract Model 1807–1808, I. Guest

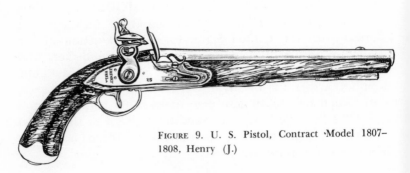

Figure 9. U. S. Pistol, Contract Model 1807–1808, Henry (J.)

98

Abraham Henry is not to be confused with James Henry, John Joseph Henry I, John Joseph Henry II, William Henry I, William Henry II, and William Henry III. Various men named Henry manufactured firearms in Pennsylvania over a long period of years, extending through the flintlock and percussion eras, and even into the age of metallic cartridges. Abraham Henry is listed here because experts are convinced that he existed, that he signed a contract, and that he may have manufactured Model 1807–1808 Pistols. Anything beyond that is left to future research.

A pistol made by "J. Henry," who probably was Joseph Henry of Philadelphia, is described below. Other pistols made by members of the Henry family are described in the chapter on U. S. Secondary Martial Flintlock Pistols.

U. S. PISTOL, CONTRACT MODEL 1807–1808, HENRY

(J.), made by J. Henry, Philadelphia. Cal. .54, with 10-inch, round, smoothbore, pin-fastened barrel marked "J. HENRY PHILᴬ", with the "A" in "PHILA" raised above the "L". The proofmarks are an eagle head and a "P" within the same oval. The lock plate is marked "U S" between the hammer and the frizzen spring, and also marked "J. HENRY PHILᴬ" behind the hammer, with the "A" in "PHILA" raised. The total length is 16 inches and the weight 2 lbs., 9 oz. This pistol is illustrated in Figure 9.

Brass-mounted. Full-length walnut stock extends to 0.25 inch from muzzle. The trigger and the brass thimbles are pin-fastened. Flat, beveled, double-neck hammer. Iron pan with fence. Hickory ramrod. Knife-blade-type, brass front sight on barrel. No rear sight. Brass trigger guard.

The "U S" stamping on the lock plate and various design features of the pistol, together with fragmentary records of the period, indicate that this pistol was made in accordance with design or pattern specifications of the United States which approximate those of the U. S. Pistol, Model 1808, S. North. However, this Henry (J.) Contract Pistol must not be confused with other pistols made by members of the

Henry family described and illustrated in the chapter on U. S. Secondary Martial Flintlock Pistols.

LEITNER (ADAM) CONTRACT MODEL 1807–1808 PISTOL. Adam Leitner, of York County, Pennsylvania, signed a contract on May 31, 1808, with Tench Coxe, U. S. Purveyor of Public Supplies, for 100 pairs of pistols. Assuming that he carried out his contract, his pistols are U. S. martial flintlock pistols. In the past, evidence that pistols of this make, model and type were used by state troops not called into federal service made it necessary to classify them as U. S. Secondary Martial Pistols, but it is apparent that those made and delivered under the federal contract definitely belong in the major classification. The author has never seen a pistol which could be identified as a Model 1807–1808 made by Adam Leitner.

McCORMICK (ROBERT) CONTRACT MODEL 1807–1808 PISTOL. Robert McCormick, of Philadelphia, has been listed repeatedly by many experts as one of the contractors for the Model 1807–1808 Pistol. Curiously enough, some of the authors of magazine articles and books on U. S. Martial and U. S. Secondary Martial Flintlock Pistols who have included him among the makers of 1807–1808 Model Pistols also have mentioned that he failed financially, closed his business in July, 1801, and was imprisoned for debt. Therefore, it is difficult to believe that he was given a contract to make the Model 1807-1808 Pistols.

An investigation of this subject by the author of this text resulted in the discovery that Samuel E. Smith, Markesan, Wisconsin, has in his collection the pistol illustrated in Figure 2 of this chapter and correctly described as U. S. PISTOL, CONTRACT MODEL 1797–1800, ROBERT McCORMICK, PHILADELPHIA.

U. S. PISTOL, CONTRACT MODEL 1807–1808, JOHN MILES, cal. .58, with 9.75-inch, round, smoothbore, pin-fastened barrel marked "MILES PHILAD$_A$", with the letter "A" at the end of "PHILADA" below the line. Total length

15.5 inches. Full-length walnut stock. Brass-mounted. Flat, double-neck hammer. Iron pan with fence. Hickory ramrod. Flat lock plate marked "MILES PHILA" within an oval, between the hammer and the frizzen spring. A specimen of this description has been described and illustrated in many editions of *The Gun Collector's Handbook of Values* as a U. S. Secondary Martial Flintlock Pistol.

Although there is no known record of John Miles having a contract to make *pistols* for the United States, he did have contracts to make muskets for the United States and it is believed that he made and sold both muskets and pistols to the various states, to privateers, and to individuals.

In addition to the specimen described above, John Miles made a martial-type flintlock pistol sometimes called an officer's pistol, and also called a militia pistol, which was probably used by both officers and enlisted men of the federal forces. This variation resembles U. S. Pistol, Model 1805 (1806), Harpers Ferry, except that it is usually pin-fastened and with a full-length stock. The known specimen is cal. .62, smoothbore barrel, 9.5 inches long, with a total length of 15.5 inches, and a weight of 2 lbs., 5 oz. The lock plate is marked "MILES" over "PHILA" in curving lines. The barrel is marked "MILES PHILADA". It is brass-mounted with a band to reinforce the tip of the stock. Figure 10.

MILES PISTOL, cal. .69, with 10.5-inch, round, smoothbore, pin-fastened barrel marked "C.P", having a full-length walnut stock, has been described in *The Gun Collector's Handbook of Values* as a U. S. Secondary Martial Flintlock Pistol. It has no sights. Total length 16 inches. Lock plate marked "MILES" and marked behind the hammer "C.P." Brass-mounted. Bludgeon-type hammer. Double gooseneck hammer.

MILES PISTOL, cal. .64, with 9.375-inch, round, smoothbore, pin-fastened barrel, having a total length of 15.25 inches, and a full-length walnut stock, has also been described through many editions of *The Handbook* as a U. S. Secondary Martial Flintlock Pistol. This specimen has a gooseneck hammer, iron pan with fence, no sights, and a hickory ram-rod. The flat lock plate is marked "MILES", "C.P.", and with two vertical slashes. This "C.P." mark is believed by several eminent authorities to stand for "Commonwealth of Pennsylvania" and not for "Continental Property" as previously thought. However, some authorities believe that it may mean either "City Proof," or "City of Philadelphia."

PERKIN PISTOL, also known as PERKINS PISTOL, probably made by Joseph Perkins, also known as Joseph Perkin. He was born in England and became the first Master Armorer at the U. S. Armory, Harpers Ferry, Virginia. According to the archives of the United States, Joseph Perkin was the first Superintendent of the U. S. Armory at Harpers Ferry, probably in 1803, and he was recorded in 1813 as the United States Inspector of Arms for the New England District. As explained elsewhere in this book, the letters "I" and "J" were often interchangeable in the flintlock era, and men were not particular about the spelling of their names. Therefore, we are probably discussing the same man whether we call him I. Perkin, I. Perkins, J. Perkin, or J. Perkins.

To confuse matters, there was a Jacob Perkins listed as U. S. Inspector of the arms made by Asa Waters under contract with the United States, and we know that he was active in 1821. Also, we know that a James Perkins made muskets in Bridgewater, Massachusetts, along with Adam Kinsley, under a contract with the United States provided for by the Act of Congress of July 5, 1798. This contract was for 2,000 of the Charleville French muskets, and we know that 1,550 were supposedly delivered to the United States on or before June 10, 1801.

Furthermore, we know that a Joseph Perkins either manufactured or repaired firearms for the United States or for militia forces called into federal services, in Philadelphia, Pennsylvania, possibly between 1783 and 1789, although the only record of acceptance and payment for his work is dated 1788.

Throughout many editions of *The Gun Collector's Hand-*

book of Values, the chapter on U. S. Secondary Martial Flintlock Pistols has included an entry which reads as follows:

> PERKIN PISTOL, cal. .62; 8.875-inch, round, brass, smooth-
> bore, pin-fastened barrel, marked "I Perkin". Total length
> 14.125 inches. Full stock, walnut. Brass-mounted. Flat gooseneck
> hammer. Iron pan with fence. Brass trigger guard. Hickory
> ramrod. Lock plate marked "I Perkin".

PERKINS PISTOL, cal. .58, with 8.875-inch, round, smoothbore barrel, marked at the breech in three lines: "P M",
"R P", and "1815". No sights. Full-length stock made of
yellow birch, which is unusual. This particular pistol and
others of similar description, dated 1814 and 1815, were
made by either Rufus Perkins or N. French to arm privateers
sailing out of Massachusetts seaports in the War of 1812.
Total length 14.25 inches. Weight 2 lbs., 5 oz. The specimen
described is from the collection of Samuel E. Smith, Markesan, Wisconsin, and probably was made in Bridgewater,
Massachusetts. It definitely belongs in the U. S. Martial
Flintlock Pistol classification. Figure 11.

PICKEL PISTOL, also known as PICKELL PISTOL, also
known as U. S. PISTOL, CONTRACT MODEL 1807–1808,
made by Henry Pickel, who also spelled his name Pickell.
He was a manufacturer of muskets in York, Pennsylvania.
Working with Jacob Doll and Conrad Welshanze, he was a
contractor with the Commonwealth of Pennsylvania for making 1,000 Charleville-pattern muskets, under an agreement
signed April 17, 1801. Later, Pickel (or Pickell) contracted
with Tench Coxe, U. S. Purveyor of Public Supplies, to
deliver 100 rifles, under an agreement signed December 9,
1807. There is a belief that he made U. S. martial flintlock
pistols, but the author has never examined a pistol which
could be attributed to him. Some authorities believe that he
made pistols according to the pattern of the U. S. Pistol,
Model 1807–1808.

SHANNON (WILLIAM & HUGH) CONTRACT PISTOL,
MODEL 1807–1808. William and Hugh Shannon are among

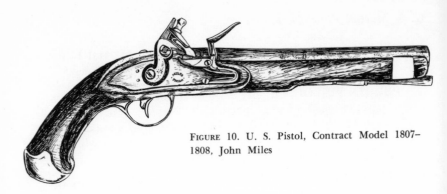

FIGURE 10. U. S. Pistol, Contract Model 1807–1808, John Miles

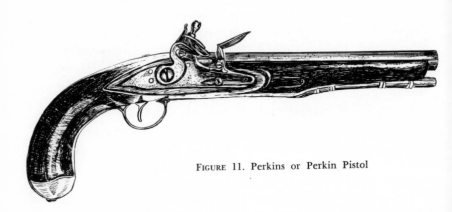

FIGURE 11. Perkins or Perkin Pistol

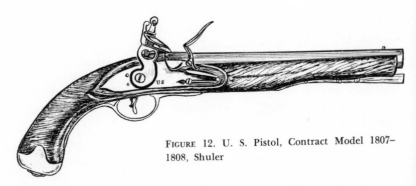

FIGURE 12. U. S. Pistol, Contract Model 1807–1808, Shuler

those frequently mentioned as contractors for the Model 1807–1808 Pistol. The author has never examined one which could be attributed to the Shannons, hence their pistol is not illustrated. We do know that William Shannon was a gunmaker in Philadelphia from 1805 to 1807; that William and Hugh Shannon worked together from 1809 to 1811; and that they also had a gun business from 1813 to 1816. William Shannon worked alone from 1817 to 1820 and Hugh Shannon worked by himself from 1819 to 1820. These facts can be found in city directories of Philadelphia and from other sources.

On November 9, 1808, W. & H. Shannon were the signers of a contract with the United States to make 4,000 muskets to be delivered during a period of five years. It is recorded that they delivered at least 1,000 on or before October 7, 1812. Therefore, they made weapons for federal use in the War of 1812 and deserve at least brief mention.

U. S. PISTOL, CONTRACT MODEL 1807-1808, SHULER, cal. .54, 9.625-inch, round, iron, smoothbore, pin-fastened barrel, marked "SHULER", although some collectors report specimens with barrels up to 10.5 inches. Total length with the conventional 9.625-inch barrel is 16 inches. Weight with the conventional barrel, 2 lbs., 5.5 oz. Full-length walnut stock extending to 0.0625 inch from the muzzle, reinforced by brass band. Brass-mounted. The butt has a brass butt cap with short, rounded, curved extensions. No back strap. Brass, blade-type front sight. No rear sight. Brass trigger guard of the loop type characteristic of the period. Beveled iron pan with fence. Double-neck hammer. Hickory ramrod. Flat, beveled lock plate marked "U S", and also with the date. The "U S" may be horizontally marked at the lower edge of the lock plate, forward of the hammer, and the date is usually marked at the rear of the lock plate, approximately at a 90-degree angle to the barrel. In other words, if the pistol were held with the barrel in a vertical position, the date would then be horizontal.

This pistol, illustrated in Figure 12, was made by John

Shuler, Liverpool, Pennsylvania, and resembles the John Joseph Henry Pistol, Model 1807–1808, made in Philadelphia, as well as other pistols of this period made under contract not only for the state troops but also for the United States. It is believed that this pistol was made as late as 1812. Undoubtedly it was used in the War of 1812 and in campaigns conducted by the armed forces of the United States after the War of 1812.

U. S. CONTRACT PISTOL, MODEL 1807–1808, SWEITZER, cal. .54, 10.5-inch, round, smoothbore, pin-fastened barrel marked with letters "C T" and an eagle inside an oval. Total length 16 inches. Weight 2 lbs., 6 oz. Full-length walnut stock extends to 0.0625 inch from muzzle. Brass-mounted. Brass, blade-type front sight, mounted on barrel. No rear sight. Brass trigger guard forks at rear to form the trigger guard in the conventional manner of the flintlock era and then extends along the forward, front edge or surface of the butt. No back strap. Straight trigger. Flat, bevel-edged, double-neck hammer. The iron pan with fence is not made integral with the lock plate but as a separate part. Hickory ramrod. Flat, bevel-edged lock plate marked "SWEITZER & CO." in two parallel lines between the hammer and the frizzen spring. The butt has a brass butt cap which has short, rounded extensions, sometimes called tangs, on the sides of the butt.

Collectors and historians believe, but do not know definitely, that this pistol was made by Daniel Sweitzer & Co., Lancaster, Pennsylvania, which publicly advertised in 1808 that it was a gunlock factory. The Sweitzer pistol resembles the U. S. Pistol, Model 1807–1808, made by other contractors, and it has been listed for many years as a U. S. Secondary Martial Flintlock Pistol. The author of this text believes it belongs in U. S. Martial Flintlock Pistol category. Not illustrated.

U. S. CONTRACT PISTOL, MODEL 1807–1808, WINNER, NIPPES & STEINMAN. The manufacturers of this pistol were Pennsylvania musket makers who had a contract with the United States, dated July 20, 1808, to make and deliver 9,000 muskets during a period of five years. We know that they made and delivered 3,900 on or before October 7, 1812. There are several bits of evidence which indicate that they were among the many contractors who made the U. S. Pistol, Model 1807–1808. For some reason, we can find many records regarding the manufacture of rifles, carbines, muskets, and musketoons, but few archives confirm the manufacture of U. S. martial pistols, possibly because pistols in that era were not regarded as important by the men who kept the records. Since no specimen has been examined by the author, there is no illustration, but we include Winner, Nippes & Steinman in the hope that future research will lead to the discovery of an authentic specimen of their manufacture.

U. S. PISTOL, CONTRACT MODEL 1808, S. NORTH, NAVY, cal. .64, round, smoothbore, pin-fastened, browned, unmarked barrel, 10.125 inches long, with no proofmarks. Full walnut stock extends to within 0.25 inch from muzzle. Total length 16.25 inches. Weight 2 lbs., 14 oz. No sights. Brass-mounted. Hickory ramrod. Iron belt hook on left, characteristic of Navy-type pistols. Double-neck hammer. Horizontal brass pan with fence. Lock plate marked "U. STATES" between hammer and frizzen spring, with an eagle, and "S. NORTH, BERLIN, CON." in three lines behind hammer. Figure 13.

This is called a Navy pistol because it was made by Simeon North under contract with the U. S. Navy to be used as a boarding pistol. The iron belt hook on the left was used to fasten the pistol to a belt, trousers, or a sash, worn by seamen or marines. Although the usual pan of a pistol of this period was made of iron, this particular Simeon North model was made of brass because it was less subject to salt-water corrosion than the conventional iron pan. Although the mountings, also called furniture, are usually described as made of brass, they were made of both brass and bronze.

There were two contracts, one of 1808 and the other of

1810. Pistols made under both contracts were used during the War of 1812. Historians often say that this was the only official, regular U. S. Martial flintlock pistol made without proofmarks on the barrel, but this statement, like all other remarks about flintlock pistols, is subject to exceptions.

After the completion of the contract for the U. S. Pistol, Model 1799, North & Cheney, Simeon North made farm tools until June 30, 1808, when he obtained the contract for the U. S. Pistol, Model 1808, S. North, Navy, which forced him to enlarge his factory, develop specialization of workmanship by letting certain men make particular parts, and thereby obtain a degree of standardization of interchangeable parts. Previously, a gunsmith usually would make all parts of a pistol, although a few men had long specialized in making barrels, stocks, and other major parts. When Simeon North started the practice of specialization, he saved time and money and produced better pistols for government use, although it meant that he had to buy all his materials in advance instead of purchasing just enough for a week or two of production.

When the contract for the Model 1808 to the extent of 2,000 Navy pistols was approved on December 4, 1810, Simeon North signed a contract with the Navy to manufacture additional pistols.

Previously, in 1808, Congress had passed laws for the arming and equipment of the militia of the states by the United States. Since the Armories at Springfield and Harpers Ferry were not able to produce enough arms, the United States continued to buy weapons from private contractors.

In this model, in addition to the barrel, the trigger, thimble, and forward portion of the trigger guard are pin-fastened. The expanded, rounded-in butt is reinforced by an iron back strap reaching from the tang to a butt-cap extension. The brass butt cap, which is sometimes described as umbrella-shaped, has a slight ridge at the forward portion and reaches a point on each side. The brass trigger guard divides at the rear to complete a streamlined oval shape. The rear extension of the trigger guard extends under the butt and comes to an end slightly forward of the butt cap. The sides of the forward end of the trigger guard are sometimes described as "pinched in," but this merely means that they were designed to be streamlined with the stock.

Pistols similar to the U. S. Pistol, Model 1808, S. North, Navy, marked with the spread eagle and "U. STATES" on the lock plate, with a lock plate of heavier construction and a slightly greater length, are sometimes mistaken for this model, but the absence of the "S. NORTH, BERLIN, CON." mark, and the physical differences, show that such pistols were made by other contractors.

U. S. PISTOL, CONTRACT MODEL 1811 (1810), S. NORTH, ARMY, cal. .69, with 8.625-inch, round, smoothbore, pin-fastened barrel marked with "V", and eagle head with letters "CT" within the same oval. Full-length walnut stock extends to within 0.25 inch from muzzle. Total length 15 inches. Weight 2 lbs., 11 oz. Lock plate 5.188 inches long and 1.05 inches wide. Brass trigger guard 6.25 inches long with pointed ends. Double-neck hammer. Brass pan with fence. Umbrella-shaped brass butt cap. Lock plate marked with eagle and "U. STATES" between hammer and frizzen spring, and marked "S. NORTH BERLIN CON." in three lines behind hammer. Figure 14.

A variation of this pistol is made with one band, whereas the standard model is pin-fastened. The barrel in the variation is slightly longer. The stock in the variation is almost two inches shorter and the trigger guard is very slightly longer with round instead of pointed ends.

Simeon North, Berlin, Connecticut, received a contract from the United States to make one thousand pairs (2,000) of this pistol under the Federal Act of 1808 and provided for under the contract of 1811. This required the delivery of a pistol similar to the U. S. Model 1808, S. North, Navy, but without the belt hook, in order to arm mounted troops in the War of 1812. This is the reason we use the year 1811 as the preferred model year and place within parentheses after

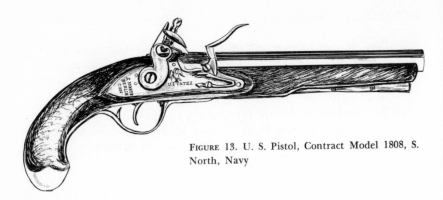

FIGURE 13. U. S. Pistol, Contract Model 1808, S. North, Navy

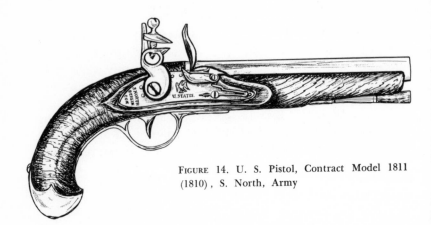

FIGURE 14. U. S. Pistol, Contract Model 1811 (1810), S. North, Army

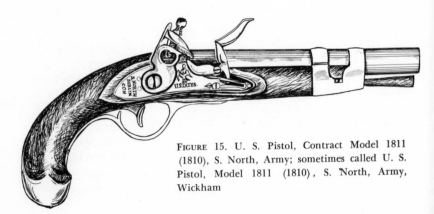

FIGURE 15. U. S. Pistol, Contract Model 1811 (1810), S. North, Army; sometimes called U. S. Pistol, Model 1811 (1810), S. North, Army, Wickham

1811 the year 1810, which is the model year erroneously
given this pistol by some collectors, dealers, and authors in
the past.

The contract was between Tench Coxe, U. S. Purveyor of
Supplies, acting for the War Department, and Simeon North.
It is not of tremendous importance whether the contract was
signed in 1810 or 1811. The important features of the contract are specifications for cavalry pistols, sometimes called
horse pistols, similar in design to the U. S. Pistol, Model
1808, S. North, Navy, except that the Army wanted the
caliber to be .69 instead of .64; the barrel was to be shorter
than the Navy model; and the pistol was to be made without
the Navy belt hook. Incidentally, the armed forces of the
United States are still arguing about the use of the same
hand and shoulder arms by the Army, Navy, Marine Corps,
Air Force, and Coast Guard.

Some historians dispute the number of pistols required
under the contract for the Model 1811 (1810). They argue
that the original contract was for about 5,000 pistols. This is
difficult to prove or disprove. However, in executing contracts in flintlock and percussion days, the manufacturer might
assemble lock plates, barrels, and other parts from an earlier
model to meet production demands and still legally comply
with contract specifications.

In the case of Simeon North, although his original plant
was at Berlin, Connecticut, he established a new factory at
Middletown, Connecticut, about the middle of 1813. It is
easy to believe that he did not discard parts made at Berlin,
but used any in stock when he assembled pistols at Middletown. This explains why all specimens are not marked the
same.

U. S. PISTOL, CONTRACT MODEL 1811 (1810), S.
NORTH, ARMY, sometimes called U. S. PISTOL, MODEL
1811 (1810) S. NORTH, ARMY, WICKHAM, is like the
U. S. Pistol, Model 1811 (1810), S. North, Army, except that
it has a double-strap band, sometimes called an improved
double front band. This pistol is illustrated in Figure 15.

Marine T. Wickham was a musket manufacturer in Philadelphia, Pennsylvania, and had a contract dated July 19, 1822, to make 5,000 muskets to be made and delivered at the rate of 2,000 per year beginning January 1, 1823. On December 6, 1823, he signed another contract to make and deliver 10,000 more muskets at a rate of 2,000 muskets per year, beginning July 1, 1824. Furthermore, he had a contract with the U. S. Navy to make and deliver muskets and an additional contract with the U. S. Army, dated January 24, 1829.

From 1811 to 1815, he was a U. S. Inspector of Arms for one of the federal ordnance districts, which was not inconsistent in that era with being at the same time a contractor making arms for the United States. Specialists in arms of this period contend that the specimen described here was not marked by Wickham, although in the past some collectors and historians have insisted on the Wickham marking to establish this particular variation.

U. S. PISTOL, CONTRACT MODEL 1813, S. NORTH, ARMY, cal. .69, 9-inch, smoothbore, round barrel with semi-octagonal breech (sometimes described as an octagonal breech), banded to the stock with two straps, the forward strap not being fluted. Barrel marked "P" and "U S". Walnut stock, usually about 12.69 inches long, ends at forward edge of barrel band. Total length 15.3 inches. Weight 3 lbs., 6 oz. Iron-mounted. No sights. Trigger guard 5.56 inches long with round ends. Brass pan without fence. Double-neck hammer. Lock plate marked "S. NORTH", followed by an eagle and "U S MIDln Con." between the hammer and the pan, with the "ln" of "MIDln" and the "on" of "Con." in lower-case letters. Figure 16.

On some specimens, the mark between the hammer and the pan is only "S. NORTH U S".

This was the first of the pistols made by Simeon North at his new and enlarged factory at Middletown, Connecticut. His first contract with the United States, dated April 16, 1813, required the delivery of 20,000 iron-mounted pistols to the armed forces of the United States, but only 1,156 pistols were delivered and accepted on or before June or July, 1815. It is believed that not more than 1,500 were manufactured.

Unconfirmed records indicate that the contract was not fully executed because the United States objected to excessive recoil. The original contract called for interchangeability of parts, but this was difficult to accomplish when gun parts were made by hand. Obviously, this contract did not provide for delivery in time to be effective during the War of 1812. A Navy model, with the belt hook on the left, is regarded by some collectors as worth more than the Army model.

In all variations of this model the double-strap band is spring-fastened by means of a stud between the two straps.

Some experts describe this pistol as having a barrel 9.0625 inches long, with a total length of 15.25 inches, but these dimensions, like others pertaining to early pistols, may be due to variations in manufacture or personal errors in measurement.

The rounded butt is reinforced by an iron back strap extending from the tang to the butt cap, which also is made of iron.

The flat lock plate is beveled at the front and somewhat rounded at the rear.

The original hickory ramrod was enlarged at the front with an iron, slotted ferrule, which is threaded internally to receive a bullet screw for removing a bullet, or for handling a cleaning patch.

As stated above, the true and original model was designed and made with a caliber .69 barrel, and fired a one-ounce round ball. Although we believe that not more than 1,500 were manufactured, some authorities state that 1,150 were delivered on or before June 22, 1815, which is not inconsistent with the idea that more were accepted later by the United States. The excessive recoil of this pistol led to the contract between the United States and Simeon North for the manufacture of the U. S. Pistol, Model 1816, S. North, Army, which had a reduced recoil because it was caliber .54 instead of caliber .69.

The Model 1813, S. North Army Pistol was used in the campaigns against the Seminole Indians, commonly called the Seminole War. However, other handguns were used in the same campaigns. Calling the series of campaigns against the Seminoles a war is a debatable point with historians, but the pistol was used by the armed forces of the United States against those who opposed them, hence it is a martial pistol.

U. S. PISTOL, CONTRACT MODEL 1815, TRYON, PHILADELPHIA, cal. .69, smoothbore, round barrel marked "PHILADELPHIA". Some specimens have an iron barrel and others have a bronze barrel. Lock plate marked "TRYON" under the pan. Full stock. English proofmarks. George W. Tryon was not the manufacturer of this pistol but a contractor who assembled the parts for the United States and delivered the completed pistols to the U. S. Arsenal in Philadelphia, Pennsylvania, in 1815, although some may have been delivered as early as 1814. The lock and barrel were definitely bought in England under a contract. Total length 14.5 inches. Figure 17.

George W. Tryon was born in 1791, of French Huguenot ancestry, came to America, and as a boy was an apprentice for Frederick W. Goetz of Philadelphia, also known as Frederick W. Getz. In 1811, when Tryon was twenty, Goetz made him a partner in his gunsmithing business. Shortly afterward, Tryon bought Goetz's interest in the firm and operated under his own name at 165 North Second Street. By 1829 his business required a larger building and he moved to 134 North Second Street, later designated 220 North Second Street. This was only the beginning. Tryon and his descendants continued to import, manufacture, repair, and sell all types of firearms well into the present century. The whole story of the Tryon family and their gun business, generation after generation, through many wars, is a fascinating one, but beyond the scope of this text. We have presented these few facts to indicate that Tryon means much more than merely a name on a lock plate.

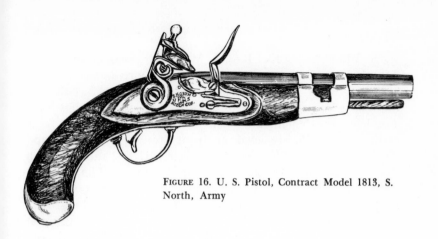

FIGURE 16. U. S. Pistol, Contract Model 1813, S. North, Army

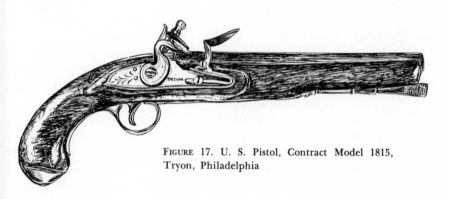

FIGURE 17. U. S. Pistol, Contract Model 1815, Tryon, Philadelphia

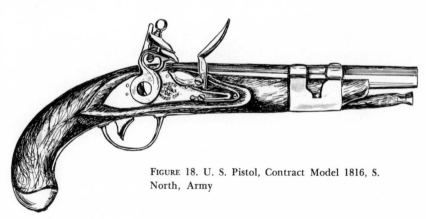

FIGURE 18. U. S. Pistol, Contract Model 1816, S. North, Army

115

U. S. PISTOL, CONTRACT MODEL 1816, S. NORTH, ARMY, cal. .54, round, 9-inch, smoothbore barrel marked "P" and "U S" with initials of either the barrel maker or the man who proof-tested the barrel. Stock 13.25 inches long. Total length 15.3 inches. Lock plate 5.25 inches long, 1.125 inches wide, flat, beveled at front, rounded at rear, and marked "S. NORTH", with an eagle, "U S", and "MIDLn Con." between the pan and the hammer. The "n" in "MIDLn" and the "on" in "Con." are lower-case letters. Weight 3 lbs., 3 oz. Trigger guard 5.56 inches long with rounded ends. Iron-mounted. Double-strap barrel band. Iron butt strap. Brass front sight. Brass pan without fence. Hickory ramrod, made with slotted iron ferrule, threaded to remove a bullet or to be used with a cleaning patch. Double-neck hammer. Figure 18.

A variation of this model has a lock plate marked "S. NORTH", an eagle, "U S", and "MIDLtn Conn.", using a "t" in the abbreviation for the town and an extra "n" in the abbreviation for the state.

Some historians contend that this Model 1816, S. North, was made in caliber .54 to reduce the recoil obtained with the Model 1813, S. North, which was caliber .69, and that otherwise the two models are very similar, overlooking the brass blade-type front sight on the Model 1816 and the fact that the flat portions at the breech of the Model 1813 were removed in the Model 1816.

As originally made, the lock and screws of the Model 1816 were casehardened to a gray color and the barrel and furniture were browned. The Model 1816 was used in the Black Hawk War (in which Abraham Lincoln served), the Seminole War, and the Mexican War.

The front sight is mounted on the forward strap of the double-strap barrel band, which in turn is held on the right side by a stud between the two straps. The rounded butt is strengthened by an iron strap extending from the tang to the butt cap, also made of iron.

In the contract for making the Model 1816, a sight was

required, the interchangeability of parts was to be followed as much as possible in an era when pistols were essentially made by hand, the tip of the stock was to extend beyond the barrel band, the stock was to be round throughout its length (that is, no part was to be hexagonal or any shape except round), the barrel was to be browned, the mountings were to be browned, and the lock was to be casehardened.

In 1850, many of these pistols were converted from flintlock to percussion and were used in the subsequent campaigns and wars of the United States, including the Civil War, when it was used in battle both by the Union Army and the Confederates.

Notice that the hammer in the illustration is of the so-called "double-neck" construction, which means that the portion of the hammer under the lower jaw has a cutaway area which is approximately oval in shape. The lower end of the hammer screw extends into this area. The reason for the so-called "double-neck" construction is that this design provides more strength than the simpler "single-neck" construction of the hammer found on many flintlock pistols. This feature is emphasized here not because it is unique in the U. S. Pistol, Model 1816, S. North, Army, but to provide a means of identifying this and other flintlock pistol hammers.

U. S. PISTOL, MODEL 1817 (1818), SPRINGFIELD, cal. .69, 11.06-inch, round, smoothbore barrel, held by a double-strap iron band with a brass sight mounted on the front strap. The barrel is marked over the breech plug "1818" and some specimens have an eagle head between "P" and "V". The lock plate is marked "SPRINGFIELD 1818" in three lines behind the hammer and "U S" under an eagle between the frizzen spring and the hammer. The word "SPRING-FIELD" is marked in the upper two of the three lines, broken into "SPRING" and "FIELD", above the year, behind the hammer. Figure 19.

In order to be classified as a conventional U. S. Pistol, Model 1817 (1818), Springfield, this pistol should have an ordinary frizzen, a lock plate with a blunt rear end, and a double-neck hammer, in addition to the markings described above.

If it has a frizzen resembling that of the French Charleville musket with turned-up toe and a lock plate resembling that of the Charleville, with a sharp teat-shaped rear end, it may be otherwise classified. Nevertheless, there is some doubt as to the actual issue of the Model 1817 (1818) Springfield to the armed forces, although it was assembled at the U. S. Armory, Springfield, Massachusetts, in 1818.

The weight is 3 lbs., 3 oz. The barrel band is held by a spring retained by a stud between the straps. The trigger guard, butt strap, and back strap are made of iron. The iron lock plate is 5.25 inches long and 1.0625 inches wide, with a beveled edge. The iron pan is forged as an integral part of the lock plate.

Although the author has not found evidence that this particular model was issued to or used by the armed forces of the United States, the fact that it was assembled at the U. S. Armory, Springfield, justifies its inclusion in this chapter.

U. S. PISTOL, CONTRACT MODEL 1819, S. NORTH, ARMY, cal. .54, round, 10-inch, smoothbore, browned barrel with brass sight on muzzle. The barrel is held by a single spring-fastened band, and it is marked "P", "U S", and with the initials of the man who proof-tested the barrel. Full-length walnut stock, 13.75 inches long. Total length 15.5 inches. Weight 2 lbs., 10 oz. Lock plate 4.625 inches long and 1 inch wide, marked "S. NORTH", with an eagle, "U S", MIDLTN CONN", between the hammer and the frizzen spring. The trigger guard is 5.25 inches long with round ends. Iron-mounted. Brass pan without fence. Double-neck hammer. Sliding safety bolt on outside of lock near hammer. The catch behind the cock on the lock plate is of a unique design. There is a rear sight. The year, which is either 1821 or 1822, is marked behind the hammer.

This Model 1819, S. North, Army, was the first U. S. Martial Flintlock Pistol which had an iron swivel ramrod built into the pistol to eliminate the problems caused by the separate hickory ramrod supplied with previous models and types. Unfortunately, the cavalrymen found that the sliding bolt made it difficult to draw the pistol from the saddle holster; hence this feature was not retained in the later models. Figure 20.

One variation bears additional marks, such as "S.N.Y.", for the State of New York.

Simeon North browned the barrels and iron mountings for this model with acid. The barrel is held by a spring-fastened, single band which resembles the lower (rear) band of a musket of that period. The flat lock plate is beveled in the forward portion and rounded at the rear. The sliding bolt behind the hammer was supposed to retain the hammer at the safety position when it was half cocked, but this feature was not successful.

This pistol with its 10-inch barrel and other features was better balanced for aiming than the Model 1816, S. North, Army, which had a 9-inch barrel. Also, the longer barrel on the Model 1819 provided an increased sighting radius (distance between sights), which improved accuracy of aimed fire. It was designed primarily as a cavalry pistol to be carried in a saddle holster by officers, enlisted cavalrymen, mounted messengers, and artillerymen armed with pistols. The swivel-type ramrod made it easier to load on horseback and the possibility of losing the old-type separate ramrod was eliminated.

Since the design and construction of this pistol provided two sights, front and rear, it is important to realize that when the commissioned officers of an organization armed with pistols supervised marksmanship practice emphasizing accuracy of aiming, the enlisted men armed with a good flintlock pistol, such as this model, could and did achieve a comparatively high degree of success with aimed fire, even when both the United States soldier and his enemy were in motion.

Troops armed with pistols having no sights, or only a front sight, and also troops armed with pistols having two sights if they had not been previously trained in pistol marksmanship could not and did not do more than aim in the general direction of the enemy.

These statements about the use of sights and marksmanship training before battle apply throughout the military and naval history of the United States. Unfortunately, many officers from colonial days up to and including World War I believed that the delivery of a shower of bullets in the general direction of the enemy was sufficient to insure that at least some of the enemy were hit. Those officers throughout the history of the United States who believed in and carried out marksmanship practice were the ones whose men suffered fewer casualties and killed more of the enemy.

U. S. PISTOL, CONTRACT MODEL 1826, S. NORTH, ARMY and NAVY, cal. .54, 8.625-inch, round, smoothbore, browned barrel held by a single spring-fastened band. The barrel has a brass sight at the muzzle. The barrel is marked "P", "U S", and with initials. Total length of pistol 13.25 inches. Weight 2 lbs., 4 oz. Full-length walnut stock. Iron-mounted. Swivel-type ramrod. No safety bolt. Double-neck hammer. Brass pan without fence. Lock plate marked "U S" and "S. NORTH", in two lines between the hammer and the frizzen spring. The year—1827 or 1828 on specimens known to the author—is marked on the lock plate behind the hammer.

This pistol has a belt hook on the left, held by a separate screw and pin. Many specimens have tinned barrels. Fundamentally, this is a Navy model because of the belt hook, the tinned barrel, and a contract known to have been executed between the Navy and Simeon North. But since this pistol also was used by the Army, we have classified it as an Army and Navy pistol, although a strict construction of the background might throw it into the Navy classification. Figure 21.

U. S. PISTOL, CONTRACT MODEL 1826, W. L. EVANS, NAVY, cal. .54, 8.625-inch, round, smoothbore, browned barrel, held by a single spring-fastened band, with brass sight

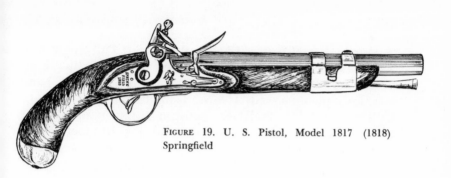

FIGURE 19. U. S. Pistol, Model 1817 (1818)
Springfield

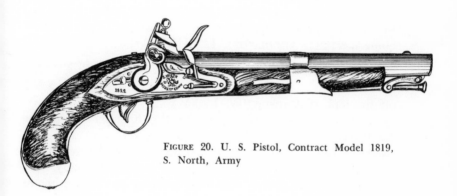

FIGURE 20. U. S. Pistol, Contract Model 1819,
S. North, Army

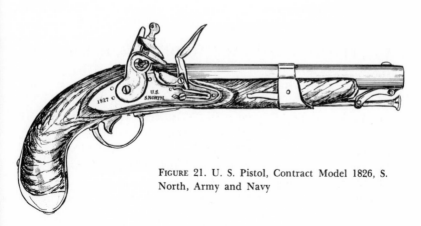

FIGURE 21. U. S. Pistol, Contract Model 1826, S.
North, Army and Navy

at muzzle. Barrel is marked "P". Rear sight. Full-length walnut stock. Total length 13.375 inches. Weight 2 lbs., 4 oz.
Brass pan without fence. Swivel ramrod. Double-neck hammer. Lock plate marked "U.S.N." behind hammer and "W.L.
EVANS" and "V. FORGE" between hammer and frizzen
spring, with the year marked behind the hammer. Some
specimens do not have the "V. FORGE" mark. Steel belt
hook on left, held by a separate screw and pin. Some specimens available today are found with a few parts tinned.

About one thousand pistols of this model, fundamentally
designed like the U. S. Pistol, Model 1826, S. North, were
made for the Navy in 1830 and 1831 by William L. Evans.
It is believed that the barrels were made at Valley Forge and
that other parts were made at Evansburg, Pennsylvania.
Some specimens are marked "E. BURG".

**U. S. PISTOL, CONTRACT MODEL 1826, W. L. EVANS,
ARMY,** same as above but marked "U.S." instead of "U.S.N."
on the lock plate over "W. L. EVANS", and with the year
marked on the lock plate behind the hammer as on the
Navy lock plate. Both the Navy and the Army models were
issued to and carried by the armed forces of the United States
until the beginning of the percussion era, when many were
converted to percussion and were used at the beginning of
the Civil War by both the Union and Confederate forces.
Figure 22 illustrates the Army version, and is dated 1830
on the lock plate behind the hammer.

**U. S. PISTOL, CONTRACT MODEL 1836, R. JOHNSON,
ARMY,** cal. .54, 8.5-inch, round, smoothbore barrel, held to
stock by single branch band, and marked "U S", "P", and
with initials. The three-quarters-length walnut stock is 11.125
inches long. Total length 14.25 inches. Weight 2 lbs., 10
oz. Flat, beveled lock plate 4.65 inches long and 1 inch wide,
marked "U S", "R. JOHNSON", "MIDDN CONN", and
the year, in four horizontal lines between the hammer and
the frizzen spring.

There is a brass front sight on the barrel. Rear sight.

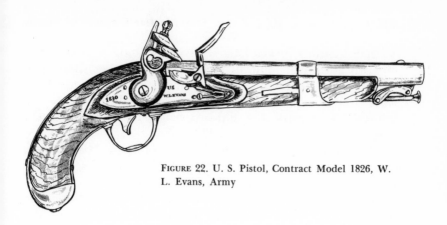

FIGURE 22. U. S. Pistol, Contract Model 1826, W. L. Evans, Army

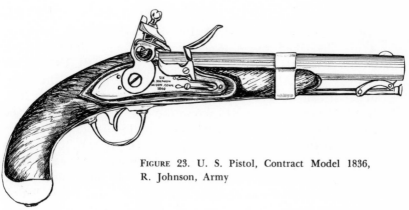

FIGURE 23. U. S. Pistol, Contract Model 1836, R. Johnson, Army

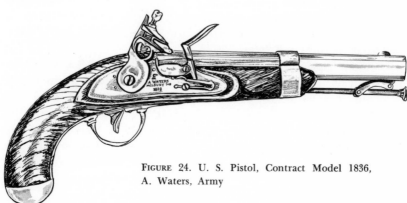

FIGURE 24. U. S. Pistol, Contract Model 1836, A. Waters, Army

123

Trigger guard 5 inches long with round ends. Polished iron mountings. Swivel ramrod. Double-neck hammer. Brass pan with fence. The barrel and all other parts, except the lock, barrel tang, and the trigger, were finished bright at the factory. Those parts not finished bright were casehardened gray.

This pistol was made by Robert Johnson, Middletown, Connecticut, from 1836 to 1844. Many of his pistols were used in the Mexican War. Figure 23.

Like many other martial flintlock pistols; many were converted to percussion and were used at the outbreak of the Civil War by both Union and Confederate forces.

U.S. PISTOL, CONTRACT MODEL 1836, A. WATERS, ARMY, cal. .54, same as U. S. Pistol, Model 1836, R. Johnson, Army, described above, except for markings. The lock plate is marked with an eagle head over "A. WATERS", which is over "MILBURY MS", and the latter is over the year, hence it can be said that the lock plate is marked with four parallel, horizontal marks, counting the eagle head and the year as two of the lines. Illustrated in Figure 24.

Asa Waters, Jr., and his son, Asa H. Waters, made this pistol at Millbury (also spelled Milbury), Massachusetts. Nineteen thousand were supposedly made and sold to the United States by the Waters family. Like the U. S. Pistol, Contract Model 1836, Army, R. Johnson, these were the last of the U. S. Martial Flintlock Pistols and were used in the Mexican War. Converted later to percussion, some were used in the Civil War.

Some specimens are marked "A. H. WATERS & CO." instead of "A. WATERS". Regardless of how they are marked, collectors value the Waters pistol slightly lower than the R. Johnson pistol, probably because the demand for the R. Johnson pistol is greater and the supply is less. Except for the markings they are as much alike as it was possible to make flintlock pistols.

CHAPTER 4

U.S. Secondary Martial Flintlock Pistols

DEFINITION

U. S. Secondary Martial Flintlock Pistols are those large-caliber, large-size, single-shot, flintlock pistols, suitable in design and construction for the use of the armed forces of the United States of America, which cannot be described accurately as U. S. Martial Flintlock Pistols and which fall into one of the following groups:

1. Pistols made by individuals, partnerships, companies, or corporations which had contracts with the United States to make U. S. Martial Flintlock Pistols, but also made pistols for the militia of the several states, volunteer military and naval organizations, officers who bought pistols from their own funds, ship officers of privateers, and state forces of various types who were not called into federal service.

2. Pistols made by contractors who did not have a contract with the United States, but were contractors with the states, or had contracts with semiofficial, volunteer military or naval organizations.

3. Pistols made by private enterprise for sale to individuals, such as officers of the federal service, the militia, and semi-official military or naval volunteer organizations, or for sale to enlisted men who bought arms from their own funds.

Pistols in this group were made by individuals, partnerships, companies, or corporations not known to have had contracts with either the United States or any of the states.

4. Pistols sold to owners, officers, and members of the crews of privateers by manufacturers who did not have contracts with either the United States or the government of any state. A privateer is an armed, privately owned vessel, authorized by a sovereign power to go to sea against either vessels of war or merchant vessels of the enemy and destroy or capture them. Privateers usually sailed with letters of marque and reprisal in possession of the captain of the privateer. Originally, these letters were granted by a sovereign as authorization to seize the subjects of an enemy ruler and to seize and keep the property (including vessels, of course) belonging to the enemy ruler or his subjects, supposedly in reprisal for alleged wrongs.

Shortly before the United States came into official existence as a nation, some of the American colonies issued such letters of marque and reprisal. After the Revolution began, and especially after the Declaration of Independence was signed, both the United States and individual states issued such letters. Throughout the American Revolution, private individuals were commissioned in this manner to arm their own vessels, arm their crews, and cruise the seas as privateers (sometimes called corsairs) for the purpose of capturing enemy vessels and cargo, and also to bombard enemy ports.

The Declaration of Paris, signed by several of the leading nations of the world at Paris, France, April 16, 1856, stated that privateering "is and remains abolished by the signatory powers." The United States of America did not sign this document, but after 1856 the United States never again commissioned privateers, or issued letters of marque and reprisal. However, both individual states of the Confederacy, and the Confederate States of America commissioned privateers for action against the United States directly and for running the Union blockade.

5. Pistols in this group were experimental, speculative, or

sample weapons, made by manufacturers who did not have contracts with either the United States or any of the states, who hoped to obtain a contract, or who anticipated the sale of pistols to semiofficial military or naval organizations, or to civilians.

6. Pistols in this group are those which by tradition or legend were used by the armed forces of the United States, about which there is not sufficient evidence to classify them as United States Martial Pistols.

GENERAL COMMENTS ON U. S. SECONDARY MARTIAL FLINTLOCK PISTOLS

1. The presence of the "U S" or similar United States mark on a pistol does not necessarily mean that it is a United States Martial Pistol, nor does its absence mean that it must be classified as a U. S. Secondary Martial Flintlock Pistol. Each pistol must be judged on its own merits by examining it as a whole rather than relying upon one or two characteristics.

2. The pistols described and illustrated in this chapter are those generally accepted by experienced collectors, dealers and historians as U. S. Secondary Martial Flintlock Pistols. Undoubtedly, there are many pistols not mentioned here which future research will bring into this classification. In a similar manner, evidence obtained in the future may advance some of these pistols to the U. S. Martial classification.

3. Flintlock dueling pistols of martial caliber and size were sometimes carried into battle and fired at the enemy, even though they were not intended by design or construction for the rough usage of warfare. Dueling pistols used in battle cannot be classified either as U. S. Martial or U. S. Secondary Martial Pistols. This applies to both flintlock and percussion dueling pistols; hence we classify such martially used pistols as Semi-Martial and place them in a chapter on Dueling Pistols.

4. Single-shot Kentucky pistols of martial size and caliber, both flintlock and percussion, unless they meet the require-

ments set forth for U. S. Martial or U. S. Secondary Martial Pistols, are described and illustrated in a chapter on Kentucky Pistols, because they are *semi-martial,* but not U. S. Martial or U. S. Secondary Martial Pistols.

5. Confederate pistols òf martial size and caliber obviously cannot be given a "United States" designation, either as U. S. Martial or U. S. Secondary Martial Pistols; hence they are regarded as semi-martial from the United States viewpoint and placed in a chapter of their own. This applies to both flintlock and percussion pistols.

However, many United States Martial Pistols and United States Secondary Martial Pistols, both flintlock and percussion, were in the possession of the Southern states before they revolted; many were captured on the field of battle; and a surprisingly large number were bought in the North after the Civil War began, and shipped to the Confederacy. In addition, machinery, tools and parts captured at Harpers Ferry were used by the Confederacy, hence it is often difficult to identify accurately Confederate arms as weapons made or used by the Confederacy. Confederate marks by themselves do not justify identifying arms as Confederate.

COMMITTEE OF SAFETY AND CONTINENTAL ARMY AND NAVY PISTOLS

After the Battle of Lexington in 1775, the various British colonies which later became the United States of America began to form Committees of Safety for the purpose of acquiring arms, ammunition, and equipment for the soldiers, sailors, and marines organized to fight the British.

Since the early effort was started by colonies or provinces, the weapons which they bought or had made cannot, in the strict sense of the term, be regarded as United States arms. They are properly classified as Committee of Safety weapons.

Those authorized by the Continental Congress, before there was a United States of America, also can be placed in the secondary category. However, this is a field of overlapping which is subject to revision as we learn more about our early weapons. Many of the pistols formerly classified as U. S. Secondary Martial Flintlock Pistols have been advanced in this text to the U. S. Martial group.

ORDER OF LISTING SECONDARY MARTIAL FLINTLOCK PISTOLS

The dearth of reliable records showing when colonies or provinces signed contracts for the manufacture of martial pistols, the absence of records showing when manufacture began, and other gaps in our early history require the grouping of U. S. Secondary Martial Flintlock Pistols more or less alphabetically. But when there is some shred of evidence indicating the year of the contract or the year of manufacture of the pistol, we place it earlier in the chapter than the name of the maker would otherwise warrant.

COMMITTEE OF SAFETY PISTOL. This pistol of large size and martial caliber was probably made in accordance with a Resolution of the Continental Congress in 1776 providing that a committee "provide arms for 3,000 horse," which would mean 6,000 pistols. Contracts were let in York and Lancaster, Pennsylvania, in the region famous for the development and manufacture of Kentucky flintlock pistols and rifles. The crude workmanship of the specimen illustrated in Figure 1 is not consistent with the quality of the so-called "Kentucky" pistols and rifles. The reason is probably the haste with which the Committees of Safety operated to arm the American forces.

This is a cavalry-type pistol, cal. .60, with a 9.5-inch, smoothbore barrel. The total length is 15.5 inches and the weight is 1 lb., 12 oz. It has thin brass mountings, a brass fore tip (front end of stock), and a full-length maple stock. It was found in an attic in York, Pennsylvania, in 1953, and is now in the collection of Samuel E. Smith, Markesan, Wisconsin, who has identified it as a Committee of Safety Pistol even though it is unmarked.

BIRD & CO. PISTOL. C. Bird & Co. were gunsmiths from about 1812 to about 1820. Many experts believe they were basically specialists in the manufacture of lock plates, but there is a pistol with a lock plate marked in three horizontal lines between the hammer and the frizzen spring: "C. BIRD & CO.", "PHILADa", and "WARRANTED". The last letter in "PHILADa" is a lower-case "a" dropped below the horizontal line on which the capital letters rest. This pistol is cal. .58, with a 12-inch, round, tapering, smoothbore, pin-fastened, brass barrel marked "Philadelphia" on some specimens, while others have an unmarked barrel. The total length is 17 inches and the weight is 2 lbs., 5 oz. It has an iron pan with a fence, an iron trigger guard, and iron mountings in general. The hammer is of the gooseneck type. There is a full-length walnut stock and a hickory ramrod. This pistol is not illustrated in this chapter because a pistol exactly like this with Confederate marks is illustrated in Chapter 10, "Confederate Pistols."

BOOTH PISTOL (Figure 2), cal. .58, with an 8-inch, brass, round, tapered, smoothbore, pin-fastened barrel without sights, marked on top "PHILADELPHIA". Total length 13.5 inches. Weight 2 lbs., 5 oz. Brass-mounted. Iron pan with fence. Brass trigger guard. Full-length walnut stock extends to within 0.125 inch from muzzle. Hickory ramrod. Gooseneck hammer. The flat lock plate is flush with the stock and marked "BOOTH" under the pan between the hammer and the frizzen spring, but the name on the specimen available is so faint that it cannot be shown accurately in the illustration.

William Booth, who made this pistol, was active as a gun manufacturer from 1797 to 1816, and it is known that he had a shop in Philadelphia from 1798 to 1816. He made martial pistols and also made and rented dueling pistols. The specimen illustrated was probably used in the War of 1812 and later.

CHERINGTON PISTOL, cal. .45, 12.25-inch, octagon, pin-fastened, smoothbore barrel, marked "T.P. CHERINGTON". Total length 17.75 inches, although sometimes given as

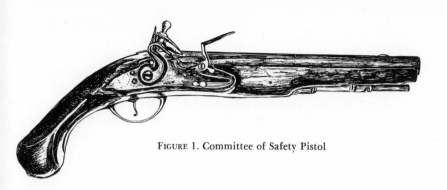

FIGURE 1. Committee of Safety Pistol

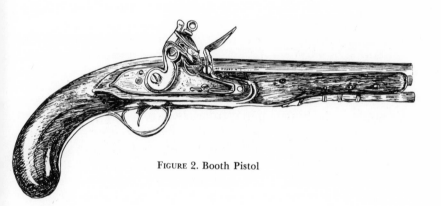

FIGURE 2. Booth Pistol

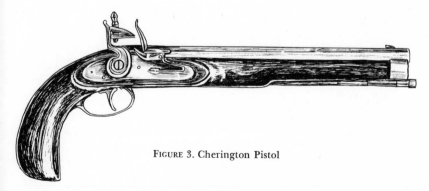

FIGURE 3. Cherington Pistol

17.625 inches. Weight 3 lbs., 1 oz. Full-length walnut stock has brass end cap near muzzle. Brass thimbles, front sight, and pan with fence. Iron trigger guard. Flat gooseneck hammer. Hickory ramrod, brass-tipped. Flat lock plate marked "T.P. CHERINGTON" between the hammer and the frizzen. Bird-shaped butt without back strap or butt cap.

Thomas P. Cherington made pistols and rifles at Cattawissa, Pennsylvania, during the flintlock era.

He is not to be confused with his son, Thomas P. Cherington, Jr., who made pistols and rifles at the same place during both the flintlock and the percussion periods. The absence of date and other information on this pistol makes it difficult to classify, but traditionally it has been regarded as a U. S. Secondary Martial Flintlock Pistol.

It is illustrated in Figure 3, but the marking on the lock plate is not shown because on the specimen available the marking is too faint to be reproduced accurately.

CONSTABLE PISTOL. Richard Constable, who had a gun business in Philadelphia from 1816 until 1851, imported parts from England and assembled them into arms at his shop. A flintlock pistol attributed to him is caliber .50, with a 10-inch, pin-fastened, round, smoothbore barrel marked on top "Philadelphia". The total length is 15.5 inches. Originally it had a brown finish. Brass-mounted. Walnut stock to within 1 inch from muzzle. Gooseneck hammer. Lock plate is marked "R. CONSTABLE". There is some reason to believe that this pistol was used after the War of 1812. It is not illustrated in this text.

COUTTY PISTOL, cal. .58, has a 7.75-inch, tapering, brass, pin-fastened, smoothbore barrel, without sights, marked "Philadelphia" with proofmarks. Lock plate marked "COUTTY" under the pan. Total length 13.5 inches. Weight 1 lb., 12 oz. Full walnut stock. Iron pan with fence. Gooseneck hammer. Brass trigger guard. Hickory ramrod.

Samuel Coutty worked for the Commonwealth of Pennsylvania from 1781 to 1788; hence his period extends from before the close of the Revolutionary War to a few years later. This particular specimen is a beautifully made holster pistol, the type carried by officers, wealthy enlisted men of the militia who were permitted to own and carry their own pistols in some organizations, and possibly by civilians who wanted a pistol for traveling on horseback.

This pistol is illustrated in Figure 4 but the name "COUTTY" under the pan on the lock plate is too faint on the available specimen for accurate reproduction in the picture.

W. L. EVANS PISTOL. U. S. Pistol, Contract Model 1826, W. L. Evans, was formerly classified as a U. S. Secondary Martial Pistol but in this book it is described and illustrated in Chapter 3 as a U. S. Martial Pistol.

GOLCHER FOUR-SHOT, SINGLE-BARREL PISTOL. This is not a single-shot pistol and there is not enough evidence to classify it as any type of martial pistol, although in the past it has been grouped with U. S. Secondary Martial Flintlock Pistols simply because collectors and dealers erroneously gave it this classification for many years.

GRUBB PISTOL, cal. .44, 8.75-inch, round, brass, key-fastened, smoothbore barrel marked "T. GRUBB". Some specimens have a barrel which is octagonal for the rear 4.375 inches and round for the front half. Total length 14.375 inches. Pin-fastened thimbles. Silver-mounted. Iron barrel tang. Horn-tipped walnut stock extends to 0.125 inch from muzzle. Silver front sight but no rear sight. Silver trigger guard forks at the rear to form a curl. The bird's-head butt has ornamental silver inserts and a silver butt cap. Flat gooseneck hammer. Iron pan with fence. Horn-tipped hickory ramrod. The flat lock plate is not marked, a peculiarity because the pistol is otherwise so carefully and elaborately made and ornamented.

This pistol is the type personally purchased by sea captains, officers of the militia, and wealthy men who wanted a holster pistol for horseback traveling. Its caliber and size place it in the martial type and although *there is no known record of its martial use,* it is tentatively classified as a U. S. Secondary Martial Pistol.

T. Grubb was a Philadelphia gunsmith who started in business at least as early as 1820. In addition to the flintlock holster pistol described here, he made at least one Kentucky (Pennsylvania) flintlock rifle with beautiful silver ornamentation and mountings. He also made flintlock Kentucky (Pennsylvania)-type dueling pistols in pairs, also beautifully mounted and ornamented with silver.

Since there is doubt about its martial use, the pistol is not illustrated in this text although future research may determine its classification.

HALBACH & SONS PISTOLS

HALBACH & SONS PISTOL, cal. .50, has a 6.75-inch, rifled, bronze barrel, part octagonal and part round, with cannon-type muzzle. The barrel is pin-fastened to the stock. Total length 12 inches. Bronze-mounted with brass butt cap ornamented with an American spread eagle, an American-type shield, and 13 stars. Flat, gooseneck hammer. Iron pan with fence. Lock plate marked "HALBACH & SONS". The stock is carved and there is a horn-tipped fore end. This specimen is described and illustrated in *The Gun Collectors Handbook of Values,* where it is listed as made about 1780, in Baltimore, Maryland, although some experts believe it was not made before 1785.

HALBACH & SONS SMOOTHBORE, BRASS-BARREL PISTOL, cal. .63, 7.675-inch, round, brass, smoothbore barrel. Total length 13.25 inches. The details generally correspond to those of the cal. .50, rifled-barrel specimen described above, except as to the use of brass instead of bronze, the lack of rifling, the barrel length, the total length, and the fact that the barrel is round throughout instead of being part-round, part-octagonal like the other specimen. The carved stock is characteristic of all known Halbach & Sons specimens.

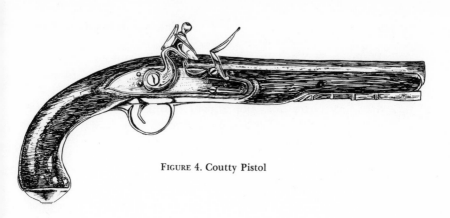

FIGURE 4. Coutty Pistol

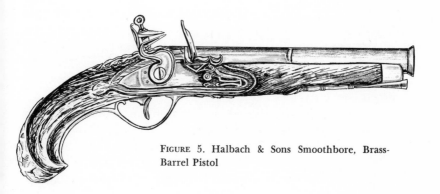

FIGURE 5. Halbach & Sons Smoothbore, Brass-Barrel Pistol

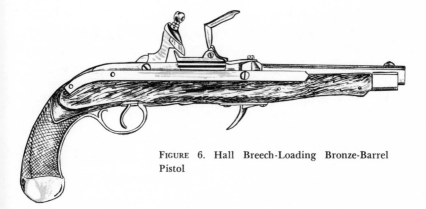

FIGURE 6. Hall Breech-Loading Bronze-Barrel Pistol

Halbach & Sons were listed in the Baltimore, Maryland, and in the Washington, D. C., city directories as manufacturers of cutlery and firearms as early as 1785. The fact that a directory entry does not appear before a certain date does not mean anything in itself, although it is often the best evidence available.

<h2 style="text-align:center">HALL BREECH-LOADING PISTOLS</h2>

HALL BREECH-LOADING BRONZE-BARREL PISTOL, cal. .50, has a 5.625-inch, bronze, octagon, smoothbore, pin-fastened barrel without marks. Total length 14.625 inches. Weight 2 lbs., 13 oz. Full-length walnut stock, capped with brass end band, and extending to within 0.25 inch from the muzzle. The butt is rounded and checked and has a brass butt cap. Brass, oval, pin-fastened trigger guard with the rear forking to complete the trigger-guard oval and then extending down the butt.

The specimen illustrated in Figure 6 has a brass butt cap, but some specimens have no butt cap. The pan is part of the bronze breechblock. Steel hammer and frizzen and iron or steel side straps or side plates. Bronze latch frame. The steel-blade front sight is set into the barrel by means of a wedge and is offset to the left to provide for correct aiming because of the construction of the hammer and pan. The trigger is offset to the right of the usual position. There is no rear sight. There is no mark on this pistol except a serial number on the right side of the breechblock.

Despite the lack of markings, this pistol was undoubtedly made by John H. Hall, because it is similar in design to the U. S. Rifle, Model 1819, John H. Hall Breechloader, which is one of the U. S. Martial Shoulder Arms. John H. Hall, of Yarmouth, Maine, obtained a U. S. patent for a breech-loading firelock (flintlock), March 21, 1811, and made a few shoulder arms and pistols based on his breech-loading principle between 1811 and 1816, at Portland, Maine. It is believed that this bronze-barrel pistol was made during this period, possibly in 1814. The lack of markings may indicate that it was one of his early experimental or pattern productions. In addition to the accompanying drawing, this pistol also is illustrated in *The Gun Collector's Handbook of Values.*

HALL BREECH-LOADING IRON-BARREL PISTOL, cal. .50, has a 7.125-inch, iron, octagon, key-fastened, rifled barrel. Total length 16.25 inches. Weight 2 lbs., 15 oz. Full walnut stock extends to within 0.625 inch from the muzzle, and is strengthened near the forward end by a silver band. The barrel is held to the stock by two keys. The oval-shaped butt is checked and is flat at the bottom end, where a silver butt plate is set into the wood so that it is flush with the surrounding wood. The iron pan is an integral part of the iron breechblock and not a separate unit. The silver trigger guard forks at the rear to complete the oval for the trigger guard and then extends along the forward surface of the butt. A brass-blade front sight is offset to the left to provide for aiming, which otherwise would be impossible because of the location of the hammer and pan along the center line. There is no rear sight. The breechblock is marked "John H. Hall Patent". Figure 7.

Like the Hall Breech-Loading Bronze-Barrel Pistol, this model, type, or variation is similar in operation to the U. S. Rifle, Model 1819, John H. Hall Breechloader, which is classified as one of the U. S. Martial Shoulder Arms. It was probably made later than the Bronze-Barrel Pistol, possibly in 1815.

In both specimens described, a locking catch or spur release in front of the trigger guard is pushed to the rear and upward to tip the breechblock upward to expose the chamber for loading. Figure 7 shows the left-side view of the iron-barrel pistol, but it also gives an excellent idea of how the bronze-barrel pistol looks from the left, allowing for minute variations between the two breechloaders.

U. S. SECONDARY MARTIAL FLINTLOCK PISTOLS MADE BY

HENRY FAMILY

In Chapter 3, we described and illustrated the U. S. Pistol, Contract Model 1807–1808, Henry (J.), made in Philadelphia by J. Henry, who may have been John Joseph Henry, as a U. S. Martial Flintlock Pistol. We also mentioned the fact that Abraham Henry was one of those who signed a contract with Tench Coxe, U. S. Purveyor of Public Supplies, on December 9, 1807, to deliver 200 pairs of pistols, but lacking evidence that Abraham Henry made any pistols in fulfillment of the contract, we did not describe or attempt to illustrate a pistol made by him.

The Henry pistols described and illustrated below must be classified as U. S. Secondary Martial Flintlock Pistols until such time as new evidence is discovered which will qualify them for upgrading to the U. S. Martial Flintlock Pistol classification.

J. HENRY PISTOL (Figure 8), cal. .62, with a 10-inch, octagonal, smoothbore, key-fastened barrel. The total length is 15.75 inches. It has a full-length walnut stock, extending to about 0.25 inch from the muzzle. In Figure 8, the hickory ramrod is not shown in place in order to illustrate the appearance of a martial flintlock pistol with its ramrod removed. However, the hollow brass tube under the forward portion of the stock indicates how the ramrod was guided from near the front of the muzzle, through the hollow tube, and into the stock when the ramrod was inserted. The pistol is brass-mounted. All versions have a brass butt cap and brass trigger guard. Some specimens have a brass front sight but the one illustrated was made without any sight. There is a flat, gooseneck hammer and an iron pan with a fence. The lock plate is marked "J. HENRY" between the hammer and the frizzen spring, and behind the hammer the lock plate is marked with two vertical slashes. It is possible that this pistol was made by the same J. Henry who made the U. S. Pistol, Contract Model 1807–1808, Henry (J.), but the ab-

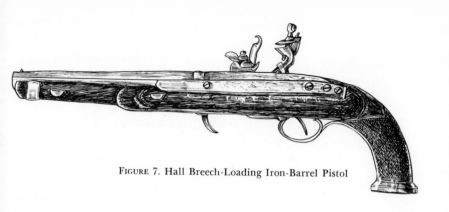

FIGURE 7. Hall Breech-Loading Iron-Barrel Pistol

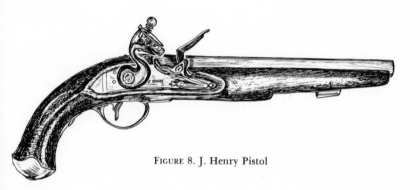

FIGURE 8. J. Henry Pistol

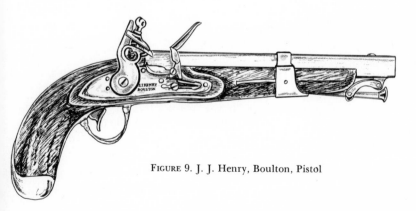

FIGURE 9. J. J. Henry, Boulton, Pistol

139

sence of federal marks and other indications of federal use combined with the knowledge that a J. Henry did make martial flintlock pistols for other than federal use place this specimen in the Secondary Martial group.

J. J. HENRY, BOULTON, PISTOL, SIMILAR TO U. S. PISTOL, CONTRACT MODEL 1826, S. NORTH, ARMY AND NAVY, AND U. S. PISTOL, CONTRACT MODEL 1826, W. L. EVANS.

This pistol is also known as the "J. J. Henry (Boulton) Pistol, Contract Model 1826 Type." The word "type" in this method of naming the pistol is used by some experts to indicate that they do not consider that the pistol was made for federal use but belongs in the U. S. Secondary Martial group, even though it superficially resembles the Contract Model 1826 Pistols made by S. North and W. L. Evans. Figure 9.

It is cal. .54, with an 8.5-inch, round, smoothbore barrel held to the stock by one band. Total length 13.5 inches. Weight 2 lbs., 4 oz. The band holding the barrel to the stock is spring-fastened and shaped like the lower band of a flintlock martial musket of that period. There is a low, knife-blade-type, brass front sight near the muzzle. The front end of the walnut stock is near the swivel of the swivel-type steel ramrod. The stock is sometimes described as "full-length" but Figure 9 clearly shows that it is impossible to have a walnut stock that is actually full-length when the pistol is equipped with the swivel for the ramrod. The butt is sometimes described as forming almost a 90-degree angle with the main portion of the stock, but such is not the case in the specimen illustrated.

An iron barrel tang, in which a large, open rear sight is cut, follows the curve of the upper portion of the stock as it slopes downward to form the round butt and it ends where it joins a very short extension of an iron butt cap.

The lock plate is flat. It has a beveled edge on its front portion. The rear of the lock plate on some specimens is rounded, but it comes to a sharp end on the specimen illustrated, although this does not mean that it has the so-called "teat" shape found on some martial flintlock lock plates.

The brass pan is tilted upward very slightly at the rear and it is made without a fence. The double-neck hammer with a rounded face is one of the salient points of identification of this model.

The steel, swivel-type ramrod at its small rear end is internally threaded to fit either a wiper head (to hold a cleaning patch) or a ball screw to remove a bullet.

The lock plate is marked in two lines, in capital letters, "J. J. HENRY" over "BOULTON", as shown in Figure 9. This indicates that the pistol was made by John Joseph Henry, at Boulton, Pennsylvania, although the Henry family also had a shop or factory in Philadelphia, which was the headquarters of the business. This was a militia pistol.

J. J. HENRY, BOULTON, PISTOL. The J. J. Henry, Boulton, Pistol illustrated in Figure 10 is entirely different from the one shown in Figure 9. It is cal. .58, with an 8.875-inch, round, smoothbore barrel, octagonal at the rear, and pin-fastened to the stock. Total length 14.5 inches. Weight 2 lbs., 3 oz. The full-length walnut stock extends to the muzzle. There is a low, blade-type, brass front sight. There is no rear sight. Brass-mounted. The brass butt cap has short, rounded extensions, often called spurs, on both sides of the butt for reinforcement. There is no back strap on this model.

The brass trigger guard forks at the rear to form the trigger-guard oval, but the upper rear portion of the oval does not touch the stock in the specimen illustrated.

There is a flat, gooseneck hammer with a beveled edge. The iron pan has a fence. The frizzen spring has a roller to reduce friction as explained earlier in this text in describing the function of the roller. The presence of the roller indicates clearly that this specimen was made in the latter part of the flintlock era. There is a hickory ramrod with an enlarged forward end (swell tip).

The flat lock plate with a beveled edge is marked in two lines between the hammer and the frizzen spring "J.J.

HENRY" over "BOULTON". There is a medium amount of engraving on the lock plate and the hammer.

The three vertical objects on the barrel and four vertical objects on the ramrod are wire, iron or steel reinforcing bands found on the specimen illustrated although other specimens examined do not have these reinforcements; hence they are not necessarily parts of the pistol as made originally.

C. KLINE PISTOL (Figure 11), cal. .48, with a 9.25-inch, round, pin-fastened, smoothbore barrel. There is a front sight mounted on the barrel near the muzzle, but there is no rear sight. Total length 16 inches. Brass-mounted. The walnut stock extends to the muzzle but at the rear it does not have the pronounced curve found in most martial flintlock pistols. Instead, it has an ugly-looking butt. There is no back strap. The brass butt cap is thin and has no side extensions (spurs). The brass trigger guard forks to form a loop with a shape much different than that of most martial flintlocks.

The gooseneck hammer is shown without the flint between the jaws in Figure 11. There is an iron pan with a fence. The hickory ramrod has an enlarged forward end (swell tip).

The lock plate is marked in capital letters "C. KLINE" between the hammer and the frizzen spring. There is no mark on the barrel or on any other part except the lock plate.

A similar specimen is identical with the above except that it has a 7.625-inch barrel and a total length of 14.375 inches.

All we know about C. Kline is that he was a Pennsylvania manufacturer of flintlock pistols.

KUNTZ PISTOL (Figure 12), cal. .62, with a 9-inch, round, iron, smoothbore, pin-fastened barrel which is marked on top "KUNTZ PHILADEL". Total length 12.75 inches. The walnut stock extends almost to the muzzle, although it is sometimes erroneously described as "full-length." The butt has a shape known to collectors as "bird's head." The flat, gooseneck hammer is shown in Figure 12 without a flint between the jaws. The iron pan has a fence. The brass trigger guard forks at the rear to form an oval, but the oval is longer fore and aft than on most martial flintlock pistols. There is

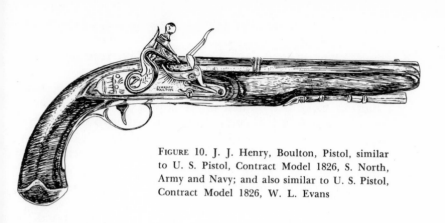

FIGURE 10. J. J. Henry, Boulton, Pistol, similar to U. S. Pistol, Contract Model 1826, S. North, Army and Navy; and also similar to U. S. Pistol, Contract Model 1826, W. L. Evans

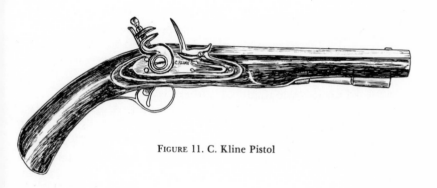

FIGURE 11. C. Kline Pistol

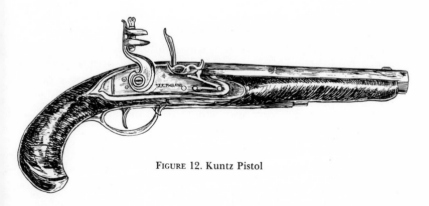

FIGURE 12. Kuntz Pistol

a low, brass, blade-type front sight, but no rear sight, and there is no back strap. There is a shallow, brass butt cap without extensions. The specimen illustrated does not have a hickory ramrod mounted on it and apparently the pistol was not constructed to carry a ramrod, although other specimens were.

The lock plate is marked "J.K. PHILADEL" between the hammer and the frizzen spring, and also marked with two vertical slashes behind the hammer. The rear end of the lock plate is teat-shaped.

A somewhat similar specimen, which is not illustrated, is cal. .48, with a 7.625-inch, round, pin-fastened, smoothbore barrel, octagonal at the rear but round in front, marked on top "KUNTZ PHILAD". The total length is 12.75 inches, the same as the total length of the specimen described above, despite the fact that the specimen described first has a barrel length of 9 inches and this one has a barrel only 7.625 inches long. The explanation is that the barrel is mounted farther forward on the one made in caliber .48.

The caliber .48 specimen is brass-mounted and there is a brass cap at the fore end (forward end) of the stock, flush with the muzzle. The lock plate is stamped "T. KETLAND & CO.", which probably means that it was imported from the English Ketlands, already marked, but the lock plate on some specimens of caliber .48 is marked "J.K. PHILADEL", like the one in Figure 12.

Jacob Kuntz, sometimes listed as Jacob Kunz, and also erroneously listed as either I. Kuntz or I. Kunz, was a Philadelphia gunsmith and dealer who made flintlock pistols and rifles from about 1819 to about 1829. His pistols probably were used by militia during that span of years and even up to and during the percussion era. Which of his pistols were entirely made by him and which were merely assembled in his shop is difficult to determine.

LAWRENCE PISTOL, cal. .61, although some specimens measure cal. .62. It has a 9-inch, round, iron, pin-fastened, smoothbore barrel, marked on top "PHILAD^A^", with the final "A" raised above the horizontal line of the other letters. Total length 15 inches. Flat, gooseneck hammer. Brass-mounted. The lock plate is marked in capital letters "LAWRENCE" between the hammer and the frizzen spring. Hickory ramrod with an 'enlarged forward end (swell tip). The walnut stock extends almost to the muzzle. The brass butt cap does not have side extensions. The brass trigger guard forks at the rear to form the usual oval.

Lawrence made flintlock holster pistols of cavalry size like the one illustrated in Figure 13. He was listed in the city directories of Philadelphia from 1821 to 1829 as a gunsmith, but directory listings do not necessarily prove or disprove the era in which a gunsmith produced arms. This is true because "gunsmith" has been loosely used for centuries to describe a man who made, assembled, repaired, or often only sold firearms. Nevertheless, Lawrence pistols belong with the others of this chapter.

McKim Brothers Pistols

McK BROS. PISTOL, also listed as McKIM & BROTHER PISTOL, cal. .54, 10-inch, smoothbore, pin-fastened, part-round and part-fluted barrel, which is round for first third of distance from muzzle and fluted with two flutes, one on each side of barrel, to the breech. Two brass thimbles. No back strap. Marked on flat lock plate: "Mc K BROS. BALTI-MORE" in capital letters except for "c" in "Mc" with "Mc K BROS." over "BALTIMORE". This mark is that of McKim & Brother, who made martial pistols in Baltimore, Maryland, during the flintlock period. Figure 14.

A variation of this pistol is described thus:

McKIM & BROTHER, BALTIMORE, PISTOL, cal. .60, 10.375-inch, part-round, part-octagonal, pin-fastened, smooth-bore barrel, without marks. Total length 15.5 inches. Brass-mounted. Full-length walnut stock extends to about 0.375 inch from the muzzle, and is made smaller forward of the front thimble, probably to make it easier to remove the brass-tipped hickory ramrod, although this type of design is unusual. A very small brass butt cap is set into the butt. The brass, oval-shaped trigger guard forks at the rear to complete the trigger-guard oval and then extends along the forward side of the butt, like many other flintlock pistols. There is no back strap.

In some specimens, "Mc KIM BROTHERS" is marked on the lock plate in one horizontal line, with "BALTIMORE" in another horizontal line beneath. In other specimens, the lock plate is marked in three horizontal lines: "Mc KIM &", "BROTHER", and "BALTIMORE", but the exact method of marking is not a controlling factor in identification. This is a holster pistol carried by cavalrymen and mounted officers of the state troops during the War of 1812, and in later campaigns, both in caliber .54 and caliber .60.

McNAUGHT PISTOL. This has been classified erroneously for many years as a U. S. Secondary Martial Flintlock Pistol, but it is only a pocket pistol and if it was used by the armed forces during flintlock days, it was merely a privately purchased pocket weapon. It is cal. .41, with a 3-inch, round barrel, rifled near the muzzle and smoothbore at the rear. The total length is 6.5 inches. The trigger folds into the grip but is fully exposed at full cock. A slide on top of the stock holds an apron or cover over the pan to prevent accidental discharge. It was made by James McNaught, Richmond, Virginia, probably between 1800 and 1812. McNaught advertised in the *Richmond Enquirer* in 1821 that he made, sold, or both, pistols, rifles, fowling pieces (shotguns), dueling pistols, and other firearms. It is not illustrated.

MEACHAM & POND PISTOL, not illustrated because it was not available to the author when this book was written, although he has examined several authentic specimens. It is cal. .54, with an 8.5-inch, round, pin-fastened, smoothbore barrel. The total length is 13.25 inches. A full walnut stock extends to within 0.125 inch from the muzzle. It is brass-mounted and has an iron pan with a fence. The rounded butt

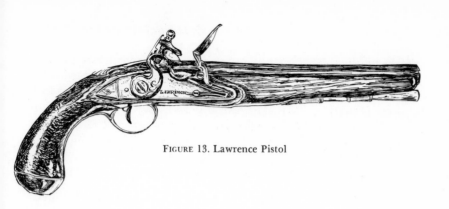

FIGURE 13. Lawrence Pistol

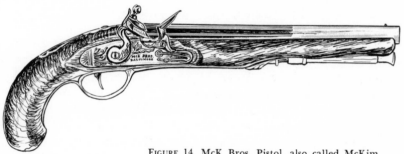

FIGURE 14. McK Bros. Pistol, also called McKim & Brother Pistol

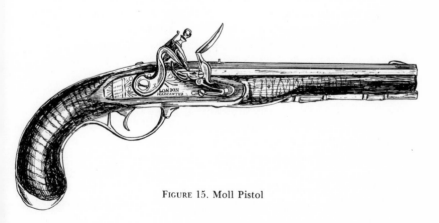

FIGURE 15. Moll Pistol

147

has neither a back strap nor a butt cap. The hammer is of the flat, gooseneck type. There is a hickory ramrod with an enlarged forward end (swell tip). The flat, beveled-edge lock plate is marked "MEACHAM & POND WARRANTED", in three horizontal lines between the hammer and the frizzen spring. This pistol probably was made in Albany, New York, before 1825. It could have been used as a U. S. Secondary Martial Pistol during campaigns after the War of 1812.

MOLL PISTOL (Figure 15), cal. .38, with an octagon, rifled, pin-fastened, brass barrel, 8.375 inches long, and marked on top "P. & D: MOLL HELLERSTOWN" in script. It is rifled with eight grooves. The total length of the specimen examined is 13.5 inches although some specimens are reported to have a total length of 14 inches. The weight is 1 lb., 15 oz., although some specimens weigh 2 lbs., 2 oz. It has a full-length, tiger-striped, maple stock, extending to the muzzle. It is brass-mounted. A brass, blade-type front sight is mounted near the muzzle and there is an open, V-shaped rear sight. The hammer is of the gooseneck type. The rounded butt has a brass butt cap. The iron pan has a fence and is forged integral with the lock plate. The brass trigger guard forks at the rear to form the conventional trigger-guard oval and then continues downward on the forward surface of the butt for reinforcement. It has a hickory ramrod.

The flat, beveled-edge lock plate is marked in two lines between the hammer and the frizzen spring, in capital letters, "LONDON" over "WARRANTED", which definitely indicates that the lock plate was imported from England.

This pistol was made by Peter and David Moll, Hellerstown, Pennsylvania, to equip a troop of cavalry known as the Sawken Light Horse, and also as the Sawken Light Horse Cavalry, which served during the War of 1812.

Peter and David Moll began making firearms before 1812 and continued after 1833, the exact dates being uncertain. They made elaborately ornamented Kentucky (Pennsylvania) rifles; U. S. Secondary Martial Flintlock Pistols, like the one in Figure 15; and specialized in making "tiger-striped" stocks for both pistols and shoulder arms.

"Tiger striping" was accomplished by wrapping a heavy, tarred twine around the stock, setting fire to the twine, and thus artificially producing the appearance of naturally curly maple. Since there was not enough maple available with the tiger-stripe pattern, the tiger-striping process was merely one of the accepted methods of ornamenting stocks; it was not intended to deceive anyone.

THE MOORE PISTOL (Figure 16), cal. .70, with a 10-inch, smoothbore, iron barrel, octagon for a distance of 3 inches from the breech, and then round to the muzzle. Brass-mounted. Hickory ramrod. The full-length walnut stock extends to the muzzle. The hammer is of the gooseneck type. The brass butt cap has gracefully rounded extensions on each side for reinforcement. The brass trigger guard forks at the rear in the conventional manner to form the trigger-guard oval, but a distinctive feature is a lanyard ring mounted in front of the trigger-guard oval for attaching a lanyard (cord) so that if the soldier let go of the pistol, he would not lose it. This is generally regarded as a feature of cavalry pistols, but the use of a lanyard has continued into modern times even for infantry; hence it is not historically accurate to give the impression that only mounted forces used lanyards.

The Moore Pistol is an example of a comparatively high degree of craftsmanship which is rare for a martial flintlock pistol intended for combat. By this we mean that some carefully made and elaborately decorated pistols were intended only for show purposes, although they could be fired effectively when necessary. The elaborate carving on the stock forward of the lock plate, clearly shown in Figure 16, and the decorative markings on the lock plate indicate that the specimen illustrated was probably made for and carried by a mounted officer of state troops. The total length is 16 inches.

The lock plate on Figure 16 is marked in capital letters in three horizontal lines, as follows: "J.P. MOORE", "NEW YORK", and "WARRANTED"; but the artist was unable to reproduce these words accurately on the drawing, although they are on the specimen illustrated.

John P. Moore, working either alone or with others, made muskets and pistols from about 1820 to about 1840. He started working for himself in New York City in 1823, after several years of service as an apprentice and journeyman in shops owned by other gunsmiths. The pistol illustrated was probably made sometime between 1823 and 1840.

Firearms by a company known as John P. Moore's Sons, consisting of George G. Moore, the son of John P. Moore, and two grandsons of John P. Moore, were made as late as 1885, which was during the cartridge period.

POND PISTOL, cal. .56, with a 9-inch, octagonal, smoothbore, brass, key-fastened barrel which is marked "ALBANY" The total length is 15 inches and the weight is 3 lbs. The flat lock plate is engraved "POND & CO." between the hammer and the frizzen spring. The full-length apple' stock extends to the muzzle. There is a gooseneck hammer and an iron pan with a fence. There is no back strap. A brass butt cap reinforces the rounded butt. The brass trigger guard follows conventional lines. There is a brass, cone-type front sight but no rear sight. There is an ordinary hickory ramrod. The frizzen spring has a roller, which indicates that the pistol was made comparatively late in the flintlock era in Albany, New York. It is not illustrated because the only unique feature is the apple-wood stock.

RICHMOND, VIRGINIA, PISTOL. The so-called Richmond, Virginia, Pistol is the same as the Virginia Manufactory Pistol, two models of which are described and illustrated in this chapter.

ROGERS & BROTHERS PISTOL, cal. .54, with an 8.5-inch, half-octagonal, smoothbore, key-fastened barrel, held to the stock with two keys. Total length 14 inches. The full maple stock extends to 0.125 inch from the muzzle and has a forward brass end cap. Brass-mounted. Gooseneck hammer. Iron pan with fence. Hickory ramrod brass-tipped. Pinned thimbles. The maple stock is striped, probably artificially as explained for the Moll Pistol, in the "tiger" style. The bird's-head butt is checked and has a brass butt cap which is usually described as "shallow" because it barely covers the end of the butt, or handle. There is a large, brass front sight on the barrel but no rear sight. The frizzen spring has a roller. Not illustrated.

The flat lock plate is usually engraved, but sometimes stamped, "ROGERS & BROTHERS", and also "WARRANTED".

Historians believe that this pistol, and others very similar, were made at Valley Forge, Pennsylvania, between 1814 and 1825, thus placing this pistol in the category of those used during the campaigns conducted by the United States and the several states after the War of 1812.

John Rogers, Charles Rogers, and Evan Rogers were hardware merchants of Philadelphia from 1805 to 1846, according to the Philadelphia city directories. John Rogers bought a gunsmithing shop at Valley Forge in 1814. Other members of the family owned a Valley Forge Gun Factory until it was completely destroyed in 1843, when the property was inherited by women who eventually sold it to the State of Pennsylvania for park purposes.

RUPP PISTOL, cal. .47, with an 8.5-inch, round, semi-octagonal, smoothbore barrel, octagonal for the rear 4.25 inches, and round for the 4.25 inches extending to the muzzle. The barrel is key-fastened to the stock with two keys and is marked "JOHN RUPP". Total length of pistol is 13.75 inches. Silver-mounted. Pinned thimbles. The full-length, red-finished, maple stock terminates 0.125 inch from the muzzle.

The bird's-head-type butt is checked and has a silver butt cap which barely covers the butt. The silver trigger guard forks at the rear in the conventional manner of the flintlock period. There is a brass, blade-type front sight, but no rear sight. Gooseneck hammer. Iron pan with fence. Hickory ramrod. The flat, bevel-edged lock plate has no marks except the two vertical slashes commonly found behind the hammer on flintlock pistols of this era. Not illustrated.

John Rupp, who made this pistol, worked at Ruppville, Pennsylvania, near Allentown, about 1780, but another man named John Rupp made Kentucky (Pennsylvania) rifles about 1740; hence it is difficult to know which John Rupp made this pistol.

THE SMITH & HYSLOP PISTOL (Figure 17), cal. .58, with an 8.75-inch, round, iron, smoothbore, pin-fastened barrel. Total length 14 inches. The gooseneck hammer is designed according to a type found in the latter part of the flintlock era. The specimen shown in Figure 17 has a walnut stock extending almost to the muzzle, but in some specimens the stock reaches the muzzle. The butt is checkered.

The lock plate of the specimen shown in Figure 17 is marked "SMITH & HYSLOP", "NEW YORK", and "WARRANTED" between the hammer and the frizzen spring, but this marking is not reproduced in the drawing. The rear of the lock plate comes to a teat-shaped point. There is a brass butt cap. The hickory ramrod has an enlarged forward end (swell tip). There is a small front sight near the muzzle.

Smith & Hyslop had a plant or shop in New York City during the 1820's. A pistol very similar to the one in Figure 17 has been illustrated for many years in various editions of *The Gun Collector's Handbook of Values* and is accepted by experts as a U. S. Secondary Martial Pistol.

VIRGINIA MANUFACTORY PISTOLS

Virginia Manufactory Pistols, also erroneously called "Richmond, Virginia Pistols," are all definitely U. S. Secondary Martial Flintlock Pistols because they were made by the State of Virginia at the Virginia Manufactory for state troops and not for federal forces. There are actually only two models. The first model is sometimes called by collectors and dealers the "Big Virginia." The second model was designed and manufactured according to the pattern of U. S. Pistol, Model 1805 (1806), Harpers Ferry, which is described and illustrated in Chapter 3.

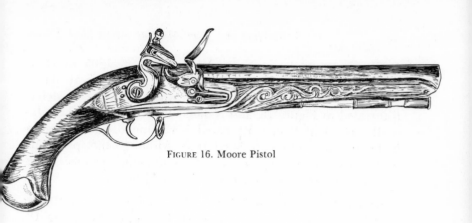

FIGURE 16. Moore Pistol

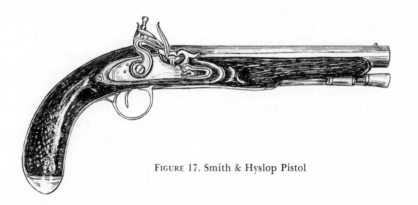

FIGURE 17. Smith & Hyslop Pistol

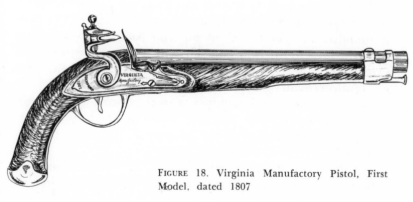

FIGURE 18. Virginia Manufactory Pistol, First
Model, dated 1807

153

The first-model pistols are all dated from 1805 to 1811, both dates inclusive. The second-model pistols are all dated from 1812 to 1815, both dates inclusive. The first model is illustrated in Figure 18, and is dated 1807. The second model is illustrated in Figure 19, dated 1812, and illustrated again in Figure 20, where it is dated 1815. Although the specimens in Figures 19 and 20 are both second-model pistols, there are obvious variations which are explained below.

VIRGINIA MANUFACTORY PISTOL, FIRST MODEL, cal. .69. The barrel of the specimen illustrated in Figure 18 is 12.0625 inches long, although authentic specimens are found with barrels ranging from 11.75 inches to 12.25 inches long. The total length of the pistol in Figure 18 is 17 inches and the weight is 3 lbs., 6 oz. When the barrel is shorter or longer than 12.0625 inches, this also affects the total length and the weight, but such variations are common in flintlock pistols.

The barrel is fastened to the stock by an iron device, sometimes called a "double-barrel band," but also called a "two-ring barrel band." Both terms mean the same thing. The barrel is round and smoothbore. There is a brass, blade-type, low front sight mounted on the rear "ring" or "band" of the "double-barrel band" or "two-ring barrel band," depending entirely on your choice of terminology. There is no rear sight.

The walnut stock is sometimes described as "full-length," but actually it ends about 0.5 inch from the muzzle. The butt is rounded and reinforced by an iron back strap extending from the tang to the iron butt cap, which has a short, rounded extension (spur) reaching upward on both sides of the butt for reinforcement.

There is a gooseneck hammer, a steel ramrod, and an iron pan with a fence. The pan and its fence are forged as an integral part of the lock plate. In general, the pistol is iron-mounted.

The barrel of most specimens has a "P" stamped on it as a proofmark, and an abbreviation for the organization to which the pistol was issued, such as "REG. 2 V", followed by the year, but there is considerable variation in barrel markings.

The flat, beveled-edge lock plate in Figure 18 is marked in two horizontal lines between the hammer and the frizzen spring. The word "VIRGINIA" is entirely in capital letters. Below it is "Manufactory" in script, with the letter "M" a capital letter and the other letters in lower case. Behind the hammer, the word "RICHMOND" is in all-capital letters formed in a distinct curve. Near the rear end of the lock plate is the year, sometimes almost straight, but often found in a very slight curve. In Figure 18 the year is 1807.

VIRGINIA MANUFACTORY PISTOL, SECOND MODEL. This pistol, as stated before, was designed and manufactured according to the pattern of U. S. Pistol, Model 1805 (1806), Harpers Ferry, described and illustrated in Chapter 3, but there are unique details which distinguish it from the pattern from which it was made.

This pistol is cal. .54, with a round, key-fastened, smoothbore barrel, 10 inches long, made without sights. There is a walnut half stock, that is, it does not extend near the muzzle because of the construction of the steel, swivel-type ramrod. The rounded butt of the stock has a brass butt cap with reinforcing extensions on each side which are inlaid flush with the butt and extend upward and forward to provide not only reinforcement but also decoration. These butt cap extensions are shorter than those on the U. S. Pistol, Model 1805 (1806), Harpers Ferry. There is no back strap.

This model is brass-mounted and has a double-neck, flat, beveled-edge hammer; an iron pan with a fence; a conventional brass trigger guard; brass ramrod thimble; and brass reinforcing band for the barrel, which is shown in both Figure 19 and Figure 20 coming down around the stock near its forward end, but above the swivel-type ramrod. The total length is 16.625 inches and the weight is 2 lbs., 13 oz.

In Figure 19, the flat, beveled-edge lock plate is marked

in capital letters "VIRGINIA" between the hammer and the frizzen spring. The word "RICHMOND" is in all-capital letters in a distinct curve behind the hammer, and below it is the year "1812", which has a very slight curve.

In Figure 20, the lock plate is marked "RICHMOND" in capital letters in a pronounced curve between the hammer and the frizzen spring. Behind the hammer in Figure 20 appears the year "1815" in a straight line.

VIRGINIA MANUFACTORY HISTORY

The State of Virginia authorized the construction and operation of the Virginia Manufactory in 1797 to make firearms only for the armed forces of Virginia. The year 1797 is significant because the passage of the federal Alien and Sedition Laws in 1798 caused Virginia and Kentucky legislatures to pass resolutions stating the right and duty of the states to halt the action of the United States Government whenever federal action violated the U. S. Constitution in the opinion of the individual states. Therefore, the seeds of civil war were planted very early in the history of Virginia, although the harvest of this thinking did not take place until 1861.

The production of firearms of various types began at the Virginia Manufactory in 1802. The production of Virginia Manufactory Pistols may have begun before 1805, but that is the earliest year found on any first-model specimens. As stated before, the second model is dated from 1812 to 1815, but the production of firearms in general did not stop until 1820, when the Virginia Manufactory became a school. It is possible that the second model was made after 1815, using lock plates dated from 1812 to 1815, but it is certain that none were made after 1820.

During the Civil War, the Virginia Manufactory operated as an arsenal or as an armory, or as a combination of both, depending on the definition you choose, but it was primarily a repair shop, first for Virginia troops only, and later for the Confederate States of America. There is absolutely no evidence that any firearms were manufactured at the Vir-

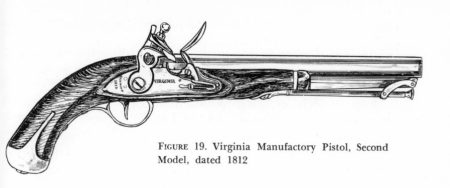

FIGURE 19. Virginia Manufactory Pistol, Second
Model, dated 1812

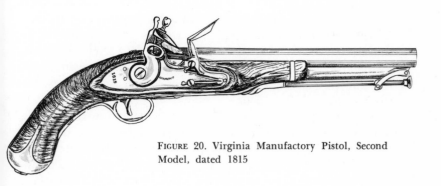

FIGURE 20. Virginia Manufactory Pistol, Second
Model, dated 1815

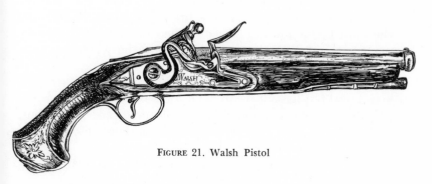

FIGURE 21. Walsh Pistol

157

ginia Manufactory during the Civil War although it is probable that parts were assembled to produce weapons in firing
condition.

Both models of Virginia Manufactory Flintlock Pistols
were used in the War of 1812 and in subsequent wars and
campaigns. At the beginning of the Civil War, Virginia and
other Confederate troops went into action with flintlocks
and any other type of firearm they could get. As soon as
possible, Confederate armorers, including those at the Virginia Manufactory, converted flintlock arms into percussion
weapons. In the chapter on Confederate arms, this subject
comes up again.

THE WALSH PISTOL (Figure 21), cal. .54. It has an 8-inch,
brass, tapering, smoothbore, cannon-shaped, pin-fastened
barrel, with a brass, cone-type, low front sight mounted on the
muzzle band. The barrel is marked "J. WALSH PHILAD"
inside an engraved panel, but this marking is not visible from
the side view of Figure 21. The total length is 14 inches, and
the weight is 1 lb., 15 oz.

A walnut stock extends to about 0.5 inch from the muzzle.
The butt is rounded but has a fishtail shape where the brass
butt cap is fastened. The brass butt cap is ornamented with
a high quality of engraving and has extensions on each side
of the butt which are set into the wood, flush with the surface.
There is a hickory ramrod with an enlarged front end
(swell tip).

There is a gooseneck hammer. The brass pan and its
fence are cast integral with the brass lock plate. Notice that
the word is *cast* and not *forged* in the case of a pan and fence
made integral with the lock plate when the whole assembly
is made of brass.

The brass trigger guard forms the conventional trigger-
guard oval but has a forward projection and also a rear projection, the latter extending along the lower surface of the butt
almost to the butt cap. The pistol is brass-mounted. There
are two pin-fastened ramrod thimbles.

The flat, beveled-edge, brass lock plate is marked "J.

WALSH" between the hammer and the frizzen spring. This marking is surrounded by decorative engraving. The specimen illustrated in Figure 21 is one of a pair of almost identical pistols in the collection of Samuel E. Smith, Markesan, Wisconsin. It is known that this pair was carried into battle during the Revolutionary War.

James Walsh, who made the matched pair of pistols in the Smith collection, made complete firearms of various types for the Pennsylvania Committee of Safety in Philadelphia in 1776 and later. He also made gunlocks for the same Committee of Safety, presumably for shipment to men who assembled guns but did not make their own locks. Careful workmanship and elaborate ornamentation are characteristics of all his firearms, including his martial flintlock pistols.

From about 1777 to about 1778, he was Superintendent of Arms for the Pennsylvania Gun Repair Shop, located at Allentown, Pennsylvania. In 1779, he offered for public sale his gunsmithing tools, and there ends as much as we know of one of the very best manufacturers of U. S. Secondary Martial Flintlock Pistols.

Percussion Lock Development and Cartridge Design

TRANSITIONARY STEPS LEADING TO DESIGN OF LOCKS ON U. S. MARTIAL PERCUSSION PISTOLS

IN order to fully understand the design, manufacture and use of the firing mechanism of U. S. Martial Percussion Pistols, it is necessary to examine the transitionary steps between the firing mechanism of the flintlock and that of the percussion pistols used by the armed forces of the United States.

FORSYTH, THE FATHER OF THE PERCUSSION ERA

Early Experiments by Forsyth

The Reverend Alexander John Forsyth, a Scottish Presbyterian minister of the parish of Belhelvie near Aberdeen, Scotland, completely revolutionized the design, manufacture and use of all firearms when he developed a chemical compound that would explode when struck by a sharp blow and produce fire to ignite the powder in the bore of the barrel. This was not a substitute for gunpowder. It was an ignition agent that replaced the sparks produced when the flint struck the steel frizzen (battery) of the flintlock.

Working at his home, Forsyth made his first percussion

lock in 1805. He received his first patent in 1807 after experimenting several months in the Tower of London, an ancient fortress on the north bank of the Thames River in London, England. The Tower of London was at various times a prison, a barracks, a royal residence, and an armory or arsenal, but while Forsyth worked there, space was provided for inspectors of firearms, gunsmiths and other artisans associated with the weapons industry.

The Forsyth detonating compound depended primarily upon potassium chlorate, which is transparent, colorless and poisonous. It can be produced either as crystals or as a white powder. When ground with sulfur, sugar or any other combustible substance there is danger of an explosion or at least a fire.

Forsyth found that when he placed his detonating compound in a tube inserted in the enlarged vent of a flintlock and then struck the tube with a hammer, a flash of fire was produced that ignited the powder charge in the bore. He realized that this did away with the necessity for having a flint, a frizzen (battery), priming powder, and the priming powder pan, together with all the other details associated with the flint-and-steel ignition system. His next problem was to develop a lock mechanism for the practical application of his detonating principle, but first he secured the legal protection of a patent.

Principal Elements of the Forsyth Patent

The entire language of the Forsyth patent application is too long to quote in full, but extracts from his own words reveal this thought process:

> Instead of permitting the touch-hole or vent of the pieces of artillery, fire arms, mines, chambers, cavities or places to communicate with the open air, and instead of giving fire to the charge by a lighted match, or by flint and steel, or by any other matter in a state of actual combustion applied to a priming in an open pan, I do close the touch-hole or vent by means of

a plug or sliding piece, or other fit piece of metal or suitable material or materials so as to exclude the open air, and to prevent any sensible escape of the blast or explosive gas or vapour outwards, or from the priming or charge, and as much as possible to force the said priming to go, in the direction of the charge, and to set fire to the same and not to be wasted in the open air.

And as a priming I do make use of some or one of those chemical compounds which are so easily inflammable as to be capable of taking fire and exploding without any actual fire being applied thereto, and merely by a blow, or by any sudden or strong pressure or friction given or applied thereto without extraordinary violence; that is to say, for example, the salt formed of dephlogisticated marine acid and potash, which salt is otherwise called oxymuriate of potash; or I do make use of such of the fulminating metallic compounds as may be used with safety: for example, fulminating mercury, or of common gunpowder mixed in due quantity with any of the before mentioned substances, or with an oxymuriate salt as aforesaid, or of suitable mixture of any of the above mentioned compounds. . . .

The manner of priming and exploding which I use is to introduce into the touch-hole or vent or into a small and strong chamber or place between the said touch-hole and vent, and the plug or sliding piece, or other piece with which external communication with the air is cut off, a small portion of some or one of the chemical compounds before mentioned. . . .

And when the required discharge is to be made I do cause the said chemical compound or priming to take fire and explode by giving a stroke or sudden and strong pressure to the same.

Experiments Prior to the Forsyth Patent

Samuel Pepys, who held many high offices in England, is today most famous for his diary. Repeatedly described by authorities on literature and history as the most unique diary in the English language, it was written in a secret cipher, was truthful, and was extremely detailed regarding topics of interest to Pepys. In his entry dated November 11, 1663, he said this about detonating compounds:

At noon to the Coffee House, where, with Dr. Allen, some good discourse about physick and chymistry. And among other things I telling him what Dribble, the German Doctor, do offer of an instrument to sink ships; he tells me that which is more strange, that something made of gold, which they call in chymestry Aurum Fulmina'ns, a grain, I think he said, of it put into a silver spoon and fired, will give a blow like a musquett, and strike a hole through the silver spoon downwards, without the least force upwards; and this he can make a cheaper experiment of he says with iron prepared.

The above quotation follows the exact spelling, punctuation and grammar of the Pepys Diary. In 1665, in addition to other honors, titles and positions, Samuel Pepys was elected a Fellow of the Royal Society, the members of which experimented with what Pepys described as "Aurum Fulminans" by loading it into a hollow steel ball, throwing the ball against a stone wall, and otherwise flirting with sudden death. There is no record that any of them were killed, but they abandoned their experiments, probably because they found that pure fulminate of gold, silver, or mercury detonated so suddenly that it would scatter loose powder without setting fire to it.

Forsyth's Application of Theory to Practice

The "oxymuriate of potash" mentioned by Forsyth in his patent application was what we call today potassium chlorate. A fulminate of any element by itself is not a useful detonating agent, and a chlorate is equally impractical, but when combined, as they were by Forsyth, they formed a substance that led to the evolution of not only the United States Martial Percussion Pistols, but also the later self-contained metallic cartridge, and the practical manufacture of breech-loading firearms. Second only to the discovery of gunpowder was the work of the Reverend Alexander John Forsyth.

Forsyth made a lock for shoulder arms which was one of the experiments leading to application of his principle to pistols. This early lock had a revolving magazine which moved around a nipple projecting from the weapon at the touchhole or vent on the flintlock. One side of this revolving magazine was a tube holding twenty charges of the detonating powder. The opposite side of the revolving magazine had a spring-actuated striker (something like the firing pin on modern hand and shoulder arms). This striker was called a "piston," hence the early Forsyth lock was called a "piston lock."

The magazine was revolved until a charge of detonating powder fell into the hollow nipple. The magazine was then revolved back through 180 degrees to bring the spring-actuated striker above the nipple charged with detonating powder. When the trigger was pulled, the hammer fell and drove the piston into the detonating charge and fired the main charge in the bore. It is obvious that this was a crude and dangerous mechanism. When he began to make pistols, Forsyth abandoned the early piston lock and simplified his firing system.

FORSYTH FIRST MODEL PISTOL (Figure 1) is cal. .45, with an octagon barrel 5 inches long, a brass-tipped ramrod, a walnut stock, an engraved lock plate, an engraved hammer, and a total length of 11 inches. There is a small, bead-type front sight, and a trigger guard which lacks the usual oval shape but has a fairly straight line at the bottom of the trigger guard proper and then curves sharply upward and to the rear.

In Figure 1, the hammer is resting on the piston (striker or firing pin). In front of the piston is the screw cap which covers a brass "charger" underneath. This brass charger is the magazine holding either fulminating powder or fulminating pellets. The shooter had to move the charger with his hand to bring under the piston each quantity of charging powder, or each pellet (depending upon whether powder or pellets were loaded into the charger), before firing a shot. Like the early Forsyth shoulder arm, this pistol was inefficient and dangerous. It was made before Forsyth formed his own company.

FORSYTH SECOND MODEL PISTOL (Figure 2), sometimes called the Forsyth Pill-Lock Pistol. The barrel is marked "Forsyth & Co., Gunmakers, London", and is 7 inches long. The total length of the pistol is 12.25 inches. The lock plate is engraved in a curve "FORSYTH & CO." over "PATENT", which also is curved, but not as much as the upper line of letters. Figure 2 shows that the priming mechanism, hammer, and trigger guard, as well as the lock plate, are decorated with engraving of a high quality.

The short, nearly horizontal slide extending back from the bottom of the hammer is a safety bolt to prevent accidental discharge. Attached to the hammer is a slide on which a small primer magazine operates.

The butt of the pistol is checkered to prevent slipping when the pistol is held in the hand. There is a brass butt cap.

In order to fire the pistol, the main charge of powder and the ball are rammed down the bore by means of the steel swivel-type ramrod which rests under the forward portion of the stock when not in use. The hammer is cocked. This causes the magazine to drop a priming pellet, also called a pill, into a hole. A firing pin on the face of the hammer crushes the pill (or pellet) when the hammer falls after the trigger is pulled. This ignites the main powder charge in the bore and discharges the pistol.

In more technical language, the magazine is connected by a link to the hammer. The magazine is free to slide on rollers along a bar. Cocking the pistol draws the magazine over the vent (or touchhole) to let the pellet or pill drop into place. Pulling the trigger causes the hammer to fall, the magazine is returned to its original position, the pellet or pill is exposed, the firing pin on the face of the hammer strikes the pellet, and the pistol is discharged. This pistol was made after Forsyth left the ministry and organized Forsyth & Co. in London, probably in 1812.

FORSYTH SCENT-BOTTLE, PILL-LOCK PISTOL (Figure 3), called the "Scent-Bottle Type" because the priming magazine is shaped something like early scent bottles which

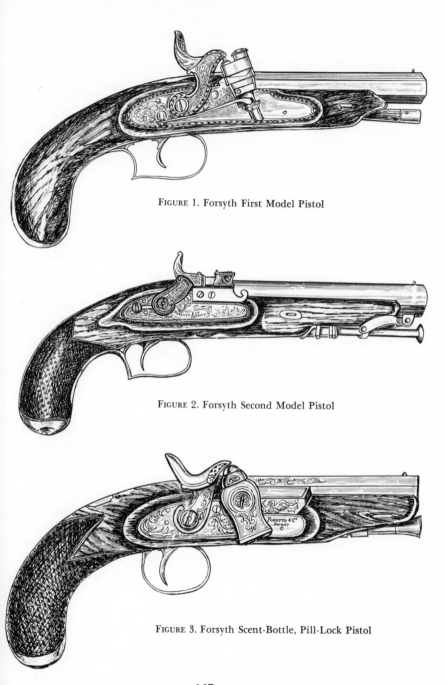

FIGURE 1. Forsyth First Model Pistol

FIGURE 2. Forsyth Second Model Pistol

FIGURE 3. Forsyth Scent-Bottle, Pill-Lock Pistol

contained sweet-smelling, aromatic substances. The barrel is 3.75 inches long, octagonal in shape, with "FORSYTH & CO. LONDON" inlaid on top in letters of gold. The lock plate is elaborately engraved. Forward of the magazine, the lock plate is engraved "FORSYTH & Co." over "PATENT". The "F" in "FORSYTH" is larger than the other letters. The primer magazine and all other metal parts are beautifully engraved.

There is a full-length walnut stock. The total length is 9 inches. The ramrod is an ordinary hickory ramrod with a swell-tip front end made of brass. The butt is checkered.

In order to fire this pistol, the main charge of powder and the ball were first rammed into the bore. The hammer was cocked. The priming magazine ("scent bottle"), which was removable for reloading, was turned so that the pill would fall into the vent leading to the bore. The priming magazine was then given a half turn, back to its original location. A firing pin was held by a spring under tension. When the trigger was pulled, the hammer fell, the tension on the spring holding the firing pin was released, the firing pin hit the pill, and the detonation of the pill ignited the main powder charge in the bore.

JOSEPH MANTON TUBE-LOCK PISTOL. Joseph Manton, one of the most outstanding arms manufacturers of the flintlock and percussion eras, was already well established in business when Forsyth & Co. was organized. Manton sent one of his best gunsmiths, James Purdey, who later became famous in his own right, to help Forsyth improve his firearms.

Manton was not satisfied with the Forsyth firing mechanism. He developed the Joseph Manton Tube-Lock Pistol (Figure 4). Manton obtained a patent for the tube-lock principle in 1818. He used a copper tube about 0.625 inch long, with an external diameter of 0.0625 inch, filled with fulminate of mercury as a detonating compound. This tube was open at both ends and was placed partway in the vent of the pistol or shoulder arm, where it was held by a spring clip. The outer or upper end of the tube rested against a small anvil fastened to the lock plate. A blow from the hammer smashed the tube, causing a detonation which sent fire into the powder charge in the bore.

The Manton pistol in Figure 4 has an octagonal barrel 10.25 inches long and a total length of 16.25 inches. The lock plate is engraved elaborately and "JOSEPH MANTON PATENT" is in one straight line near the lower edge. It has a so-called "half-length" walnut stock, a checkered butt, and a brass trigger guard of conventional shape. The hickory

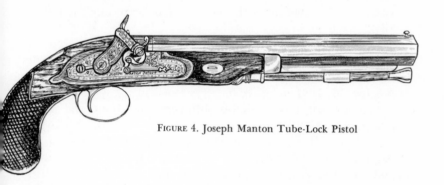

FIGURE 4. Joseph Manton Tube-Lock Pistol

ramrod has a brass "swell tip." There is a small bead sight mounted near the muzzle. Almost all of the exterior of the lock mechanism is elaborately engraved.

The invention or development of the tube-lock mechanism by Joseph Manton was second in chronological order in the progress of percussion ignition, counting Forsyth's "pill lock" ("pellet lock") as the first practical step after Forsyth abandoned the use of loose detonating powder. Joseph Manton made many martial pistols, dueling pistols, fowling pieces (shotguns), and other types of firearms with his tube-lock mechanism, some of them as early as 1811.

BRITISH ADOPTION OF PERCUSSION SYSTEM

The Forsyth detonating system and the Manton tube lock were regarded as highly dangerous, inefficient and unsuited to martial requirements by the British armed forces for many years, although British sportsmen accepted both systems early in the nineteenth century. By 1825, various inventors had improved on the designs of Forsyth and Manton to the extent that the *percussion copper cap,* described later, came into general use on privately owned firearms.

The British retained their old flintlocks until the percussion system was officially adopted by the armed forces in 1836. All of the so-called "Brown Bess" flintlock muskets in the armed forces were gradually converted to the percussion system of ignition until the last of them were modified about 1842.

It is an interesting sidelight on history that percussion rifles were first used in action by the British Second Border Regiment, at Amoy, later a part of French Indo-China, on August 26, 1841.

We do not have reliable information about the actual official adoption of percussion pistols by the British armed forces, but it is assumed that the year 1836 marked the beginning of the conversion of flintlock pistols to percussion and the first year when plans were discussed for the future manufacture of British martial pistols as percussion handguns.

Ironically enough, Alexander John Forsyth received little recognition during his lifetime for what he had done to revolutionize the whole concept of firearm ignition, but the British Parliament, after much debate, awarded Forsyth the sum of five thousand pounds sterling, to be paid in installments. However, the first installment was not delivered until the day of his death, when it was presented to his widow.

REVIEW OF IGNITION METHODS

Ignition Methods Used Prior to the Forsyth Lock

Figure 5 is a simplified drawing of fire applied by a torch or hot rod held at the vent of a *hand cannon.* Figure 6 is a sketch of the matchlock firing mechanism in which the glowing end of a match (cord or wick) is brought to the vent

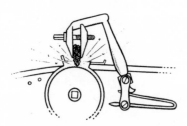

FIGURE 5. Hand cannon ignition

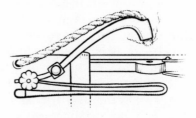

FIGURE 6. Matchlock ignition

FIGURE 7. Wheel-lock ignition

FIGURE 8. True flintlock ignition

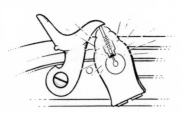

FIGURE 9. Forsyth lock hitting the "piston"

FIGURE 10. Detonation of a pill, pellet, disc, or section of tape holding detonators

by means of a "serpentine." This shows the spring which was an improvement over the first crude *matchlock* design.

Figure 7 is a sketch of a *wheel-lock* firing mechanism at the instant that the pyrite clamped between the jaws of the "cock" is being held against the revolving, notched steel wheel, throwing sparks into the priming pan.

Figure 8 is a *true flintlock* shown at the instant that the flint strikes the steel frizzen (battery) and at the same second uncovers the priming pan so that the sparks will ignite the priming powder.

Ignition Methods from Forsyth to the Modern Cartridge

Figure 9 is a sketch of one of the Forsyth locks in which the hammer is hitting the "piston," which, in turn, crushes grains of fulminate of mercury.

Figure 10 is a simplified sketch of the detonation of a *pill, pellet, disc, or a section of tape holding a pill or pellet,* but the important feature of the sketch is that the detonating substance is in a *tube* leading through the vent to the powder charge in the bore. In other words, this is a generalized drawing to show a transitional stage in percussion lock development and not a picture of any particular make or model.

Figure 11 shows both the detonating pellet and the powder charge loaded into a hollow area at the base of a bullet. This is merely a variation of the detonating principle and does not necessarily represent a distinct step in development of the percussion system.

Figure 12 represents the *metallic cartridge* having the primer in its base, the powder charge in its case, and the bullet inserted at the front of the case. Although this drawing does not belong in the percussion era from the viewpoint of a gun collector, it does show the culmination of the long line of progress from Forsyth to the present.

Detonating Powder, Pellets, Caps and Tubes

Figure 13 shows on the left a pile of loose detonating

powder, representing the loose powder used in the early Forsyth weapons. The little balls on the right are the *pills or pellets* later used in the Forsyth firearms.

Figure 14 shows *percussion caps and tubes*, each containing a small quantity of detonating substance.

The Cap Lock

The true *cap lock* was an improvement over the tube-lock system of Joseph Manton because tube-lock firearms tended to blow the tubes out of the vents, causing powder gases to escape at the breech, thus loosing power, accuracy, and safety.

A few so-called *cap-lock* firearms of the earliest form were made with a platinum *disc* (also spelled *disk*) perforated to communicate with the breech and allow an escape of gas, but this was found undesirable and few weapons with this feature were made after 1835.

In the United States, Captain Joshua Shaw, also famous as an artist, obtained a patent in 1822, although his original application was made in 1814. He originally tried a thimble-shaped cup holding a small quantity of detonating powder which was placed on a hollow nipple leading through the vent to the powder charge in the bore. In its first form, the cap was made of either iron or steel, but in 1815 he made his caps of pewter. In 1816, he perfected the *copper cap* and this was the *primer* copied by various inventors and manufacturers and used in the U. S. Martial Percussion Pistols and U. S. Secondary Martial Percussion Pistols. It was also used in martial shoulder arms and in all other percussion arms.

The credit for the invention of the *perfected copper cap* has been the subject of controversy for many years. British historians have said that one or more of the famous English gunmakers, such as Joseph Manton, James Purdey, or Joseph Egg, invented the copper cap in its final form. However, Charles Ffoulkes, Master of Armouries, Tower of London, said in his famous book, *Sword, Lance & Bayonet:*

At first the detonating was effected by inserting small tubes or primers in place of Forsyth's somewhat elaborate magazines, and in or about 1836 a copper cap by Westley-Richards was introduced, based on the previous invention of Captain Shaw of Philadelphia.

Captain Joshua Shaw, whose biography can be found in many standard references on painters of his period, was born a British subject and became a citizen of the United States by naturalization. The argument about whether Shaw or one of the famous English gunmakers invented the copper cap used in U. S. Martial Percussion Pistols and other percussion weapons is merely of academic interest, although gun collectors like to write and talk about it. The important thing is that a perfected copper cap was invented and successfully used during the percussion era, as we understand the term today.

The Tape Primer

Figure 15 shows a strip of paper or fabric which encloses a large number of detonating pills, pellets, or caps. The detonators could be fed successively to the firing position by the action of the lock. This was similar in design to the toy "repeating cap pistols" used by children.

It is logical to assume that the *tape primer,* and the firing mechanism in which it was used, known in firearms history as the *tape lock,* was developed or invented as the next step in ignition improvement after the pill lock or pellet lock, but its invention is credited by American historians to Edward Maynard, Doctor of Dentistry, who obtained his basic patent in 1845. Doctor Maynard, who lived and worked in both Washington, D. C., and Chicopee Falls, Massachusetts, obtained a U. S. patent, No. 8,126, on May 27, 1851, for the Maynard breech-loading system, and was issued another U. S. patent, No. 26,364, on December 6, 1859.

Doctor Maynard delivered 400 carbines manufactured according to his system to the United States on December 25, 1857. These were shipped from Chicopee Falls and it is

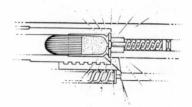

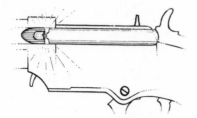

FIGURE 11. Detonating pellet and powder loaded into base of bullet

FIGURE 12. Metallic cartridge with primer in its base, powder in case, and bullet at front of case

FIGURE 13. Loose detonating powder and pellets or pills of Forsyth pistols

FIGURE 14. Percussion caps and tubes, each containing a small amount of detonating substance

FIGURE 15. Tape primer

FIGURE 16. Disc (or disk) primers

175

assumed that they were manufactured by the Maynard Arms Co. (also called Maynard Gun Co.), although subcontractors may have been employed to make parts or subassemblies. A whole book could be written about Doctor Maynard and his contributions to firearms development, but it is sufficient to say here that pistol collectors are interested in the Maynard tape primer because it was built into U. S. Pistol-Carbine, Model 1855, Springfield Armory, one of the important U. S. Martial Percussion Pistols issued to the armed forces. In addition, the U. S. Pistol-Carbine, Model 1855, Harpers Ferry Armory, was manufactured as pattern or experimental models for trial in the field, but there is no record of its production at Harpers Ferry in quantity. Details regarding these pistols are given in the chapter on U. S. Martial Percussion Pistols.

Disc Primers, Also Called Disk Primers

Disc primers, also called *disk primers* (Figure 16), were thin metallic foil discs, usually made of copper, which contained a detonating substance. This type of primer was used in some breech-loading percussion firearms. In the drawing, the picture at the left shows how the primers were piled up in a magazine from which they were fed, one at a time, as each shot was fired.

Cup Primer

The *cup primer* is illustrated in Figure 17. The picture on the left shows the metallic cartridge case. The picture on the right is a view of the base of the cartridge case, which was concave in shape and contained the detonating substance.

Bullet Containing Both Detonator and Powder

Figure 18 illustrates in more detail the bullet at the left of the principal portion of the drawing in Figure 11. The picture on the left in Figure 18 portrays the bullet, which had a hole in its base. Both powder and a detonating substance were loaded into this hole, thus eliminating any need for a

FIGURE 17. Cup primer

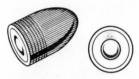

FIGURE 18. Bullet containing both detonator and powder charge

FIGURE 19. Teat (tit) cartridge

FIGURE 20. Crispin cartridge

FIGURE 21. Lip-fire cartridge

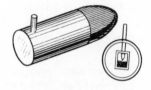

FIGURE 22. Pin-fire cartridge

FIGURE 23. Rim-fire cartridge

FIGURE 24. Center-fire cartridge

cartridge case when the bullet was fired in a mechanism like that in Figure 11.

Teat ("Tit") Cartridge

Figure 19 shows a *teat-type cartridge*. Our ancestors were not always skilled in spelling, hence the early records often refer to the "tit cartridge," and also to the "tit-fire" weapons. Even today, educated collectors and dealers often use the word "tit," either through ignorance of its significance or to follow the traditional designation. The teat or tit was filled with the detonating substance. When the weapon was loaded, the cartridge was placed so that the hammer, or a firing pin driven by a hammer, smashed the teat, thus setting fire to the powder in the metallic cartridge case.

Crispin Cartridge

Silas Crispin received U. S. patent No. 49,237 on August 8, 1865, for the cartridge illustrated in Figure 20, which his patent application refers to as follows:

> The cartridge constructed as described, that is to say, with the fulminate placed within a projecting annular recess or rim, which is formed at a point between the ends of the cartridge case.

Although this cartridge belongs in the *metallic cartridge* era which followed the percussion period, it demonstrates one of the many efforts to improve ammunition.

Lip-Fire Cartridge

The *lip-fire cartridge* (Figure 21) contained the fulminate in a small projection, called a "lip," extending outward from what would otherwise be a perfect circle at the base of the cartridge. The cartridge is shown at the left and an outline of the base of the cartridge is at the right.

Pin-Fire Cartridge

The *pin-fire cartridge* (Figure 22) is typical of the *first type of metallic cartridge case* which contained a primer detonated by means of a pin struck by the hammer. The cartridge is shown at the left and a cross-sectional view is at the right. A blow from the hammer forces the pin inward against the fulminate in the percussion primer (cap), thereby detonating the primer and igniting the powder in the cartridge case.

Rim-Fire Cartridge

The *rim-fire cartridge* (Figure 23) has a hollow rim filled with the detonating substance (referred to frequently as the "fulminate" in descriptions of earlier ammunition) which is exploded when the rim is pinched between the firing pin of the modern rifle and the face of the chamber of the rifle. The same principle is applied in a modern pistol made to fire rim-fire cartridges. Crushing the rim explodes the detonating material and ignites the powder in the cartridge. "Rim-Fire" is abbreviated either "R.F." or "r.f." in many catalogs and texts.

Center-Fire Cartridge

The *center-fire cartridge* (Figure 24) has the primer in the center of the base of the cartridge case. The picture at the left in Figure 24 shows the cartridge and the one at the right the base of the cartridge. "Center-Fire" is abbreviated either "C.F." or "c.f."

In order to manufacture the rim-fire cartridge, the cartridge case must be made of a softer brass than that which can be used in making the center-fire cartridge. Therefore rim-fire cartridges are generally restricted in use to the smaller loads that develop less pressure when fired, and center-fire cartridges are used in firearms of greater power. Modern martial cartridges are all center-fire.

Figure 25 consists of cross-sectional views of a large *center-*

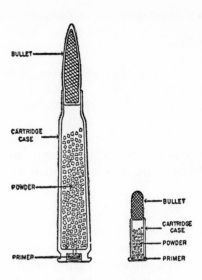

FIGURE 25. Cross-sectional views of large center-fire cartridge and small rim-fire cartridge

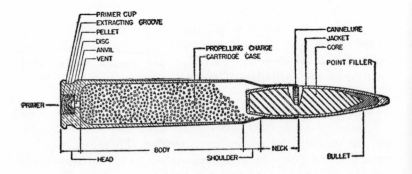

FIGURE 26. Cross-sectional view of component parts of a modern cartridge

fire cartridge on the left and a small *rim-fire cartridge* on the right, both as they appear standing on their bases.

Figure 26 is a cross-sectional view of the *component parts of a cartridge.* This is a side view of a rifle cartridge but the nomenclature and design principles apply to a pistol or revolver cartridge of modern manufacture.

Figures 5 to 24 were drawn by Herschel Logan. Figures 25 and 26 are reproduced by courtesy of the National Rifle Association of America.

All Firearms from Forsyth to Modern Cartridges Fundamentally Based upon Percussion Principle

The review of percussion lock development and cartridge design has taken us from Forsyth to the modern metallic-case cartridges in order to present in an unbroken line the transitionary steps in the improvement of the methods of ignition and the development that led to the modern metallic cartridges.

Fundamentally, all firearms, whether single-shot pistols, revolvers, rifles, muskets, musketoons, carbines, semiautomatic pistols, semiautomatic shoulder arms, automatic shoulder arms, or machine guns, from the days of Forsyth until the present, are based upon the *percussion principle* first employed practically by the Reverend Alexander John Forsyth. However, in Chapter 5, the U. S. Martial Percussion Single-Shot Pistols go back to the use of the *separate primer,* often called a "cap," invented either by Captain Joshua Shaw or one of the famous English gunmakers we mentioned previously.

ADOPTION OF PERCUSSION ARMS BY UNITED STATES

Although men began to convert flintlocks to percussion fire shortly after Forsyth started making his weapons commercially, and percussion firearms were in general use in Europe and the United States by 1825, the United States of America did not officially adopt the percussion method for its martial weapons until 1842.

There were several reasons for the delay by the United

States in officially sanctioning percussion arms. These were:

1. A vast number of flintlock arms, both pistols and shoulder arms, were in the possession of the armed forces of the United States, being manufactured under contract between the United States and private gunmakers or at the National Armories.

2. The early manufacturers of the separate primers, used in what collectors designate as percussion firearms, did not always use a good grade of copper and there was a tendency to load the primers with too heavy a charge of detonating substance. These two factors resulted in many accidents, some of them fatal.

3. During a war or campaign, on land or sea, the armed forces frequently exhausted their supply of primers, which could not be improvised but had to be made in factories. This made percussion arms contrast unfavorably with flintlocks which depended only on a supply of pieces of flint. Although it is true that a source of flint was not always accessible, it was a natural substance and not one that had to be made usable by precision tools and machinery.

4. The last and yet the most logical reason for the delay in adopting percussion arms was the basic reluctance of the armed forces of the United States to accept weapons of a new and radically different design. Throughout all the campaigns and wars of the United States, each new and improved method of fighting has met with violent opposition. This was true when the steam-driven ships of war, the diesel-driven vessels, the airplane, and the nuclear weapons were first proposed. The basic tendency of the United States is to fight each new war with the weapons of the previous war.

CHAPTER 6

U. S. Martial Percussion Pistols

CLASSIFICATION

U. S. Martial Percussion Pistols are single-shot percussion pistols made at both the U. S. Armory at Harpers Ferry, Virginia, and the U. S. Armory at Springfield, Massachusetts. In addition, those single-shot percussion pistols of martial caliber and size which were made under contract with the United States by private manufacturers for use by the armed forces of the United States belong in this classification.

Historically recognized contractors who made U. S. Martial Percussion Pistols include Henry Aston, the reorganized firm of H. Aston & Co., and Ira N. Johnson, all of Middletown, Connecticut; William Glaze & Co., Columbia, South Carolina, operating as the Palmetto Armory; N. P. Ames, Springfield, Massachusetts; and Henry Deringer, Jr., Philadelphia, Pennsylvania.

MODEL YEARS

If we disregard signal pistols and the U. S. Pistol, Navy Contract Model 1837, U. S. Martial Percussion Pistols are designated as Model 1842, Model 1843, and Model 1855. Collectors, dealers, and historians argue among themselves about model years. Some want to give a pistol a model year which represents the first year it was produced, even though the first pistol was an experimental or pattern model, produced before a contract was signed between the private manufacturer and the United States. Others wish to take the year stamped on some part of the pistol although it represents merely the year during which that part and not the whole pistol was made.

A few specialists in the collecting of U. S. Martial Percussion Pistols want to use as the model designation the year during which a patent was issued by the United States to the inventor of one or more parts, subassemblies, or assemblies. Closely related are those who wish to use as the model reference the year during which an inventor obtained a U. S. patent for a completely new pistol design.

In this text, we avoid the pitfalls inherent in these various methods of selecting the model year. We use as the model year for U. S. Martial Percussion Pistols the first year of official production of pistols by either the U. S. Armory at Harpers Ferry or that at Springfield. In the case of pistols made under contract between the United States and private manufacturers, we use the year the contract was signed.

Whenever there is any possibility of doubt about a model year, the one the author considers correct is given first and this is followed within parentheses by the model year which reputable experts prefer. This explanation is repeated in several chapters because it is extremely important to specialists in United States Martial and Semi-Martial Pistols.

Actually, model years in themselves are merely labels, but many dealers in listing pistols for sale do not give complete descriptions and vary among themselves in the choice of model years.

Conversion of Flintlocks to Percussion

In the previous chapter, reasons were given for the delay by the United States in officially adopting the percussion system of ignition for the firearms issued to the armed forces of the federal government. Also, it was stated that 1842 was the year when the percussion system became official. However, a law or a Congressional resolution is one thing and obedience to the law or resolution by the armed forces is something else. The reason is that the desire of the Congress of the United States, even when expressed as a law signed by the President and placed in the United States Statutes, must go down through military and naval channels of command until it reaches even the smallest outpost stationed in a foreign land and all the ships at sea.

Then when "all hands get the word," to use a nautical expression of ancient vintage, the orders of the federal government slowly begin to take effect. Evidence of the truth of this line of thinking is found in the fact that in 1848 all flintlock weapons were ordered inspected by officers and civilian employees of the United States. This order, in itself, shows that although the percussion system became official in 1842 for the armed forces, there were flintlocks on hand in 1848.

The order of 1848 provided that flintlocks suitable for military and naval use were to be converted to the percussion system. This order was interpreted to mean that if parts could be salvaged from partially defective arms and assembled into usable weapons, such reassembly of parts into firearms of martial effectiveness should be accomplished.

Those flintlocks found unserviceable, including those having parts not worth salvaging for reassembly into percussion arms, were sold to civilians in accordance with the order of 1848.

PERCUSSION ARMS IN WARS AND CAMPAIGNS

Mexican War

The Mexican War (1846 to 1848) was caused principally by the annexation of Texas (1844 to 1845), Mexico's refusal to accept the Rio Grande as boundary between the two nations, American determination to acquire California, offenses against Americans living in Mexico, the seizure or destruction of American property, and the desire of many men in the Southern states to add territory to the United States in which Negro slavery could be extended.

Accepting 1842 as the first year during which percussion firearms were officially adopted by the U. S. armed forces but bearing in mind that in 1848 it was necessary to issue an order to conduct an inventory and convert all usable flintlocks to percussion, it is logical to accept the opinion of the overwhelming majority of historians that *during the Mexican War, the U. S. armed forces were principally armed with flintlock muskets, rifles, and pistols.*

Comparatively few percussion firearms were used in the Mexican War and none were what we classify as U. S. Martial Percussion Pistols.

Civil War

The Civil War was fought from 1861 to 1865. Southern authors often refer to it as the War Between the States. The author remembers that when he was a small child a neighbor who had served in the Union Navy as a carpenter aboard a warship always referred to the Civil War as "the War of the Rebellion." This term is found in many books by Northern authors up to 1898. The causes of the Civil War are numerous and well known, but it is necessary to recognize that this war has several names in order to conduct research into firearms history. For example, the British refer to it as "the American Civil War" to distinguish it from the several civil wars in their own history.

At the outbreak of the Civil War, U. S. Martial Percussion Single-Shot Pistols, as they are defined in this text, were used by both Union and Confederate forces. Furthermore, the Confederates went into battle at the beginning of the Civil War with anything that would shoot, including flintlocks.

Genuine U. S. Martial Percussion Single-Shot Pistols are comparatively rare because percussion revolvers were the principal handguns used by both the Union and Confederate forces. It is true that U. S. Martial Percussion Single-Shot Pistols were used enough to be of importance to collectors and historians, but it is equally true that weapons firing metallic cartridges were used to some extent in the Civil War.

However, the end of the war terminated the martial usefulness of both percussion single-shot pistols and percussion revolvers. And it was the beginning of the adoption of cartridge
revolvers by U. S. armed forces.

Minor Wars and Campaigns

Black Hawk War

There have been several *minor wars* in the history of the
United States. For example, there was the Black Hawk War,
1831 to 1832, between the Sac and Fox Indians. It was named
after Black Hawk, an Indian war leader of great ability.
Abraham Lincoln served in the Black Hawk War as an
officer. During this minor war, all firearms depended upon
flintlock ignition.

Texas War for Independence

Another example is the Texas War for Independence,
which legally started on March 2, 1836, when Texas declared
its independence from Mexico at a convention held at a town
called Washington-on-the-Brazos. Four days later, on March
6, 1836, Antonio López de Santa Ana, President of the Republic of Mexico, personally commanded the soldiers who
captured the Alamo, where about 180 men under Colonel
William B. Travis died fighting. Other battles followed, but
on April 21, 1836, Texans under the command of Sam
Houston attacked and defeated the Mexican army near Harrisburg on the San Jacinto River, and took President Santa
Ana prisoner.

The Republic of Texas existed as a sovereign nation for
about nine and one-half years. It was recognized as a Republic
by the United States, Belgium, France, and Great Britain.
The United States officially annexed Texas as a state on
December 29, 1845. On February 19, 1846, President Anson
Jones of the Republic of Texas ordered the Lone Star Flag
of Texas lowered and the colors of the United States hoisted

over the capitol at Austin. He turned over the government of Texas to J. Pinckney Henderson, first Governor of the State of Texas.

In view of these facts, it is obvious that we cannot strictly describe any of the firearms used by Texas before its annexation to the Union as "U. S. Martial." But in the broader sense their war was our war and their guns were our guns.

At the beginning of the Texas War for Independence, flintlocks were in general use, but gradually Texans acquired single-shot percussion pistols and even a few percussion revolvers. How they got into Texas is beyond the scope of this book, but Texans did use United States Martial Flintlock Pistols, United States Secondary Martial Flintlock Pistols, United States Martial Percussion Pistols, and United States Secondary Martial Percussion Pistols before Texas became a state.

Campaigns

The word *war* is difficult to define. It may be conflict between two sovereign nations whether there is a formal declaration of hostilities by either nation or not. When hostilities exist between a sovereign nation's central authority and a subdivision of that nation, it is a *civil war* and the subdivision of the nation is in a state of rebellion. Therefore, what some Southern authors like to call "The War Between the States" was a rebellion and it was a civil war. Likewise, the Texas War for Independence was a rebellion from the Mexican viewpoint because Texas was part of the Republic of Mexico.

Since war has several definitions, only two of which we have given, the phrase *minor war* is equally difficult to define. The word *campaign* is often used to mean the same thing. Originally, a campaign signified the time armed forces were kept in the field of operations. Later dictionaries defined it as a series of military or naval engagements forming a distinct stage in a war.

Wars and Campaigns of the United States Marine Corps

Even U. S. dictionaries overlook the fact that the U. S. Marine Corps—founded on November 10, 1775, when the Continental Congress ordered two battalions of Marines raised for service as landing forces with the fleet—has participated not only in all the major wars of the United States but also in far more than 300 landings on foreign shores. Although most of these Marine invasions do not meet the professional dictionary definition of a campaign, they have been recognized repeatedly by the issuance of medals.

Between the official adoption of the percussion system of ignition and the eventual substitution of cartridge arms for percussion weapons, United States Martial Pistols were used not only in minor wars and campaigns but also in action against the American Indians.

Before discussing the technical features of United States Percussion Pistols, it is necessary to say that when a pistol in this classification is referred to as a "Navy" model or type, it is assumed that the United States Marine Corps used it as well.

It is also important to emphasize that the Marines have used "Army" models and types, because in all U. S. wars and campaigns, the Marine Corps has been either "First to Fight" or close to it. As the elite, shock-troop branch, the Corps has had to use any weapons available at the moment of crisis.

CONVERSION OF U. S. PISTOL, CONTRACT MODEL 1819, S. NORTH, ARMY, FROM FLINTLOCK TO PERCUSSION

General Procedure for Conversion

The U. S. Pistol, Contract Model 1819, S. North, Army, described and illustrated in the chapter on United States Martial Flintlock Pistols, provides the frame of reference for explaining the conversion from flintlock to percussion ignition.

The priming pan, frizzen, frizzen spring, and the flintlock-type hammer were removed. The original hammer was replaced by a percussion-type hammer—a hammer in the common sense of the term and not a device for holding a piece of flint between jaws. The nipple, a hollow cone sometimes called a "teat," erroneously spelled "tit" by some writers, provided access to the bore of the barrel and replaced the old vent or touchhole. A separate primer, sometimes called a detonating cap, was placed in the nipple. The phrase *separate primer* is used to emphasize that the primer (cap) was not part of a cartridge. The nipple was fastened to the barrel in any one of the forms acceptable to the United States.

Nonmartial Conversion

Figure 1 illustrates what most collectors regard as a nonmartial conversion. A cylindrical drum with a nipple, sometimes described as a cylinder lug containing a cone, was screwed into the right side of the barrel at the vent after the vent had been plugged. The hammer on some specimens converted in this manner is of a martial type, in which case the pistol can be classified as a U. S. Martial Percussion Pistol if it has the correct markings, especially if it has the markings or initials of U. S. inspectors.

When a sporting-type hammer is used, the conversion generally is not regarded as a U. S. Martial Percussion Pistol, despite the markings. In fact, extremely conservative experts hesitate to classify any pistol converted by the above procedure as "martial," regardless of the type of hammer and the markings.

No markings are shown in Figure 1 because the purpose of the illustration is to emphasize the conversion and not the pistol as a whole.

Martial Conversion

Figure 2 is an outline drawing of the pistol emphasizing a martial method of conversion. The vent was plugged. Then

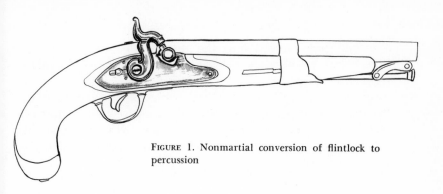

FIGURE 1. Nonmartial conversion of flintlock to percussion

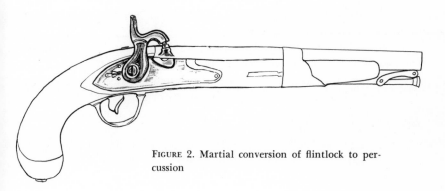

FIGURE 2. Martial conversion of flintlock to percussion

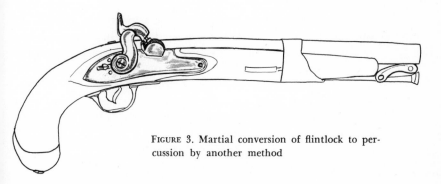

FIGURE 3. Martial conversion of flintlock to percussion by another method

191

a nipple was screwed into the top of the barrel, over the breech but to the right side. The hammer was offset to the right side to allow it to strike the primer placed in the nipple at the right-side location. Some experts contend that this was the most martial method of converting a flintlock pistol to a percussion weapon, but other experts argue that a method of conversion was "martial" if it was acceptable to U. S. inspectors.

Another Martial Conversion

Figure 3 is an outline drawing of the same pistol but with emphasis on another martial conversion. A bolster, also called a bolster lug, with a nipple was brazed on the right side of the barrel over the vent.

In the conversion of many flintlock muskets and some flint-lock pistols, the rear end of the barrel was cut off. Then a new breech, forged integral with the bolster and the nipple, was screwed into the threaded rear portion of the original barrel.

In both Figures 2 and 3, the bolster is not only called a bolster lug but also a "cone seat," "nipple seat," "teat seat," or "tit seat." This is merely another example of the failure of historians, collectors and dealers to settle on one name for a simple part.

Necessity for Repetition of Nomenclature

An advanced collector may find the constant repetition of synonyms for gun parts boresome, but a beginner is frequently confused when he reads a catalog, magazine or book and finds terminology which he has not encountered before. Since it is a common practice of gun collectors and dealers to look in a gun book for only the weapon that interests him at the moment, instead of reading the entire text, the author has attempted to describe each gun and each technique as completely as possible under each heading.

U. S. Pistol, Navy Contract Model 1837, C. B. Allen, Elgin Cutlass Pistol

Variation in Designation

This U. S. Martial Percussion Pistol was invented and patented in 1837 by George Elgin. It was made by Cyrus Bullard Allen, a gun manufacturer, with the assistance of Nathan Peabody Ames, a manufacturer of firearms and swords and other edged and pointed weapons. The business was conducted under the name of C. B. Allen.

Sometimes this pistol is called the Elgin Cutlass Pistol. It is referred to by some experts as the C. B. Allen, Elgin Cutlass Pistol, and it has many other names, all referring to the same pistol. There are variations in design and marking which are not important enough to take a pistol out of the U. S. Martial Percussion Pistol classification, but also there are some pistols which are superficially similar but belong in another classification, as explained later.

Description of Illustrated Specimen

The specimen illustrated in Figure 4 is cal. .54. It has a 5-inch, smoothbore octagonal barrel with a blade-type, iron front sight so low that it is barely visible in the drawing because the leather scabbard is drawn at an angle behind the pistol. There is no rear sight. The barrel is marked "ELGIN'S PATENT", "P M", "C B A", and 1837, together with a serial number which is the same as the serial number on the left side of the blade and also on the left side of the frame in this and all other authentic specimens. The total length is 15 inches for the specimen illustrated. Some authentic specimens have a cutlass blade 11.5 inches long and 2.063 inches wide, fastened in front of the trigger guard under the barrel. When an authentic specimen has a blade of this description, the total length is 15.75 inches, and the weight is 2 lbs., 7 oz. Obviously, when the total length is 15 inches, the weight is less.

The left side of the iron frame is stamped "C.B. ALLEN SPRINGFIELD MASS", without commas. The blade, trigger guard, and the very large oval portion in the rear of the trigger guard, sometimes called "hand guard" or "knuckle guard," are all made of tempered steel and manufactured "integral"; that is, they are not separate parts but constitute one subassembly of the pistol.

There is a side hammer, an iron back strap, an iron frame, and walnut grips. Originally, the leather scabbard (shown behind the pistol in Figure 4) was designed to hold both the pistol and a brass-tipped, iron or steel ramrod, which fitted into the top of the scabbard illustrated.

This pistol was loaded with loose powder and a ball and fired by a copper primer (cap) inserted in the nipple (cone, teat or tit) which provided a channel for the fire from the detonation of the primer to enter the bore and ignite the powder charge. This was not a unique feature; it followed the design principle of all of the fairly early U. S. Martial Percussion Pistols.

Some authentic specimens made later than the one illustrated do not have a scabbard designed to carry the ramrod.

In connection with the manufacture of the blade portion of this pistol, read the "Historical Background" in the explanation of the U. S. Pistol, Contract Model 1843 (1842), N. P. Ames, in this chapter.

Historical Justification for Classification

When George Elgin invented and patented this pistol in 1837, he wanted to obtain a contract with the U. S. Navy and other branches of the armed forces having vessels, such as the Revenue Service which preceded the present U. S. Coast Guard. He hoped his pistol would replace both pistols and cutlasses by combining a percussion pistol with an edged and pointed blade.

The U. S. Navy bought and issued exactly 150 of these pistols to personnel under the command of Lieutenant Charles Wilkes, who was responsible for several comparatively small vessels collectively known in history as the Wilkes Exploring Expedition. This venture was authorized by a Congressional law requiring a naval cruise around the world to obtain information about navigation and other subjects which would promote commerce between the United States and foreign countries.

Lieutenant Wilkes' vessels sailed from Hampton Roads, Virginia, in August 1838 and concluded the cruise on June 9, 1842, at New York City.

The Wilkes Expedition spent nearly four months—from May to August, 1840—surveying 154 islands, 50 detached reefs, and several harbors. The base of operations for this part of the expedition was at Ovelou in the Fiji Islands.

On July 24, 1840, at Malolo, Lieutenant J. A. Underwood and Midshipman Henry Wilkes were ambushed and murdered by native cannibals. Landing parties later burned two towns, killed fifty-seven natives who resisted the landing, and then forced two native chiefs to apologize before their assembled followers for the conduct of the natives, beg for mercy, and surrender.

During this and other actions of the Wilkes Exploring Expedition, officers and enlisted men carried and used what we describe as U. S. Pistol, Navy Contract Model 1837, C. B. Allen. There can be no doubt that this is a U. S. Martial Percussion Pistol. This is in the Smith collection. The serial number of his pistol is 149.

Nonmartial Variations

Distinctly different versions of this pistol, especially those having blade lengths and shapes that vary greatly from the above description, and more especially those marked "MOR-RILL MOSMAN & BLAIR AMHERST MASS", or marked with the name of some other manufacturer of similar pistols, are described and illustrated in the chapter on U. S. Secondary Martial Pistols. A few specimens do not meet the requirements of the U. S. Secondary Martial classification. These are classified correctly by collectors and dealers as "bowie-knife pistols" and are grouped with freaks and oddities.

U. S. PISTOL, CONTRACT MODEL 1842, H. ASTON, ARMY

Army Model

The U. S. Pistol, Contract Model 1842, H. Aston, Army (Figure 5) is cal. .54, with a smoothbore, round barrel, 8.5 inches long, with a brass, blade-type front sight. The barrel is marked "U S", "P", and with the initials of someone who may have been a U. S. inspector or may have been the man who made the barrel. The initials are probably those of a U. S. inspector. The barrel is marked on the tang with the year the barrel was made, which may or may not have been the year the pistol was assembled.

The walnut stock is described by collectors as a "three-quarters-length stock." It extends almost to the steel, swivel-type ramrod. The stock is 11 inches long. The total length of the pistol is 14 inches and the weight is 2 lbs., 12 oz.

The pistol is brass-mounted. The flat, beveled-edge lock plate is marked "U S" over "H ASTON & CO" in two parallel, horizontal lines in front of the hammer. The lock plate is marked behind the hammer in three lines which are horizontal when the barrel is pointed upward vertically. These marks behind the hammer are "MIDDtn" over "CONN". The year of manufacture, which is 1851 on the specimen illustrated, is under "CONN". The last two letters in "MIDDtn" are in lower case.

The lock plate is 4.8 inches long and 1.25 inches wide. The barrel is held to the stock by means of a single-branch band fastened to the stock on the left side by a forward side screw. Marks made by a U. S. inspector are on the left side of the stock. There is no separate back strap. Instead, a long extension from the brass butt cap on some specimens serves as a back strap. The total length of the trigger guard with its extensions along the stock, sometimes called "trigger-guard spurs," is 5 inches. The ends of the trigger guard are rounded.

FIGURE 4. U. S. Pistol, Navy Contract Model 1837, C. B. Allen, Elgin Cutlass Pistol

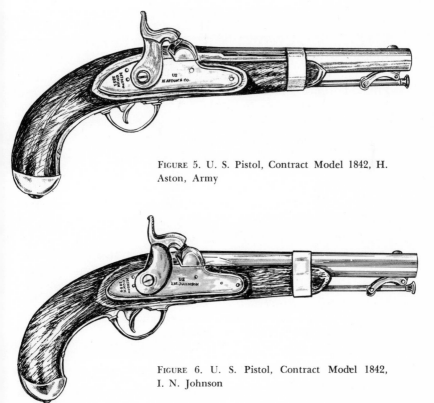

FIGURE 5. U. S. Pistol, Contract Model 1842, H. Aston, Army

FIGURE 6. U. S. Pistol, Contract Model 1842, I. N. Johnson

The swivel-type ramrod is threaded, at the end which is to the rear when the ramrod is not in use, to receive either a screw for removing a bullet or a device for holding a cleaning patch.

In its original condition, the trigger is blued and all other parts are finished bright, but firearms which have been used in combat extensively are not found in their original finish or color.

This pistol was designed at the U. S. Armory, Springfield, Massachusetts, and the pattern was copied by manufacturers having contracts with the United States.

Henry Aston came to the United States from England about 1819, worked for Simeon North at Middletown, Connecticut, and obtained a contract to make this pistol on February 25, 1845. Pistols made before 1851 are stamped "U S" and "H ASTON" in two parallel, horizontal lines on the lock plate, in front of the hammer. Those made in 1851 and 1852 are stamped "U S" and "H ASTON & CO" as shown in Figure 5. The difference in the marking between those made before 1851 and those made in 1851 and 1852 is explained by the fact that Aston's original company, organized about 1843, was reorganized and renamed in 1851.

This U. S. Pistol, Contract Model 1842 was also made under contract between the United States and Ira N. Johnson, Middletown, Connecticut. The same pattern was followed by the Palmetto Armory, operated by William Glaze & Co., Columbia, South Carolina, in the manufacture of pistols for the State of South Carolina.

The reorganized firm of H. Aston & Co. consisted of Henry Aston, Peter Aston, Ira N. Johnson, Peter Ashton, Sylvester C. Bailey, and John North. Johnson left the company in 1851 when he obtained his own contract to manufacture the pistol described and illustrated in this chapter as U. S. Pistol, Contract Model 1842, I. N. Johnson.

Navy Model

Some specimens of the Army model made by Aston have an

anchor stamped at the rear of the barrel. They may be marked with either the "H. ASTON" lettering or the "H. ASTON & CO." lettering. The presence of the anchor on the lock plate, together with any initials of U. S. inspectors who inspected for the Navy (which may or may not be found on the pistol) justify collectors in calling this Navy version "U. S. Pistol, Contract Model 1842, H. Aston, Navy" if they· desire, but the Army and the Navy versions are the same except for markings.

Martial Use

Since this pistol was made between February 25, 1845, and sometime in 1852, and possibly even later, under contract with the United States, it was available for use by the armed forces of the United States during small wars and campaigns after production started—during the Mexican War (1846 to 1848) and at the beginning of the Civil War.

U. S. Pistol, Contract Model 1842, I. N. Johnson

The U. S. Pistol, Contract Model 1842, I. N. Johnson (Figure 6) is the same as U. S. Pistol, Contract Model 1842, H. Aston, Army, described above and illustrated in Figure 5, except for the markings and those mechanical variations which can be expected in the manufacture of early American firearms before the interchangeability of parts became a standardized practice. It is cal. .54.

The barrel is marked "U S", with the proofmark "P", and initials, probably those of a U. S. inspector, but possibly those of the man who made the barrel.

The flat lock plate with a beveled edge is marked in two approximately horizontal lines "U S" over "I.N. JOHNSON" in front of the hammer. The lock plate is marked behind the hammer in three parallel lines which are horizontal if the pistol barrel is pointed vertically upward. The top line is "MIDDtn" with the "MIDD" in capital letters and the "tn" in lower case. The middle line is "CONN." The bottom line is "1854" on the specimen illustrated. These markings are found on the pistol shown in Figure 6, but on some authentic specimens the lock plate has "MIDDTN" in all-capital letters, and the year marked behind the hammer is different. The initials of an inspector are on the left side of the stock.

As mentioned before, Ira N. Johnson was a member of H. Aston & Co., formed in 1851. However, Ira N. Johnson obtained his own contract from the United States on March 8, 1851, providing for the manufacture of 10,000 pistols of the Model 1842. Therefore, he left H. Aston & Co., started his own business, and made pistols which obviously cannot be dated before 1851.

U. S. Pistol, Model 1842, Palmetto Armory

U. S. Pistol, Model 1842, Palmetto Armory (Figure 7) is not called a Contract Model because it was manufactured by the Palmetto Armory, operated by William Glaze & Co., Columbia, South Carolina, for the State of South Carolina. It is called U. S. Pistol, Model 1842, for two reasons. First, the state forces of South Carolina for whom it was made and issued were called into federal service to some extent and this pistol was used in battle by federal forces. Second, it is Model 1842 because it is almost identical in design and construction with U. S. Pistols, Model 1842, manufactured by contractors who made pistols for the United States according to the pattern and specifications established at the U. S. Armory, Springfield, Massachusetts. It is cal. .54.

This is a "contract pistol," but not a "U. S. contract pistol" because the contract was between the Palmetto Armory, operated by William Glaze & Co., and the State of South Carolina.

The barrel is marked "Wm. GLAZE & Co.", with the proofmarks "P" and "V", a palmetto tree, and the date on the tang of the barrel, which is 1853 on the specimen illustrated. However, these barrel markings are not visible in a side-view drawing such as Figure 7.

The lock plate is marked with a palmetto tree, surrounded by "PALMETTO" on the left, "ARMORY" on the right, and "S.C." at the bottom. "PALMETTO" and "ARMORY" are in distinct curves. Between the "S" and the "C" under the palmetto tree, there is a mark which resembles a small star. These marks are in front of the hammer. Behind the hammer, the lock plate is marked in two, slightly curved lines—"COLUMBIA" over "S.C. 1852" on the specimen illustrated. All these lock-plate markings are clearly shown in Figure 7.

For several years specimens of the U. S. Pistol, Contract Model 1849, H. Aston, Army, have been re-marked on the lock plate and elsewhere in order to cover up or remove the Aston marks and substitute the marks of U. S. Pistol, Model 1842, Palmetto Armory. The purpose has been to obtain a higher price because collectors and dealers assign a greater value to the Palmetto Armory Pistol than they do to the H. Aston Pistol.

All of the experienced antique arms dealers and most of the advanced collectors in the United States know about this faking. For some reason or other, very little has been said about it in magazines and newspapers of large circulation.

As we have said elsewhere in this text, the buyer should know the reputation of the seller when he buys the Palmetto Armory Pistol or any other gun collector's item having a comparatively high value.

Furthermore, there are Palmetto Armory Pistols, both genuine and counterfeit, to which Confederate marks have been applied within the last few years in an effort to deceive the buyer into thinking that he is buying a Palmetto Armory Pistol which can be classified not only as a U. S. Martial Percussion Pistol but also as a Confederate States of America Percussion Pistol.

If collectors read advertisements by certain gunsmiths and gun dealers they will find very cleverly worded insinuations that "reproductions of any firearm part you want" can be produced. On the surface, this means that they are offering to sell new parts to replace missing old parts, but if you buy enough reproduced parts you can assemble, or have a gunsmith assemble, a counterfeit firearm that will fool beginners and even some advanced collectors.

U. S. PISTOL, CONTRACT MODEL 1843 (1842), N. P. AMES

Historical Background

This U. S. Pistol was made under contract with the United States by Nathan Peabody Ames, Jr., supposedly at Springfield, Massachusetts. Nathan Peabody Ames, Jr., was born near Lowell, Massachusetts, in 1803, the son of Nathan Peabody Ames, Senior, who founded the Ames Manufacturing Company, originally located at Chelmsford (now Lowell), and moved in 1829 to Chicopee Falls, Massachusetts, a few miles north of Springfield.

In 1831 the company was incorporated legally as the Ames Manufacturing Company and obtained a contract with the United States to manufacture swords. About 1834, the company moved its office and business to Cabotsville, Massachusetts. In 1841, the company bought the factory and machinery of the Chicopee Falls Co. and then moved its machinery back to Chicopee Falls. In 1881, the Ames Sword Company was established at Chicopee Falls as a wholly owned subsidiary of the Ames Manufacturing Company after the acquisition of the adjacent Gaylord Manufacturing Co.

The Ames Manufacturing Company made the blade for the U. S. Pistol, Navy Contract Model 1837, C. B. Allen, Elgin Cutlass Pistol, described and illustrated earlier in this chapter.

Throughout its long existence under the leadership of Nathan Peabody Ames and his son, the company made edged tools, cutlasses, swords, bayonets, carbines, civilian pistols, and civilian revolvers. It had many contracts with both the U. S. Army and the U. S. Navy, but here we are primarily interested in its manufacture of a United States Martial, Single-Shot, Percussion Pistol.

Model Designation

The author does not think it important whether the con-

tract with the Ames Manufacturing Company was signed by
Nathan Peabody Senior or Nathan Peabody Junior, but it is
known that this pistol was made under contract with the
United States and also that it was made according to a pattern and a set of specifications made at the U. S. Armory,
Springfield, Massachusetts. Furthermore, it was made and
issued to the U. S. armed forces and used by them before
the issue and use of the U. S. Pistol, Contract Model 1842,
H. Aston Army (including the Navy version); U. S. Pistol,
Contract Model 1842, I. N. Johnson; the U. S. Pistol, Model
1842, Palmetto Armory; or any other U. S. Martial Percussion Pistol, Model 1842.

Some specimens are definitely Navy models because the
barrel of each of these pistols is stamped "U S N" and the
lock plate is dated with the year, starting with 1842 and end-
ing with 1845. Aside from recognition of the fact that some
were made for the Army and some for the Navy, the fact that
Navy specimens are dated as early as 1842 reinforces the
argument that this pistol should be called *U. S. Pistol, Contract Model 1842, N. P. Ames.*

Much against his own judgment, the author has given this
pistol a designation as Contract Model 1843 (1842). This is
done because the majority of collectors, dealers and historians
have been calling it the "Model 1843" so long that giving it
the correct designation as "Model 1842" would confuse the
public. It is a direct violation of the policy followed in this
text of giving the preferred model year first and the model
year used erroneously in the past within parentheses.

In some specimens the barrel is stamped "U S R", the
initials representing the U. S. Revenue Service, the predecessor
of the U. S. Coast Guard. The U. S. Revenue Service was not
under the Navy Department, although historically, in time
of war, the United States always has had the authority to
order the U. S. Coast Guard and the organizations which
preceded it to serve with and under the command of the
Navy.

The Ames Manufacturing Company delivered 2,000 pistols
of this model to the United States. How many the Army got,

how many the Navy received, and how many the U. S. Revenue Service obtained, we leave to future research.

Technical Description

This pistol is cal. .54. It has a 6-inch, round, smoothbore barrel without sights, originally browned when manufactured. The barrel of all authentic variations carries the proofmark "P", the initials of the inspector or the barrel maker, and the year.

This is called a "box-lock pistol" because the percussion lock is made with the base of the hammer inside the lock plate to facilitate a fast draw. This is why some collectors and dealers refer to the pistol as the "N. P. Ames Box-Lock, Single-Shot, Percussion Pistol." The lock and hammer are casehardened.

Figure 8 is the right-side view of the pistol. The flat lock plate 4.3 inches long and 1.25 inches wide, is marked in capital letters in three horizontal lines near the middle: "N.P. AMES" (top), "SPRINGFIELD" (middle line), and "MASS" (bottom line). The specimen illustrated is marked near the rear of the lock plate "U S R" over "1843".

The trigger guard, including extensions (spurs) is 4.75 inches long. It has square ends on the extensions.

The walnut stock is usually described as "three-quarter length," but it is longer proportionately than most stocks having this description. It is 10.625 inches long and extends to the swivel of the steel, swivel-type ramrod. Near the forward end of the stock there is one brass band which holds the barrel to the stock. A rounded brass butt cap, sometimes called a butt plate, is countersunk and not visible in Figure 8.

The pistol is brass-mounted. The total length of specimens examined by the author is 11.625 inches, but some pistols are described as being 11.75 inches long. The difference in total length could be in the pistol but it is probably due to the accuracy of measurement. The weight is always reported as 2 lbs.

Although the typical, authentic specimen in original con-

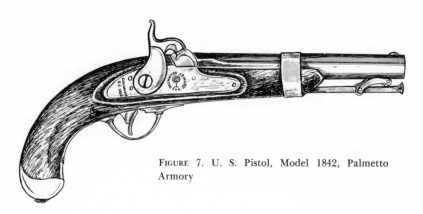

FIGURE 7. U. S. Pistol, Model 1842, Palmetto Armory

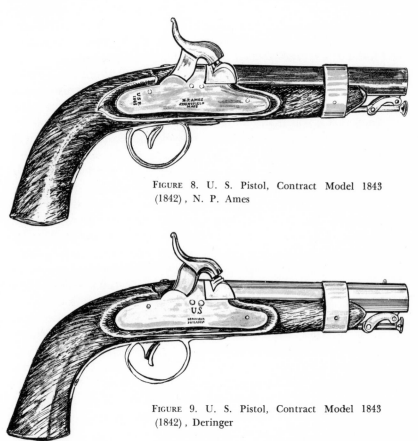

FIGURE 8. U. S. Pistol, Contract Model 1843 (1842), N. P. Ames

FIGURE 9. U. S. Pistol, Contract Model 1843 (1842), Deringer

205

dition does not have sights, some specimens are found with a low, brass, blade-type front sight, which may have been added after the pistol left the factory. None have a rear sight.

No specimens have been reported with distinctive Army markings. Although the one illustrated has "U S R" near the rear of the lock plate, those issued to the Navy may be found with "U S N" at the same place.

U. S. PISTOL, CONTRACT MODEL 1843 (1842), DERINGER

Historical Background

The U. S. Pistol Contract Model 1843 (1842), Deringer (Figure 9) is almost identical with U. S. Pistol, Contract Model 1843 (1842), N. P. Ames, described previously, except that the Deringer pistol usually is not dated; there is an easily apparent difference in markings; the Deringer pistol was made either smoothbore or rifled with seven grooves; the Ames pistol was made without sights; and the Deringer pistol, when made with a smoothbore barrel, had no rear sight and it was made either with or without a brass, blade-type front sight. When the Deringer pistol was made with a rifled barrel, it left the factory with both front and rear sights.

It is generally accepted that 1,200 were contracted by Henry Deringer, Jr., but less than one-half that number were delivered. This delivery, like the delivery of U. S. Martial Percussion Pistols bearing the model year 1842, was accomplished after the acceptance and use by the armed forces of the United States of the U. S. Pistol, Contract Model 1843 (1842), N. P. Ames. Therefore, there is no objection on the part of the author of this text to using 1843 as a model year in accordance with the well-established custom of authors, collectors, and dealers.

Henry Deringer, Jr., was the son of Henry Deringer who made the U. S. Flintlock Pistol, Contract Model 1807 (1808), described and illustrated in the chapter on United States Martial Flintlock Pistols. The son made firearms as an apprentice in Richmond, Virginia, until he moved to Philadelphia, where he worked first with his father and then for himself until he died on February 6, 1868.

During his lifetime, Henry Deringer, Jr., made both flintlock and percussion pistols, muskets and rifles for U. S. armed forces, firearms for U. S. distribution to Indians under treaties with various tribes, and all kinds, types and models of flintlock and percussion firearms for civilian sale. He made Kentucky (Pennsylvania) rifles and pistols, both flintlock and percussion, and also dueling pistols in matched pairs, both flintlock and percussion. On the day of his death, men whom he had trained in the manufacture of firearms were making cartridge weapons. Therefore, his life spanned the three great ignition eras of flintlock, percussion and cartridge weapons.

Deringer's fame is so great that his last name has become a common noun, spelled *derringer* in dictionaries and gun books. This refers to his short-barreled pocket percussion pistols of large caliber. Unfortunately, one of his "derringers" was used by John Wilkes Booth to murder President Abraham Lincoln.

The Derringers, father and son, and the firearms they made, are described and illustrated in detail in *The Complete Book of Gun Collecting, The Gun Collector's Handbook of Values, Guns of the Old West,* and other gun books by this author.

Technical Description

The U. S. Pistol, Contract Model 1843 (1842), Deringer, is cal. .54. The lock plate of the specimen illustrated in Figure 9 is stamped in three parallel lines, at about the middle of the lock plate, with a very large "U S" at the top, "DERINGER" below in all-capital letters, and "PHILADELₐ" in capital letters at the bottom. The last "A" in "PHILADELA" is a capital "A" but made smaller than the other letters in this abbreviation. On some specimens, the last letter appears to be a lower-case letter, hence it reads "PHILADELa", but repeated polishing has made it difficult to read the marking on many authentic pistols of this model.

On some specimens, the lock plate is marked similar to that of U. S. Pistol, Contract Model 1843 (1842), N. P. Ames, at the rear of the lock plate. This means that it may be stamped "U S N" with the year, but such marking is rare.

The barrel of some specimens is marked "DERINGER", together with "PHILADELA", both words in all-capital letters, except that the last "A" in "PHILADELA" on a barrel may be a capital "A" made smaller than the other letters, as on the lock plate. Also, the last letter may be a lower-case "a", as on the lock plate.

The barrel may be stamped with the letters "R P" and nothing else. Many barrels have no marking of any kind. When there is a date on the lock plate or on the barrel, it is 1847 on all specimens examined by the author or reported to him by reliable collectors and dealers.

RIFLING

Rifling was not a unique feature of the Deringer pistol. Rifling—cutting spiral grooves in the bore (barrel interior) to give the bullet a spin and thus increase its accuracy—was invented in Europe, probably in Leipzig, Germany, or Vienna, Austria, sometime between 1450 and 1500.

The grooves in many of the earliest rifles were straight. This has caused some arms historians to say that the original purpose of rifling was to make it easier to remove the fouling of the bore produced after firing the black powder of that era.

On the other hand, the principle of stabilizing the flight of a projectile by forcing it to revolve on its axis was used in the construction of some arrows and bolts shot from crossbows in China long before 1400, and in many parts of Europe before the hand cannon was developed as the first ignition type. These facts, together with the existence of many early rifles with spiral grooves, support the opinion of many arms experts that rifling was invented both to give the bullet a spin and to make it easier to clean the bore.

RAMRODS

Previously we have mentioned both wooden and steel ramrods used on flintlock and percussion pistols. A ramrod originally was intended to ram down the ball. Later, it was made so that either a screw for removing a bullet from the barrel or a device for holding a cleaning patch could be attached to one end, which was threaded to receive either the screw or the patch holder. When rifled pistols came into use, wooden ramrods broke easily due to the tight fit of the bullet and the difficulty of ramming it down the rifled bore. Therefore the wooden ramrods were replaced on many pistols by steel ramrods.

When a soldier armed with a muzzle-loading weapon lost his ramrod in battle, he was helpless until he could get another ramrod—unless, of course, he carried a pair of pistols. This led to the design and construction of the steel swivel-type ramrod described and illustrated previously. With the swivel-type ramrod, there was no danger of loss because it was permanently attached to the pistol.

U. S. PISTOL-CARBINE, MODEL 1855, SPRINGFIELD

Principal Technical Features

The U. S. Pistol-Carbine, Model 1855, Springfield, is illustrated in Figure 10, which is an artist's conception and not a mechanical drawing. In explaining the principal technical features it must be remembered that any side-view drawing of a firearm cannot portray all the details, even if it is a mechanical drawing. This applies to all firearms illustrated in this and all other books on guns.

It is cal. .58, with a 12-inch, round barrel rifled with three wide grooves. There is a low, blade-type front sight and what is technically described as a "triple-leaf rear sight." This rear sight is graduated in its markings to a range of 400 yards, with a peep sight to be used at a range of 300 yards.

The specimen illustrated in Figure 10, as all authentic specimens, has a barrel marked "P", "V", the customary proofmarks of the U. S. Armory at Springfield, Massachusetts, the head of an eagle, and the model year, which is 1855, the latter being stamped on the tang of the barrel.

The total length of the pistol when the detachable shoulder stock is not mounted is 17.75 inches, although some experts list it as 18 inches. The weight of the pistol without the detachable shoulder stock is 3 lbs., 13 oz. The detachable shoulder stock, which is 11.5 inches long, is illustrated in Figure 11, drawn by Herschel C. Logan and presented here through the courtesy of Herman P. Dean, owner of the copyright. The upper surface of the brass butt plate for the detachable shoulder stock is marked "U S". The brass butt cap of the pistol and the brass band (yoke) of the detachable shoulder stock were marked with the same serial number, either at the U. S. Armory, or later in the field.

The pistol is brass-mounted. The brass trigger guard has a total length of 5.25 inches, including extensions (spurs). The extensions have rounded ends. There is one brass band holding the barrel to the stock. It is located slightly more than one-half the distance from the front end of the lock plate and the front end of the stock. Fastened to this brass barrel band is a swivel ring for attaching a lanyard if desired, especially for carrying the pistol without the shoulder stock attached. But a more important use of the swivel ring is its function for attaching a leather strap or sling when the shoulder stock is mounted on the pistol.

The oil-finished walnut stock of the pistol itself is described as "full-length," although it actually does not extend to the front end of the barrel because of the presence of the steel-swivel-type ramrod. The stock is reinforced at its front end with a brass cap, sometimes called a "stock tip," and otherwise known as a "fore-end cap."

The Detachable Shoulder Stock

The detachable shoulder stock also is made of walnut and oil-finished. It is 26.5 inches long, without the pistol attached. There is a swivel ring fastened to the lower end of the butt for use with a leather strap or sling when the pistol and detachable stock are joined. The detachable shoulder stock is easily attached to the steel back strap of the pistol itself and tightened by means of a round nut. When the stock is attached, the total length of the pistol-carbine is 28.25 inches, and the total weight of the pistol attached to the stock is 5 lbs., 7 oz. The weight of the detachable stock alone is 1 lb., 11 oz.

In any description of a pistol-carbine it is important to distinguish between the stock of the pistol itself and the detachable shoulder stock. The failure of some experts to do this in the past has caused unnecessary confusion.

When the pistol and the detachable shoulder stock are assembled, there are three swivel rings. One is on the brass barrel band of the pistol stock, one is fastened to the butt cap of the pistol, and the third is on the lower surface of the detachable butt. This is clearly shown in Figure 10. However, when an artist or photographer illustrates the assembled pistol-carbine, if one of the swivel rings is not in a position perpendicular to the main fore-and-aft axis of the weapon, it appears to have an oval shape. This is possible because the swivel rings are not rigidly attached, but are mounted so that they can swing right and left.

The Use of a Lanyard or a Strap (Sling)

When the pistol and stock are joined, the strap or sling can be fastened between the ring on the barrel band and the ring on the butt of the detachable stock, in a manner similar to the use of a strap or sling on any shoulder firearm, including modern military rifles equipped with slings or straps.

When the pistol is carried without the detachable stock, the lanyard can be attached to the ring fastened to the pistol butt. This is the practical and normal method of attaching a lanyard. Obviously, the ring fastened to the barrel band could be used when the pistol is carried without the shoulder stock attached, but this is an improbable use of the barrel-band swivel ring.

This pistol-carbine was designed, manufactured and issued for mounted men. Hence the lanyard, even when the pistol is used without the detachable shoulder stock, is important. More important still is the use of a strap or sling extending between the barrel-band ring and the swivel ring in the butt of the detachable stock.

The purpose of the lanyard when the pistol is used by itself has been explained in discussing other handguns, but it is well to realize that its function is to prevent the loss of the pistol if the soldier takes his hand off the butt for any reason.

The strap or sling used when the pistol-carbine is assembled has two functions: First, it can reduce the possibility of losing the weapon. Second, it can be used to steady the aim, although in practice few men in the U. S. armed forces have ever used a strap or sling to steady a shoulder arm for aiming during the heat of battle. Only after long and careful training in the use of the sling or strap, and then only when closely supervised by officers and noncommissioned officers, have our soldiers, sailors and marines made proper use of a sling or strap on a shoulder weapon. The only exception to this statement is that many snipers use the sling or strap without supervision, principally because they would not be detailed as snipers unless they were already skilled in marksmanship.

Lock-Plate Identification

The flat, bevel-edged lock plate is marked in two parallel, horizontal lines on the forward surface with "U S" over "SPRINGFIELD". Behind the hammer, the lock plate is marked either 1855 or 1856. Normally, the year is stamped in a horizontal line, but in the specimen illustrated in

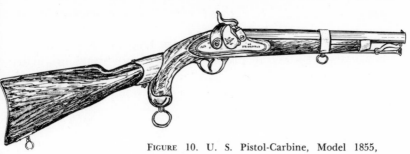

Figure 10. U. S. Pistol-Carbine, Model 1855, Springfield

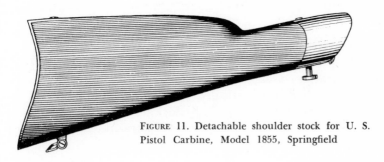

Figure 11. Detachable shoulder stock for U. S. Pistol Carbine, Model 1855, Springfield

Figure 12. U. S. Pistol-Carbine, Model 1855, Harpers Ferry

Figure 10 the year 1856 was stamped at an angle with the horizontal axis of the pistol. The lock and barrel originally were *finished bright;* that is, they were not browned, blued, or otherwise colored. A spread eagle is stamped on the Maynard primer recess cover.

The Ramrod

The steel, swivel-type ramrod has a button at its front end with a conical recess for seating the conical (more or less pointed) bullets supplied for this weapon. The rear or small end of the ramrod, not visible in Figure 10, has a thread inside for attaching either a bullet screw or a wiper head to hold a cleaning patch.

The Maynard Tape-Priming System

The pistol has a Maynard tape-priming system for ignition. This is briefly described and illustrated with a simple sketch in Chapter 5. On the U. S. Pistol-Carbine, Model 1855, Springfield, a coiled roll of paper tape, containing percussion primers, is fed automatically, one primer at a time, to the nipple (cone, teat or tit) of the lock mechanism. The tape is fed from a covered primer recess (magazine compartment) inside the lock mechanism, with the portion of the tape containing one primer coming into place each time the hammer is cocked. The cover for the primer recess in Figure 10 can be recognized by the spread eagle stamped on its surface.

The coiled roll of paper tape was available either with twenty-five or fifty primers. In some publications, the primers are called "pellets" and in others they are referred to as "caps," but these words mean the same thing.

In addition to the use of the Maynard tape-priming system on this pistol-carbine, it was applied to many muskets altered from flintlock to percussion: the U. S. Rifled Musket, Model 1855 (Maynard), which was made under contract with the United States by various contractors, the U. S. Rifle, Model 1855 (Maynard), and other firearms.

Priming Without the Maynard System

The pistol, whether or not it was attached to the shoulder stock, could be fired by means of ordinary, separate, individual, copper primers (caps or pellets), without depending in any way upon the Maynard tape-primer mechanism. However, this was awkward for mounted troops; hence the pistol usually was fired with the Maynard ignition mechanism.

Production Figures

Official records of the United States show that 2,710 of these pistol-carbines were made at the U. S. Armory, Springfield, Massachusetts, in 1856; and that 1,311 were manufactured there in 1857. This makes a total of 4,021 manufactured at the Springfield Armory.

Shoulder-Arm Classification

This pistol-carbine is treated in some publications as a pistol and in others as a shoulder arm. It was both. It was a pistol when used without the shoulder stock and a shoulder arm when the detachable stock was mounted; hence it is separately listed and described in *The Gun Collector's Handbook of Values* under both classifications.

When the pistol was used without the detachable stock, it was carried in a leather holster on the saddle of a mounted soldier. When the stock was attached, it could be fired either from horseback or on foot, but historically it usually was fired by horsemen after they dismounted and began to fight on foot. Tactically, it was employed as though it were a carbine (short rifle).

When equipped with shoulder arms, including this pistol-carbine, a cavalry squad of four men would halt in the rear of the line on which they intended to deploy. One man from each four-man squad would take the four horses for which he was responsible to the rear, under cover from enemy fire as much as possible. The other three would go on the firing line.

CAVALRY AND DRAGOONS

Historians make a distinction between cavalry and dragoons on the basis that dragoons were essentially mounted infantry, otherwise known in the early history books as "light cavalry," trained to ride to the battlefield and there dismount and fight as infantry.

This treatment of the subject is misleading because all mounted men, throughout U. S. history, have been trained to fight either on foot or on horseback. At various periods in our national life, mounted men have been required to carry shoulder arms, handguns, and also sabers. In addition, when what Americans regard as machine guns came into general martial use, the United States Cavalry had troops that carried machine guns on horseback. When ready to fire the machine guns, the men not assigned to hold horses would mount the gun on the tripod, arrange the belts of ammunition, and bring up water cans if they were using water-cooled machine guns.

A Britisher reading this text might be perplexed if we did not explain that Americans regard automatic rifles fired from the shoulder (or at the side of the hip) as shoulder arms, whereas the Britisher usually refers to them as machine guns. However, the Britisher may refer to automatic rifles as "light machine guns" and our tripod-mounted machine guns as "heavy machine guns." This explanation is offered not only for British readers but also for Americans who may try to understand British books on firearms.

Returning to the tactical use of United States Martial Single-Shot Pistols by mounted soldiers: In the early days when the comparatively primitive single-shot pistols were the principal firearms for use on horseback, the cavalry or dragoons would ride by the enemy, each man firing a shot from each of a pair of pistols (if he had a pair). The soldiers would then go to the rear while another line of cavalrymen shot at the enemy, reload and come back for another attack. The advent of the Maynard tape-primer system of ignition increased the speed of ignition activity, but the pistol was still a single-shot muzzle-loader; there was no fundamental change in tactics.

UNPOPULARITY OF PISTOL-CARBINE

The U. S. Pistol-Carbine, Model 1855, Springfield, like almost all combination-type weapons adopted by the armed forces, was unpopular with many soldiers and was superseded gradually by conventional types of firearms. Cavalry regiments hated it although regiments designated as dragoons generally liked it.

There were two reasons why soldiers did not like the pistol-carbine. A pistol fired from the hand is aimed differently than one mounted on a detachable stock and fired from the shoulder. The other reason was that a pistol mounted on a shoulder stock is an inadequate substitute for the shocking power that can be delivered by firing a shoulder arm with a comparatively long barrel.

CALIBER CHANGE IN 1855

In 1855, the United States officially took action to have all shoulder arms made in the future bored to caliber .58, instead of using the caliber .69 shoulder arms then in the hands of the armed forces.

The U. S. Pistol-Carbine, Model 1855, Springfield, cal. .58, was intended to supplant the cal. .69 musketoon (short, smoothbore musket) then carried by mounted men. The pistol-carbine was regularly issued to U. S. cavalry organizations, including those designated as dragoons, as fast as the U. S. Armory at Springfield could produce these weapons. They were in general use in 1856.

U. S. PISTOL-CARBINE, MODEL 1855, HARPERS FERRY

Historical Background

The U. S. Pistol-Carbine, Model 1855, Harpers Ferry, is generally regarded by experienced collectors, dealers and historians as an experimental or pattern weapon made at the U. S. Armory, Harpers Ferry, Virginia, but not intended for mass production. A small number was manufactured but exact figures are not available. Even the year of manufacture is uncertain but all locks on authentic specimens are dated either 1855 or 1856. Figure 12.

It is known that the U. S. Army appointed a Board to study the caliber of small arms (handguns and shoulder arms) in 1853 and assigned officers of the Ordnance branch of the Army to this Board. As a result of their work, the adoption of caliber .58 for small arms became official for the Army in 1855, and this resulted in the production of the U. S. Pistol Carbine, Model 1855, Springfield, in quantity at the U. S. Armory, Springfield, Massachusetts.

These facts support the theory that the pistol-carbines made at Harpers Ferry were merely "trial" or experimental weapons which led to the pattern and specifications for the pistol-carbines made at Springfield. If this is a logical conclusion, then it is possible that the Harpers Ferry specimens may have been made sometime during 1853 or 1854 to open the way for production at Springfield. On the other hand, the fact that all known specimens of Harpers Ferry pistol-carbines have lock plates dated either 1855 or 1856 throws us back where we started.

Technical Description

The U. S. Pistol-Carbine, Model 1855, Harpers Ferry, is cal. .58. It has a 12-inch, round, rifled barrel, semioctagonal at the breech. The barrel is marked "P", "V", and with the head of an eagle. The barrel is rifled with three wide grooves. The pistol without the detachable shoulder stock is 18 inches long, whereas the Springfield Pistol is 17.75 inches long.

The total length of the Harpers Ferry Pistol-Carbine (Figure 12) is 28.5 inches when assembled, whereas the total assembled length of the Springfield Model is 28.25 inches. It is obvious that the addition of 0.25 inch to the length of the Harpers Ferry Pistol accounts for the fact that it is 0.25

inch longer when assembled than the Springfield Model. The length of the detachable shoulder stock of the Harpers Ferry Model is 11.5 inches, which coincides with the length of the Springfield detachable shoulder stock. Both models are brass-mounted and have the steel, swivel-type ramrod.

The Harpers Ferry Model has a steel, knife-blade-type front sight fastened to the barrel by brazing. Unlike the Springfield Model, there is no rear sight. The specimen illustrated in Figure 12 has a lock plate marked "HARPERS FERRY" near the lower edge of the middle portion. It is marked "U S" behind the hammer to read vertically when the pistol is pointed upward with the barrel in a vertical position. The lock plate of the illustrated specimen was originally marked "PISTOL CARBINE" near the front, but repeated polishing has almost removed these words and they are not shown in the drawing.

One of the most distinguishing features of all known specimens of the U. S. Pistol-Carbine, Model 1855, Harpers Ferry, is that the lock plate is not cut away for the Maynard tape-primer magazine recess.

It is apparent that this pistol-carbine is one of the mystery guns in U. S. military history. We know where it was made, but we do not know definitely the year or years of manufacture, the quantity produced, or the true reason for making it at Harpers Ferry.

U. S. Signal Pistols

Definition

A *signal pistol* also is called a *flare pistol* because when fired the charge of powder is not used to propel a bullet, but sends into the air a *flare,* which is a blaze of fire or light. There are several different types of flares. Some are intended for signaling. This is accomplished by firing a single flare at a predetermined time or place, or by firing a flare of a particular color. Another method of signaling with flares is to fire them in various colors, the arrangement or sequence of which conveys a message according to a mutually understood code.

Other flares are designed to illuminate a large area either to reveal the presence of enemy targets or to light up the terrain in preparation for the advance.

Signal pistols are as old as firearms. The Chinese used a crude form of hand cannon to fire rockets as signals to their friends and to frighten their enemies hundreds of years before signal pistols came into use in Europe. Since the beginning of World War I, U. S. armed forces have used signal pistols to send up small parachutes which slowly descend, carrying with them flares to illuminate vast areas such as airfields. In addition, these parachute flares are used for all the other signal-pistol functions.

Very Pistols Belong to Cartridge Era

Some collectors, dealers and historians erroneously refer to flintlock and percussion signal pistols as "Very pistols." This is wrong because the Very Pistol was invented in 1877, long after the close of the percussion era.

It is named for Edward Wilson Very, who was born in Maine, entered the U. S. Naval Academy at Annapolis, Maryland, as a Midshipman in 1863, graduated in 1867, invented the Very Signal Pistol in 1877, resigned from the Navy on April 30, 1885, while he was still a Lieutenant, and died March 1, 1910, in New York City.

Although these comments are more appropriate for one of the later chapters on U. S. Martial Cartridge Pistols, they are presented here to show how easy it is to make mistakes in writing on firearms unless there is access to reliable records. The author thought for many years that Lieutenant Very was a British officer and wasted time trying to find him listed in British records, but finally turned to a book called *Register of Graduates,* published by the United States Naval Academy Alumni Association, and found the correct information on Lieutenant Very.

U. S. ARMY SIGNAL PISTOL, MODEL 1862. One version of the U. S. Army Signal Pistol, Model 1862, is illustrated in

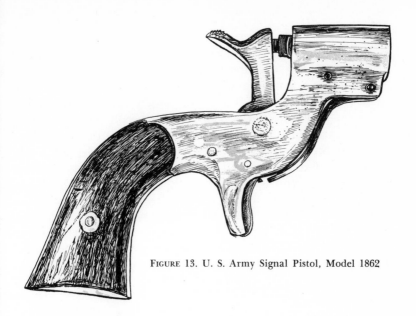

FIGURE 13. U. S. Army Signal Pistol, Model 1862

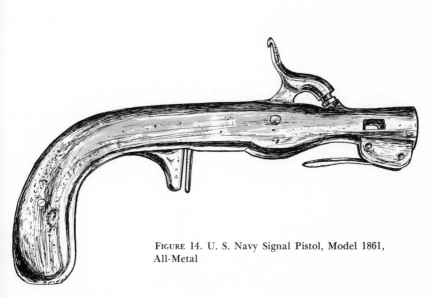

FIGURE 14. U. S. Navy Signal Pistol, Model 1861,
All-Metal

221

Figure 13. It is cal. .69, has a round, brass barrel which is 1.75 inches long, a center-hung hammer of percussion type, a spur trigger, a nipple (cone, teat, or tit) set into the rear of the barrel, and an iron lever which extends downward from the barrel along the frame and is used to hold the flare in the barrel until the shooter is ready to pull the trigger.

If this lever were not incorporated into the design of the pistol, the flare would fall out of the barrel easily because percussion-ignition flares did not fit tight in a barrel.

There is a brass frame. The grips attached to the butt frame are made of walnut. The butt strap is marked "U.S. ARMY SIGNAL PISTOL 1862" on all specimens examined by the author, but, in addition, some specimens have initials on the butt strap. The initials on the specimen illustrated are "A J M" and are the initials of a U. S. inspector. The total length is 6.5 inches.

Several specimens deviate slightly from the above description. For example, some are about caliber .75.

The model designation of 1862 is based entirely on the fact that this is the only year found stamped on U. S. Army Signal Pistols known to have been used during the Civil War. No information about the place of manufacture, the year of manufacture, or the quantity produced has been available to the author.

U. S. NAVY SIGNAL PISTOL, MODEL 1861, ALL-METAL. The U. S. Navy Signal Pistol illustrated in Figure 14 is made entirely of brass except for the hammer and the trigger, which are made of steel or iron. It has a total length of 9 inches. It is cal. .69, has a 2-inch barrel portion, a center-hung hammer, a straight trigger unprotected by a trigger guard, a nipple set into the rear of the barrel at a pronounced angle, and a brass lever which extends downward from the barrel along the frame to hold the flare in place in the barrel.

The model designation given this pistol is purely arbitrary and based on nothing more accurate than the fact that the author has never seen any specimens dated before 1861, although he has seen specimens dated as late as 1875.

U. S. Martial Use of Percussion Signal Pistols

The specimens illustrated in Figures 13 and 14 were issued to and used by U. S. armed forces during the Civil War. At the end of the war, which marked the general acceptance of cartridge revolvers, these signal pistols were still serviceable because all signal pistols known to the author, including modern cartridge signal pistols, are single-shot pistols. However, after the Civil War, some signal pistols were still fired with percussion primers, others were converted to fire metallic cartridges, and most of the remainder were sold as "war surplus" to Francis Bannerman. Bannerman founded Francis Bannerman Sons, lived from 1851 to 1918, and left his descendants Bannerman Island in the Hudson River—an island arsenal with a main building resembling an ancient Scottish castle. He also left a New York City martial-goods business that still flourishes.

CHAPTER 7

U. S. Secondary Martial Percussion Pistols

CLASSIFICATION

U. S. Secondary Martial Percussion Pistols are those large-caliber, large-size, single-shot, percussion pistols, suitable in design and construction for use by the armed forces of the United States of America, which cannot be described accurately and fall into one of the following groups:

1. Pistols made by individuals, partnerships, companies, or corporations which had contracts with the United States to make U. S. Martial Percussion Pistols, but also made pistols for the militia of the several states, volunteer military and naval organizations, officers who bought pistols from their own funds, ship officers of privateers, and state forces of various types who were not called into federal service.

2. Pistols made by contractors who did not have a contract with the United States, but were contractors with one or more of the states, or had contracts with semiofficial, volunteer military or naval organizations.

3. Pistols made by private enterprise for sale to individuals, such as officers of the federal service, the militia, and semiofficial military or naval volunteer organizations; or for sale to enlisted men who bought arms from their own funds. Pistols in this group were made by individuals, companies, or corporations which are not known to have had contracts

with either the United States or any of the individual states.

4. Pistols sold to officers, owners, and crew members of privateers authorized by the United States or any individual state to go to sea against the enemies of the United States. The explanation of privateers and their legality is given in Chapter 4, "U. S. Secondary Martial Flintlock Pistols," and applies with full force to U. S. Secondary Martial Percussion Pistols.

5. Pistols in this group were experimental, speculative, sample, or trial pistols made in the hope of obtaining a large contract or meeting with enough public approval to warrant mass production.

6. This is a catchall group for pistols which by tradition are believed to have been used to some extent by U. S. armed forces and about which there is not sufficient evidence to justify a U. S. Martial Percussion Pistol classification.

GENERAL COMMENTS ON U. S. SECONDARY MARTIAL PERCUSSION PISTOLS

1. The presence or absence of markings given in this chapter does not in itself serve as sufficient evidence for accurate identification. Each pistol must be judged as a whole.

2. The pistols classified in this chapter as U. S. Secondary Martial Percussion Pistols are those generally accepted by experienced collectors, dealers, and historians as belonging in this classification. However, there are pistols not mentioned in this chapter which future research may bring into this classification. In a similar manner, some of the pistols described and illustrated in this chapter may be advanced at a later date to the U. S. Martial Percussion Pistol classification if sufficient evidence is discovered.

3. Percussion dueling pistols of martial caliber and size, even though they were not designed or constructed for warfare, were sometimes carried into battle and used against the enemy, or used in duels against other persons in the same military or naval organization, but all dueling pistols, whether

flintlock or percussion, cannot be given either the U. S. Martial or the U. S. Secondary Martial classification. Even if used in battle, they cannot be classified as more than Semi-Martial. Hence all dueling pistols in this book are placed in one chapter.

4. Single-shot Kentucky (Pennsylvania) pistols of martial caliber and size, both flintlock and percussion, unless they meet the requirements for either U. S. Martial or U. S. Secondary Martial classification, cannot be placed in either of those groups. From the military and naval viewpoint, they are generally Semi-Martial if used in battle. Therefore, Kentucky (Pennsylvania) pistols are all placed in one chapter in this text.

5. Confederate single-shot pistols of martial caliber and size, both flintlock and percussion, are not in any sense "United States" pistols if they are primarily and fundamentally identified as "Confederate." Therefore, all Confederate pistols are in one chapter in this text. This subject is given a more detailed explanation in Chapter 4.

6. In *The Gun Collector's Handbook of Values,* Fifth Revised Edition (1960), and in previous editions of the same book, the pistols described and illustrated in this chapter as U. S. Secondary Martial Percussion Pistols are in a chapter called "American Secondary Martial Percussion Pistols" in order to avoid the implication that these are or were "United States Pistols" in the strict sense of that term. After consultation with many collectors, dealers and historians, it was decided to give this important group of single-shot percussion pistols the classification indicated by the title of this chapter.

C. B. ALLEN CUTLASS PISTOL. This pistol, sometimes called the Elgin Cutlass Pistol, when it does not comply with the description of the U. S. Pistol, Navy Contract Model 1837, C. B. Allen, Elgin Cutlass Pistol, given in Chapter 6, "U. S. Martial Percussion Pistols," must be regarded as a U. S. Secondary Martial Percussion Pistol. Since all specimens known to the author are marked "Morrill, Mosman & Blair" or with variations of the names of two or more members of Morrill, Mosman & Blair, these pistols are described in this chapter as Morrill, Mosman & Blair pistols.

CONSTABLE, PHILADELPHIA, PISTOL (Figure 1), cal. .54, with a 6-inch, smoothbore, octagonal, pin-fastened barrel marked "Philadelphia" on top. The total length is 10.5 inches. The lock plate is marked "Constable" forward of the hammer, but the name is not shown in the drawing because the marking is too faint on the pistol from which the drawing was made to be reproduced accurately. Nevertheless, all specimens examined by the author have "Constable" on the lock plate.

There is a small, iron, pin-type front sight, which is barely visible in Figure 7. There is no rear sight. The full-length walnut stock extends to the muzzle. The hickory ramrod has a horn tip. The pistol is iron-mounted.

This pistol was made about 1840 by Richard Constable, famous Philadelphia gunmaker, who had a shop at 88 South 2nd Street, Philadelphia, from 1817 to 1851. Assuming that this pistol was made in 1840, its traditional use by soldiers during the Mexican War (1846 to 1848) justifies its classification as one of the U. S. Secondary Martial Percussion Pistols.

Richard Constable made both flintlock and percussion arms, including dueling pistols and derringers. A Constable percussion dueling pistol is described and illustrated in the chapter on dueling pistols. A Constable percussion derringer is described and illustrated in *Guns of the Old West*.

DERR PISTOL (Figure 2), cal. .54, with a 10.375-inch, round, smoothbore barrel, octagonal at the rear. The barrel is key-fastened to the full-length maple stock that extends to the muzzle. There is a long, low, brass, blade-type front sight on the barrel, but it is farther back from the muzzle on the specimen illustrated than the normal location for a front sight on a single-shot pistol. There is an open, V-notch, iron rear sight. The barrel is marked on top "JOHN DERR WARRANTED"

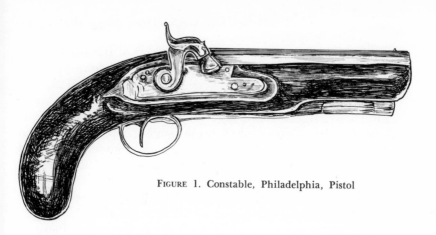

FIGURE 1. Constable, Philadelphia, Pistol

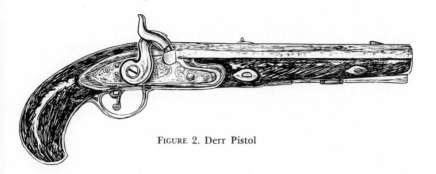

FIGURE 2. Derr Pistol

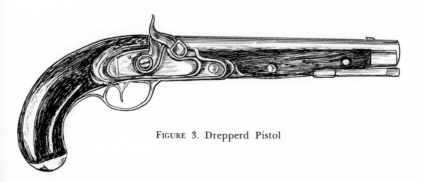

FIGURE 3. Drepperd Pistol

There is a brass cap at the forward end of the stock, sometimes called a "fore-end cap." The pistol is brass-mounted and has pinned thimbles. There is no back strap. The butt has a shape that collectors describe as a "bird's-head butt." The brass trigger guard forks at the rear after forming the loop for the trigger guard proper. The hickory ramrod is slightly larger at its forward end than throughout the rest of its length, but it is not enlarged enough to be called a "swell tip."

The flat lock plate is not marked but the specimen illustrated is elaborately ornamented with scrollwork.

This pistol was made by John Derr at Lancaster, Pennsylvania, who had shops at various locations in Berks County, Pennsylvania, from 1810 to 1831. He made both flintlock and percussion arms including both Kentucky (Pennsylvania) rifles and Kentucky (Pennsylvania) pistols.

His pistol illustrated in Figure 2 has enough of the characteristics of a Kentucky (Pennsylvania) pistol to be classified under that category but most collectors and dealers for at least thirty years have preferred to regard it as a U. S. Secondary Martial Pistol because there are records of its use as a martial pistol.

DREPPERD PISTOL (Figure 3), cal. .40, with an 8.875-inch, smoothbore, unmarked, octagonal, brass barrel, key-fastened to the stock. There is a brass, blade-type front sight and a wide, open rear sight on the tang of the barrel. The pistol is brass-mounted and has pin-fastened thimbles.

The full-length maple stock extends to the muzzle and has a brass end cap. There is no butt strap. The butt is rounded and has a brass butt cap. There is a brass trigger guard. The hickory ramrod has a horn tip.

The engraved lock plate is marked "DREPPERD LANCASTER" forward of the hammer, but this marking is not shown in the illustration because on the specimen from which the drawing was made the marking is too faint to be reproduced accurately.

This pistol has enough of the characteristics of the Kentucky (Pennsylvania) pistol to be classified in that category, but for many years it has been grouped by experts with U. S. Secondary Martial Pistols.

Although the marking is faint on the specimen from which the drawing was made, the name is definitely "DREP-PERD". Experts believe that this particular specimen was made by John Drepperd because the quality of workmanship is characteristic of that on other firearms bearing his name in full. In addition to John Drepperd, Andrew and Henry Drepperd made both flintlock and percussion arms in Lancaster, Pennsylvania.

A comparatively large number of flintlock and percussion pistols, rifles and muskets made in the section of Pennsylvania where most of the Kentucky (Pennsylvania) rifles and pistols originated are marked "Drepperd", and also marked "Dreppard", as well as "Drepert". A few are marked "Drippard". Some experts claim that each spelling represents a different gunmaker, but most authorities admit that they do not know definitely but believe that the same man often spelled his name in different ways. This was a very common practice during the flintlock period and the early part of the percussion era.

ELGIN CUTLASS PISTOL. See MORRILL, MOSMAN & BLAIR PISTOLS

Lindsay 2-Shot, Single-Barrel Pistols

LINDSAY 2-SHOT, SINGLE-BARREL PISTOL, FIRST MODEL (Figure 4), cal. .40, with a 4.875-inch, tapered, octagonal barrel marked on top "LINDSAY'S YOUNG AMERICA". It is marked "PATENT APD. FOR" on the right side, at the breech, but this marking is not visible in Figure 4. It has walnut grips, an engraved brass frame, and double spur triggers. There is a small blade-type front sight but no rear sight. Although not visible in the drawing, there are two separate triggers, one for each of the two hammers. This is the first model of the Lindsay 2-Shot, Single-Barrel

Pistol. Less than 200 were manufactured. The basic design and the operation is explained in the description of the second of Lindsay's models. One of a group of 9 different Lindsay Pistols in the Smith collection.

LINDSAY 2-SHOT, SINGLE-BARREL PISTOL, SECOND MODEL. This pistol is illustrated in Figure 5, a right-side view, and Figure 6, a left-side view. In Figure 5, only one hammer is visible in the drawing, but in Figure 6, one hammer has hit the primer in the nipple (cone, teat, or tit), while the other hammer is in the cocked position, all the way back.

This Second-Model Lindsay Pistol is cal. .45. It has a 8.25-inch, half-octagonal, smoothbore barrel with a brass, blade-type front sight. There are two nipples, side by side, hence they are not visible in a side-view drawing. The barrel is marked in front of these nipples "LINDSAY'S YOUNG AMERICA PATENTED OCT. 9, 1860" and also there is a serial number on the lower portion of the barrel which is always the same as the serial number marked on the brass frame, forward of the trigger guard. The rear sight is merely a notch in the brass frame. The total length is 12 inches. The weight is 2 lbs., 8 oz.

The grips are made of walnut. The trigger is described as being "spur type" by some experts but Figures 5 and 6 show a comparatively conventional trigger, whereas the trigger in Figure 4 is a true spur type.

A single trigger operates two centrally hung hammers. The right hammer falls on the right nipple to discharge a forward load in the barrel and then, when the trigger is given continued pressure, the left hammer falls on the left nipple to discharge the rear load. The two loads are placed with one in front of the other in a single barrel. In the strict sense of the term, this is not a single-shot pistol, and on this basis it could be eliminated from a group primarily reserved for single-shot percussion pistols. However, it has only one barrel and traditionally it has been classified by many experts for

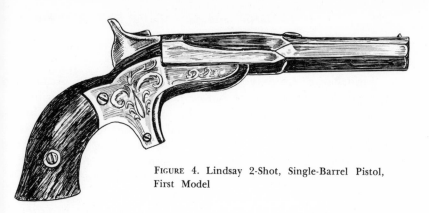

FIGURE 4. Lindsay 2-Shot, Single-Barrel Pistol, First Model

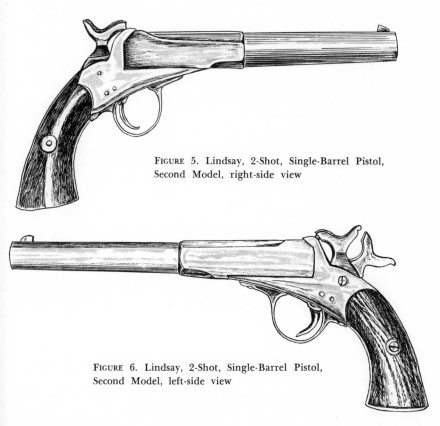

FIGURE 5. Lindsay, 2-Shot, Single-Barrel Pistol, Second Model, right-side view

FIGURE 6. Lindsay, 2-Shot, Single-Barrel Pistol, Second Model, left-side view

more than thirty years as a U. S. Secondary Martial Percussion Pistol.

John Parker Lindsay was a gunmaker at the U. S. Armory, Springfield, Massachusetts, before he decided to open his own business. It is not known when he made his first model, but he invented the mechanism patented October 9, 1860, before he organized the J. P. Lindsay Manufacturing Co. at 208 Orange Street, New Haven, Connecticut. He sold a small number of both models of his pistol and attempted to obtain a U. S. contract but his offer was rejected.

Instead, the United States bought one thousand two-shot, single-barrel, muzzle-loading percussion muskets based on the same patented mechanism in August, 1864, and issued them to the Army. The contract with the War Department was dated December 17, 1863, and the sale was made August 16, 1864.

The address of the J. P. Lindsay Manufacturing Co. was the same as that of Cyrus Manville, who was a surety named in the contract of 1863, hence it is assumed by some authorities that Manville manufactured the muskets although Lindsay was the inventor and patent owner.

The idea of loading a firearm with two or more charges of powder and ball, one placed behind another inside a barrel, was applied to weapons centuries before John Parker Lindsay obtained his patent, but he was probably the first inventor to produce a comparatively practical firearm based upon this loading theory.

Unfortunately, Lindsay faced two problems encountered by Samuel Colt when he was developing his early percussion revolving firearms. The first and more important problem was that the flash of fire from the ignition of the first load fired often spread to another load. In Lindsay's case, a man firing his two-shot pistol ran the risk of discharging only two loads at the same time, but in the very early Colt revolving firearms the flash of fire could discharge five or six charges almost instantaneously.

The second and much less difficult problem was that the

canal (channel) conducting the fire from the nipple holding the primer to the load inside the barrel was easily fouled after a few shots had been fired.

There is an unverified legend that collectors like to perpetuate to the effect that John Parker Lindsay was inspired to invent his two-shot, single-barrel mechanism because his brother was killed by Indians in an attack on an Army detachment. According to this story, the Indians first lured the soldiers into firing their muzzle-loading, single-shot muskets and then charged the soldiers before they had time to reload. Whether or not the legend relates to Lindsay's brother, it is a fact well known to students of American Indian warfare that this was a tactic developed by the Indians early in their relationship with white settlers in America.

MARSTON BREECH-LOADING PISTOL (Figure 7), cal. .36. It has a 5.75-inch, rifled, blued barrel, round at the front and octagonal at the rear, with a brass, blade-type front sight, and a V-notch, iron rear sight. The barrel is marked "W.W. MARSTON PATENTED NEW YORK" on top, and it is marked "CAST STEEL" on the right surface of the octagonal portion of the barrel, although this marking is not shown in the illustration. The same serial number is on the barrel and the bronze frame. The total length is 10.75 inches and the weight is 1 lb., 12 oz.

The walnut grips were shellacked when they left the factory. The iron trigger guard has a pronounced oval shape. The "side hammer" is offset to the right side, and is engraved. The bronze frame is engraved and was silver-plated when manufactured. The barrel was produced with a dark blue finish. The hammer, the operating lever for working the sliding breechblock, and the trigger are casehardened.

The operating lever for the sliding breechblock is shown in the closed position in Figure 7, as it appears after the pistol has been loaded. The hammer is shown as it appears after it has struck the primer.

In order to load, the operating lever is moved forward manually. This opens the sliding breechblock and permits loading into the chamber a cartridge of peculiar design, having a cardboard case with a leather base for the case. A small hole in the leather base of the cartridge, at its center, permits the fire from a primer in the nipple to reach the powder charge.

After the cartridge has been placed in the chamber, the operating lever is pulled back to the position shown in Figure 7. The backward motion of the operating lever closes the sliding breechblock. When the operating lever has been returned to the position shown in Figure 7, it partially fits into and is covered by the butt of the pistol.

William W. Marston obtained U. S. patent No. 7,443 for this pistol on June 18, 1850. He made his earlier pistols with bronze frames. Later, he used iron. In addition to the 5.75-inch barrel, Marston made pistols having a barrel length of 6, 7, 8, and 8.5 inches.

Marston not only made the breech-loading pistol described here, but also pepperbox pistols, percussion revolvers, and 3-shot, superposed barrel, rim-fire, cartridge pistols, all of which are described in *The Gun Collector's Handbook of Values*.

A factory or assembly plant operated by Marston in New York City at the corner of Second Avenue and 22nd Street during the 1860's was known both as the W. W. Marston Armory and the Phoenix Armory.

McK BROTHERS, BALTIMORE, PISTOL (Figure 8), probably made by the McKim Brothers, in Baltimore, Maryland, presumably between 1800 and 1845. They produced percussion, single-shot pistols of martial caliber and size for sale to both civilians and officers of state troops during the War of 1812 (1812–1815), and it is assumed that some of their pistols were used during the Texas War for Independence and the ensuing Mexican War. However, the records are incomplete and inconclusive.

The specimen shown in Figure 8 is cal. .60. It has a 10.375-inch, smoothbore, part-round, part-fluted, pin-fastened, un-

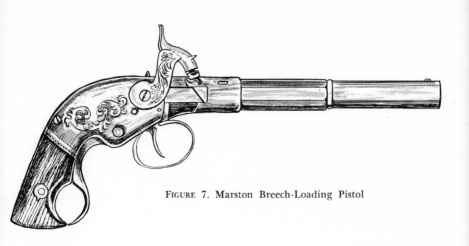

FIGURE 7. Marston Breech-Loading Pistol

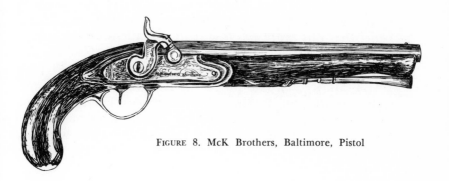

FIGURE 8. McK Brothers, Baltimore, Pistol

FIGURE 9. Morrill, Mosman & Blair Cutlass
Pistol, also called Morrill, Mosman · & Blair
Bowie-Knife Pistol, etc.

marked barrel with a very small front sight near the muzzle. The total length is 16 inches.

The walnut stock extends to within 0.375 inch behind the muzzle, hence it can be called a full-length stock. The illustration shows that there is a curved lower portion of the stock near the front. The purpose of this cut-out portion is believed to be the easier removal and replacement of the hickory ramrod with which it is equipped. The ramrod has a swell tip.

The pistol is brass-mounted. There are two pin-fastened, split, brass thimbles. There is a small, brass, rosette-shaped butt cap on the rounded butt. The trigger guard forks at the rear to form the conventional oval, and then it extends a short distance downward along the lower surface of the stock at the rear of the oval. There is no back strap. The nipple is mounted in a cylindrical side lug, which gives rise to the belief that this pistol was originally a flintlock and was then converted to percussion.

The flat, brass lock plate is marked "Mc K BROTHERS BALTIMORE" in one line forward of the hammer on the specimen illustrated, but other specimens are marked in three horizontal lines, forward of the hammer, along the lower portion of the lock plate: "Mc KIM" in the top line, "BROTHER" in the middle, and "BALTIMORE" in the bottom line.

Some specimens are cal. .69, with a 10.5-inch barrel and a total length of 16.125 inches.

MILLS PISTOL, not illustrated because it was not available when the illustrations for this book were made. It is cal. .75, and has a 10.75-inch, smoothbore, round, unmarked barrel, which is key-fastened to the stock. The total length is 16.75 inches.

The walnut stock extends about one-half the distance to the muzzle and has a German-silver end cap. The butt is rounded. There is no back strap, and no butt cap. There is an iron trigger guard. The barrel has a rib extension from the muzzle to the front end of the stock. The hickory ramrod has a brass tip.

The nipple seat is of the bolster type, hence it is probable that this was originally a flintlock and was later converted to percussion.

The lock plate is marked "B. MILLS HARRODSBURG KY", hence this pistol is sometimes listed as the "B. Mills Harrodsburg, Kentucky Pistol," which is misleading because this is not a Kentucky (Pennsylvania) type pistol.

This pistol was made by Benjamin Mills who was a gunsmith in Charlottesville, North Carolina, before he served under General Daniel Morgan, in an organization known as Morgan's Rifles, during the Revolutionary War. After the Revolutionary War, Mills made firearms in Harrodsburg, Kentucky, from about 1790 to about 1815.

Benjamin Mills supplied firearms to Colonel Richard M. Johnson's regiment of mounted Kentucky riflemen, who charged the British line at a critical moment in the Battle of the Thames River, which was fought in Canada on October 5, 1813, during the War of 1812. The attack by Johnson's regiment contributed materially to the defeat of 600 regular British soldiers and approximately the same number of allied Indians.

During this battle, Colonel (later General) Thomas Proctor commanded the British and Tecumseh, the famous war chief of the Shawnees, led the Indians. Tecumseh was among those killed.

The Mills Pistol may have been used first in the Revolutionary War as a flintlock and then converted to percussion for the War of 1812. Only the fruits of future research will reveal all the facts about the martial use of this particular pistol.

MORRILL, MOSMAN & BLAIR PISTOLS

Classification as U. S. Secondary Martial Percussion Pistols

The U. S. Pistol, Navy Contract Model 1837, C. B. Allen, Elgin Cutlass Pistol, described and illustrated in Chapter 6,

"U. S. Martial Percussion Pistols," also known as Elgin Cutlass Pistol, and otherwise as C. B. Allen, Elgin Cutlass Pistol, definitely belongs in the classification to which it has been assigned. All variations, except very minor deviations, when there is any question about conforming to the specifications for that particular pistol, belong in the group discussed here. These introductory remarks are important because some collectors and dealers, either through ignorance, carelessness, or cupidity, have sold Morrill, Mosman & Blair pistols of a somewhat similar design as C. B. Allen, Elgin Cutlass pistols.

Morrill, Mosman & Blair organized April 1, 1836, as a firm to make cutlery and various tools and machines. The original organization consisted of Henry A. Morrill, Silas Mosman, Jr., and Charles Blair. In July, 1837, Silas Mosman dropped out of the company or partnership and the original organization was thereby dissolved. Thereafter, the business was conducted by Morrill and Blair, doing business as Morrill & Blair until sometime in February, 1839, when the machines, tools, parts, and materials were sold, probably to satisfy the demands of creditors. Apparently the firm failed financially because there was a limited demand for a combination of a firearm and a blade. This is not surprising because a combination of a firearm with an edged or pointed weapon goes back in the history of firearms at least to matchlocks, and possibly hand cannon, and yet such combination weapons never have been popular.

We do not know whether the parts bought at the sale in 1839 were later assembled by the buyers to make pistols. Also we do not know whether the tools and machinery were used by the buyers to make pistols like those made by the sellers. This admission of ignorance about what was done with the parts, tools and machinery is made because it is possible that the buyers may have assembled or made some of the specimens which are hard to identify.

All genuine cutlass pistols manufactured either by Morrill, Mosman & Blair or by the reorganized firm of Morrill & Blair are rare and valuable. Historically and traditionally, these can be classified as U. S. Secondary Martial Percussion Pistols, although some collectors and dealers, when in doubt, list them among "freaks and oddities."

The use of the name Elgin on any of these cutlass pistols refers to the inventor, George Elgin. The use of the name C. B. Allen on any of these weapons can be accounted for by the possibility that either Morrill, Mosman & Blair, or the reorganized firm of Morrill & Blair, either made parts for the U. S. Pistol, Navy Contract Model 1837, C. B. Allen, or may have acquired parts from C. B. Allen.

Nomenclature

These cutlass pistols are sometimes called Bowie-Knife Pistols. This refers to the original designer or inventor of the bowie knife, James Bowie, who was born sometime between 1790 and 1796 and died on March 6, 1836, when he was killed by Mexican soldiers in their final assault on the Alamo. A town and a county in Texas are named in his honor. The knife he designed or invented was primarily a hunting knife, although it was used in warfare. The blade on the Morrill, Mosman & Blair cutlass pistols, and also on those made by Morrill & Blair, does not accurately conform to the lines of the authentic bowie knife, but there is some similarity.

Another name for these cutlass pistols is Knife Pistol. Still another name is Dagger Pistol. Such terms are more accurate from the mechanical viewpoint than "cutlass pistol," because a *cutlass* is a sword of a particular design and size, totally unrelated to the blade on U. S. Pistol, Navy Contract Model 1837, C. B. Allen or the blade on the cutlass pistols made by either Morrill, Mosman & Blair or the reorganized firm of Morrill & Blair.

Centuries ago, cutlasses were carried by crews of some merchant ships which were subject to attack by pirates, or which sailed as privateers. Cutlasses also were carried by the enlisted men of war vessels of European navies and the United States Navy to repel enemy boarders or for use in attacks on enemy sailors.

In modern times, the cutlass is worn by certain noncommissioned officers of the United States Marine Corps and by senior petty officers of the United States Navy for ceremonies.

The only justification for the word "cutlass" in connection with any of the cutlass pistols is that when George Elgin designed or invented his original cutlass pistol, he thought that it would supplant both the conventional single-shot percussion pistols of his day and also take the place of the cutlass, thereby enabling men who had been carrying two weapons in battle to be armed only with the combination weapon of his creation.

The Illustrated Specimen

The specimen illustrated in Figure 9 is cal. .34. It has a 4-inch, round, rifled barrel. The 9-inch blade is dovetailed into the lower surface of the barrel. There is a low, brass, blade-type front sight, but it is flat on top and lacks the curve of the usual blade-type front sight. The square-back trigger guard was forged integral with the blade, which was intended to be a substitute for a cutlass. The hammer is shown. The stock is made of walnut and has a curved butt but there is no butt cap.

The blade of the specimen in Figure 9 is marked in script on its right side "Elgin's Pat." within a wreathlike design. The left side of the blade, not visible in the drawing, is marked in two horizontal lines "Morrill, Mosman & Blair" over "Amherst, Mass." The total length, including the blade, is 13.5 inches.

The author has examined one specimen exactly like the one illustrated except that the blade is marked on its right side in script "Elgin's Patent".

Other Authentic Specimens

A specimen which has been described and illustrated for many years, and through various editions of *The Gun Collector's Handbook of Values,* is cal. .36, with a 3-inch, round barrel, an iron frame, and a side-hung hammer. The blade is 7 inches long and 1 inch wide. It is etched on the right side with the famous "Horn of Plenty" design and on the left side it is etched in two parallel, horizontal lines, in script, "Morrill & Blair" over "Amherst, Mass."

Another genuine specimen is cal. .38. It has a 4-inch, octagonal, rifled barrel with a brass, blade-type front sight and an open, notch-type rear sight. The weight is 1 lb., 10 oz., and the total length is 14.5 inches. The frame is made of iron. The stock is made of maple. The hammer is offset on the right side. The blade is 9.5 inches long and 1.5 inches wide, etched in script "Elgin's Patent" on the right side and etched in script "Morrill, Mosman & Blair" over "Amherst, Mass." on the left side.

Still another authentic specimen is cal. .54, with a 5-inch, round barrel. The blade is 9 inches long and etched on both sides with martial scenes. The right side of the blade is etched in script "Elgin's Pat." and the left side is etched in script "Morrill, Mosman & Blair" over "Amherst, Mass." The barrel frame and the blade were made of what was then known as "bright metal." This also applies to the trigger guard forged integral with the blade. The total length, including the blade, is 14.5 inches.

PERRY BREECH-LOADING PISTOL

Historical Background

Alonzo D. Perry obtained U. S. Patent No. 12,244 for this pistol on January 16, 1855. It was manufactured by the Perry Patent Arms Co., Newark, New Jersey, in both army and navy calibers, sizes, and types. In addition, the company made breech-loading rifles and carbines with the same Perry-type breech-loading mechanism. About 1856, the company failed financially and production stopped. Although efforts were made to obtain contracts with the United States, there is no available record of the granting of a contract. Therefore the Perry Breech-Loading Pistol comes under the classification of pistols in this chapter as an experimental, trial, or pattern pistol. It is possible that it was used as a semi-martial pistol but there is no evidence to this effect.

Technical Description

The Perry Breech-Loading Pistol (Figure 10) is cal. .52. It has a 6.5-inch, round, rifled barrel, rifled with six grooves. There is a brass, blade-type front sight. The V-notch rear sight is a groove in the barrel over the breech. The total length is 13.5 inches. The walnut stocks were oil-finished when manufactured. The hammer is offset to the right, hence is called a side hammer. The breechblock is marked on its top surface "A.D. PERRY PATENTED" and "PERRY PATENT FIRE ARMS CO. NEWARK, N.J." but this marking is not visible in a side-view drawing.

Loading Procedure

To load, the trigger-guard lever is lowered, thereby rotating the central breechblock, tilting the chamber at the breech upward so that it can be loaded either with a paper cartridge or with loose powder and ball. A projecting, beveled ring on the breechblock fits into the chamber and forms a gas-tight joint. This particular feature was an improvement on the Sharps Breech-Loading Pistol, which the Perry Pistol otherwise resembles.

When the breechblock is in the open position, the brass-tube priming (capping) magazine, which extends upward through the butt, feeds a percussion primer (cap) automatically to the nipple (cone, teat, or tit). However, all specimens do not have the automatic priming system.

Variations, Including the Buggy Pistol and the "Army Model"

One authentic specimen is exactly like the one described above, including the automatic priming system, except that it has a barrel which is 6.1875 inches long, a total length of 12.75 inches, and weighs 2 lbs., 15 oz.

Another variation is cal. .56, with a 20.25-inch, round,

smoothbore, steel barrel, and a total length of 26.5 inches. The breechblock is marked "PERRY PATENT ARMS CO. NEWARK, N.J." and "PATENTED 1855". The author has never seen a specimen of this description which was made with the automatic priming device. It is usually classified as a sporting firearm and sometimes listed as a "buggy pistol." The reason for the latter term is that one of the arguments used by salesmen for this model was that it would be a handy weapon for anyone riding around the country in a buggy.

A shorter version of the "buggy whip pistol" has a 16-inch, round, tapering, smoothbore, steel barrel. The total length is about 22.5 inches. It does not have the automatic priming mechanism.

The so-called "Perry Breech-Loading Pistol, Army Model," is cal. .44, with a 6.2-inch barrel and the automatic priming mechanism. It was offered to the War Department but the Army did not want it. This variation by itself is one of the several justifications for classifying the Perry Pistol as a U. S. Secondary Martial Pistol.

Finally, the phrases "percussion magazine," "capping device," "priming magazine," and "automatic priming mechanism" all mean the same thing, especially when applied to the Perry Pistol in all its variations.

SHARPS BREECH-LOADING PISTOL

Historical Background

The Sharps Breech-Loading Pistol (Figure 11) was manufactured by C. Sharps & Co., which consisted of Christian Sharps, J. B. Eddy, and N. H. Bolles. They had a factory in Fair Mount, later spelled Fairmount, which is now part of the city of Philadelphia, and were in business from 1859 to 1863. In 1863, William C. Hankins, of Philadelphia, who made the Hankins Pocket Percussion Revolver and other firearms, joined the firm, and it was thereafter known as Sharps & Hankins.

The most important feature of the Sharps Breech-Loading

Pistol is its lever-action, falling-block, breech-loading mechanism, for which Christian Sharps obtained U. S. Patent No. 5,763, on September 12, 1848. The same mechanism is found on Sharps breech-loading percussion rifles and carbines, including those martial shoulder arms classified by collectors as U. S. Secondary Martial Shoulder Arms.

A few specimens were made in cal. .44, offered to the War and Navy Departments of the United States, and tested by officers of the armed forces, but no contracts were issued, hence the Sharps Breech-Loading Pistols fall into the trial, pattern, or experimental group from the martial viewpoint. After the percussion pistols were rejected by the United States, a few pistols converted or modified to fire cartridges with built-in primers were offered to the U. S. Government, but these, too, were rejected and no contracts were issued.

Technical Description

The Sharps Breech-Loading Pistol illustrated in Figure 11 is cal. .38. It has a 6.5-inch, round, tapered barrel, which is rifled with five grooves. There is a small, brass, blade-type front sight. A V-notch rear sight is grooved in the frame. The total length is 11 inches and the weight is 2 lbs.

The grips are made of walnut. The back strap and the frame are made of steel. There is a side hammer, that is, a hammer offset to the right of the main axis of the pistol.

The frame is marked on the left, where it is not visible in a right-side view, "C. SHARPS & CO. RIFLE WORKS PHILA. PA. C. SHARPS PATENT 1848".

The priming mechanism incorporated into the lever-action, falling-block, breech-loading mechanism was invented by Richard S. Lawrence. Fundamentally, it consists of a tube in the frame from which primers are fed to the nipple automatically by the cocking of the hammer.

The lever, which also serves as a trigger guard, is lowered forward to operate the cylindrical breechblock and open the chamber to permit loading. After loading, the lever is pulled back to the position shown in Figure 11. The pistol could

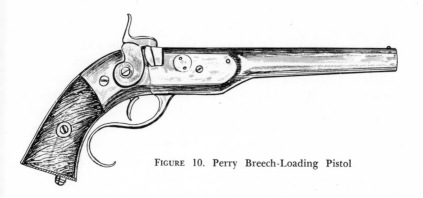

FIGURE 10. Perry Breech-Loading Pistol

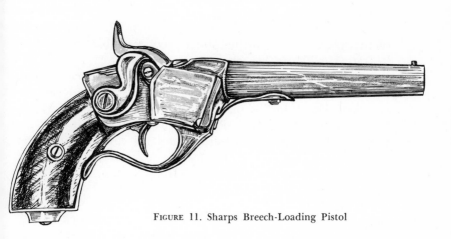

FIGURE 11. Sharps Breech-Loading Pistol

be loaded and fired either with the ordinary combustible cartridge of that era, using separate, individual primers; or with the priming mechanism invented by Lawrence.

Sharps and Perry Pistols Compared

Sharps obtained his patent for this pistol in 1848. As mentioned in the discussion of the Perry Breech-Loading Pistol, the two pistols are very much alike in many features, the most important difference being the projecting, beveled ring on the breechblock of the Perry Pistol, which fits into the chamber and forms a gas-tight joint. This feature was part of the design for which Alonzo D. Perry obtained a patent in 1855, and was a definite improvement over the Sharps design. Nevertheless, neither Sharps nor Perry obtained contracts with the United States for their pistols.

Sharps Variations

In addition to the cal. .38 pistol described in detail above, and the so-called "Army Model," Sharps produced a pistol similar to the cal. .38 version, but cal. .36, with a 6.375-inch, round, rifled barrel, rifled with five grooves. The total length of this pistol is 10.5 inches and closely resembles the one illustrated in Figure 11.

Sharps also made a cal. .31 pistol with a 5-inch, round, rifled barrel, similar in design to the cal. .38 and cal. .36 versions. The frame is marked "SHARPS PATENT MFgd. FAIR MOUNT PHILA. PA." Notice that "MFgd" has the first two letters as capital letters and the last two in lower case.

Tryon Pistol

Historical Background

The Tryon who made the Tryon Pistol illustrated in Figure 12 of this chapter is the same George W. Tryon who assembled the parts for the U. S. Pistol, Contract Model 1815, Philadelphia, described and illustrated in the chapter on United States Martial Flintlock Pistols.

The Tryon single-shot percussion pistol shown in Figure 12 has a full-length walnut stock, rounded butt with brass butt cap, a typical trigger guard of the late flintlock and early percussion period, a hickory ramrod with a swell tip, and a cal. .64, 9.25-inch, smoothbore, round, iron, pin-fastened barrel. The top of the barrel is marked "TRYON PHILADELPHIA", together with British proofmarks. The total length is 14.5 inches.

The lock plate is marked "TRYON" in all-capital letters, as shown in the illustration. The bolster-type mounting for the nipple is only one of many features which definitely indicate that this pistol was made originally as a flintlock and later converted to percussion. Whether the conversion was done by Tryon, or someone who bought the pistol from Tryon as a flintlock and then converted it, is not known, but it is a matter of record that Tryon imported the barrel from England. Whether the other parts were made by Tryon in his own factory, or bought from others, is not known definitely, but the assumption is that he made all parts except the barrel. His period of activity as a gunsmith, gun manufacturer, assembler of parts, and a contractor with the United States, extends from 1811 until 1841, hence this pistol could have been used during the War of 1812 and the Mexican War.

A. H. WATERS & CO. PISTOLS

Historical Background

Asa Waters, Senior, was born at Sutton, Massachusetts, January 27, 1742. Working with his brother, Andrus Waters, he established the Waters Armory at Sutton, Massachusetts, where firearms were made for the Continental Army during the American Revolution. Previously, Asa Waters made muskets and worked as a gunsmith for the Massachusetts Committee of Safety. Records indicate that both Asa Waters and his brother, Andrus Waters, served in the armed forces opposing the British. Although the exact military status of Andrus Waters is not known to the author of this book, he was buried at the U. S. Military Academy, West Point, New

York. After his death, Asa Waters, Senior, carried on the gun factory, although it is a matter of record that he served as a lieutenant in a company raised in Massachusetts, and also that he died on December 24, 1814.

Asa Waters, Jr., the son of Asa Waters, Senior, was born at Sutton, Massachusetts, November 2, 1769. He and his brother Elijah Waters worked in the family gun factory until they organized a partnership or company and built a gun factory called the Waters Armory. Elijah Waters died in 1814, the same year that his father died, leaving Asa Waters, Jr., who then dropped the "Jr." designation, as sole proprietor of the business.

Asa Waters received and carried out several contracts with the United States for the manufacture of shoulder arms. This is the same Asa Waters who made the U. S. Pistol, Contract Model 1836, A. Waters, Army, described and illustrated in Chapter 3, "U. S. Martial Flintlock Pistols." He had a son named Asa H. Waters. Sometime after 1843, probably in 1844, Asa H. Waters became the head of the business and incorporated it as A. H. Waters & Co.

Before proceeding to examine U. S. Secondary Martial Percussion Pistols made by A. H. Waters & Co., it is well to know that at least part of the machinery from the Waters Armory was sold in 1852 to William Glaze, who managed the Palmetto Armory at Charleston, South Carolina, and there made firearms for the State of South Carolina. This accounts for the similarity of design of some parts and even complete pistols made by the Waters family and the Palmetto Armory.

Two Distinct Models of A. H. Waters & Co. Pistols

Although the Waters family made many different types and models of firearms for the United States armed forces and for organizations armed with what we classify as U. S. Secondary Martial weapons (both pistols and shoulder arms), the two models which are recognized by experts as U. S. Secondary Martial Pistols are described and illustrated in this chapter as the A. H. Waters & Co. Pistol and the A. H. Waters & Co. "All-Metal" Pistol.

A. H. WATERS & CO. PISTOL

Technical Description

The A. H. Waters & Co. Pistol (Figure 13) is cal. .54. It has an 8.5-inch, round, smoothbore barrel, originally finished bright. There is a low, brass, knife-blade front sight and a large, open rear sight on the tang of the barrel. The barrel is marked with initials, probably those of a U. S. inspector, although possibly they are the initials of the barrel maker.

The barrel is held to the stock by a single branch band, fastened on the left side through the front-side screw, but this feature is not visible in a right-side view.

The pistol is iron-mounted. It has a three-quarter-length, black walnut stock, oil-finished when it left the factory. The pistol is iron-mounted. The back strap is formed by a long extension (spur) from the butt cap. The nipple (cone, teat, or tit) is set on a side lug. The smaller end of the ramrod, which in the illustration is the rear end and not visible when the ramrod is not in use, is threaded to be used with a wiper head (to hold a cleaning patch) or to hold a ball screw (for removing a bullet).

Superficially, this pistol resembles U. S. Martial Flintlock Pistol, Contract Model 1836, A. Waters, Army; and also U. S. Martial Flintlock Pistol, Contract Model 1836, A. H. Waters & Co., Army. Regardless of the resemblance to the flintlock pistols, the A. H. Waters & Co. Pistol, classified as a U. S. Secondary Martial Pistol, is not a conversion from flintlock to percussion. It was made as a percussion pistol for sale to officers and also to the militia of the several states. The total length is 14 inches and the weight is 2 lbs., 6 oz.

Lock-Plate Characteristics

The flintlock pistols which this model superficially resembles have lock plates with beveled edges, but the edges of the A. H. Waters & Co. Pistol, illustrated in Figure 13, are not beveled, hence the lock plate is often described as a "flat lock plate."

The lock plate is stamped in four horizontal, parallel lines, forward of the hammer, with an eagle head at the top, "A.H. WATERS & CO." in the second line, "MILBURY MASS" in the third line, and the year, 1849, at the bottom. On some specimens there is no eagle head on the lock plate.

Trigger and Trigger Guard

The trigger guard and the trigger of the specimen illustrated are made of brass, but some pistols of this model were made with iron triggers and iron trigger guards. Whether made of brass or iron, the trigger has the shape of that on U. S. Martial Flintlock Pistol, Contract Model 1836, A. Waters, Army; and U. S. Martial Flintlock Pistol, Contract Model 1836, A. H. Waters & Co., Army.

Percussion System Similar to That of U. S. Martial Percussion Pistols

Although externally the U. S. Secondary Martial Percussion Pistols made by the Waters family resemble somewhat the flintlock pistols made by the Waters family for the Army, the percussion system of these two percussion models is similar to that of the percussion system found on U. S. Pistol, Contract Model 1842, H. Aston, Army; U. S. Pistol, Contract Model 1842, I. N. Johnson; and U. S. Pistol, Contract Model 1842, Palmetto Armory. These three pistols are U. S. Martial Percussion Pistols, as explained previously.

Lock-Plate Dates

The specimen illustrated in Figure 13 is dated 1849 on the lock plate, which is the year of manufacture, but some specimens are dated 1844 on the lock plate, and other lock-plate year markings are reported. This pistol was used before and after the Mexican War, and during the opening days of

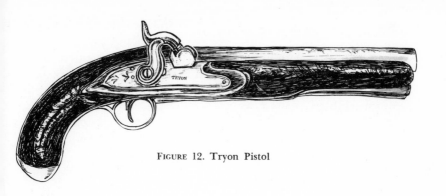

FIGURE 12. Tryon Pistol

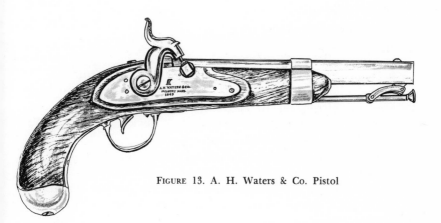

FIGURE 13. A. H. Waters & Co. Pistol

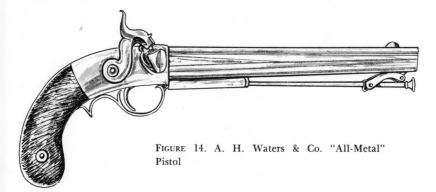

FIGURE 14. A. H. Waters & Co. "All-Metal" Pistol

253

the Civil War. Although lock-plate year markings often mean merely the year the lock plate was made, on this pistol it is the year of manufacture of the entire pistol, or the year it was assembled.

A. H. WATERS & CO. "ALL-METAL" PISTOL

The A. H. Waters & Co. "All-Metal" Pistol (Figure 14) is cal. .54. It has an 8-inch, round, smoothbore barrel. The total length is 12.625 inches. The martial-type, steel swivel is held in an iron tube, 2.5 inches long, fastened to the lower surface of the barrel. There is a rounded iron frame instead of the three-quarters-length, black, walnut stock of the A. H. Waters & Co. Pistol described above and illustrated in Figure 13.

This "all-metal" pistol has no stock. The only wooden parts are the two walnut grips fastened to the butt portion of the frame. For this reason, collectors, dealers, and historians have called this the A. H. Waters & Co. All-Metal Pistol for many years, although the presence of the walnut grips shows that it is not 100 percent metal.

It is believed that this "all-metal" pistol was made by A. H. Waters & Co. at Milbury, Massachusetts, in 1849, after the Mexican War. As we have said before, it was not bought by the United States. Seven specimens are known to be in existence. Four of them are marked on the left side of the barrel, at the flat portion, "A.H. WATERS MILBURY, MASS. 1849", and above this is the eagle head, "U S", and "P". The other three specimens have no markings of any type or kind.

CHAPTER 8

U. S. Martial Single-Shot Cartridge Pistols

HISTORICAL BACKGROUND

Civil War Theoretically Ended Single-Shot Era

THE Civil War (1861–65) ushered in the era of the revolver. First there were percussion revolvers, then percussion revolvers converted to use metallic cartridges with built-in primers, and finally cartridge revolvers. At the close of the Civil War, the single-shot pistol, even when designed and manufactured to fire metallic cartridges with built-in primers, was theoretically doomed.

These are broad, general statements which are true only when one looks at the whole picture of the use of handguns during the Civil War. As stated in previous chapters, many single-shot pistols, both flintlock and percussion, were used by both the United States armed forces and the armed forces of the Confederate States of America during the opening days of the Civil War. This is especially true of the Confederates, who had to go into battle with anything they could get in a hurry when the Civil War started in 1861.

Most of the revolvers used by both sides during the Civil War were percussion revolvers. The use of percussion revolvers converted to fire metallic cartridges with built-in primers came near the end of the war, and the number carried in combat represented only a fraction of those which were unconverted percussion revolvers. An even smaller number of cartridge revolvers, designed and made as cartridge revolvers, were fired in combat. These statements apply to U. S. Martial Cartridge Revolvers, U. S. Secondary Martial Cartridge Revolvers, and the cartridge revolvers used by the Confederate States of America. The same thing can be said for cartridge revolvers personally purchased and carried in combat by members of both Confederate and Union forces.

It is therefore something of a mystery to find that the United States ordered, purchased, accepted delivery and issued to its armed forces single-shot cartridge pistols after the end of the Civil War.

Remington Made All U. S. Martial, Single-Shot, Cartridge Pistols

There are only three U. S. Martial, Single-Shot, Cartridge Pistols. All three were made by Remington. Eliphalet Remington and his son, Eliphalet Remington, Jr., founded the Remington Arms Co., at Ilion Gorge, New York, in 1816. The whole story of the Remingtons and the corporation which still carries their honorable name is beyond the scope of this book, but it is sufficient to know that the Remington Arms Company was incorporated in 1865 when it hired Joseph Rider, one of the greatest inventors in firearms history. In 1866, the Remington Arms Co., Inc., failed financially and it was reorganized, taking the original name of Remington Arms Company, and passing under the control of Schuyler, Hartley & Graham, 19 Maiden Lane and 22 John Street, New York City, who described themselves as "Military Furnishers" in their 1864 catalog. The Remington family dropped out of control in 1866. The newly organized firm continued in business until 1902 when there was a merger with the Union Metallic Cartridge Company, but any further comments would carry us far past the era in which we are interested for the purpose of discussing U. S. Martial Single-Shot Cartridge Pistols.

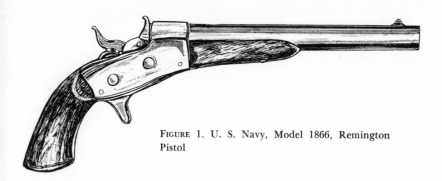

FIGURE 1. U. S. Navy, Model 1866, Remington Pistol

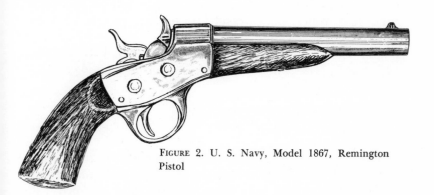

FIGURE 2. U. S. Navy, Model 1867, Remington Pistol

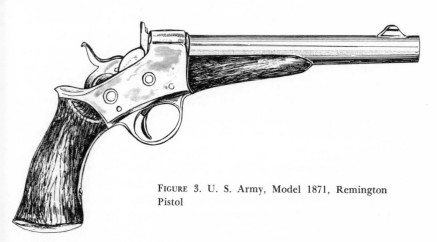

FIGURE 3. U. S. Army, Model 1871, Remington Pistol

The Three Remington Models

The three U. S. Martial, Single-Shot, Cartridge Pistols made by Remington are: (1) U. S. Navy, Model 1866, Remington Pistol; (2) U. S. Navy, Model 1867, Remington Pistol; and (3) U. S. Army, Model 1871, Remington Pistol. These are illustrated in Figures 1, 2, and 3 of this chapter.

Some collectors, dealers and historians refer to these as U. S. Navy, Model 1865, Remington Pistol; U. S. Navy, Model 1870, Remington Pistol; and U. S. Army, Model 1871, Remington Pistol. In other words, they agree with the designation of the third pistol used by the author of this book, but prefer other model years for the first two listed. From the practical viewpoint, these differences in designation of model years are of minor importance so long as everyone concerned knows which pistol he is describing or identifying.

U. S. NAVY, MODEL 1866, REMINGTON PISTOL

Technical Description

The U. S. Navy, Model 1866, Remington Pistol is illustrated in Figure 1. It is cal. .50, rim-fire, with an 8.5-inch, round barrel, rifled with three grooves, and stamped with an anchor. It was blued when it left the factory. There is a blade-type front sight with a round base. The rear sight is a V-shaped notch cut into the upper portion of the breech-block. The total length of the pistol is normally 13.25 inches, although specimens have been found with a total length of only 11.25 inches. The weight of the pistol of normal length is 2 lbs., 4 oz. Although the barrel was blued, the breech-block, hammer, and trigger were casehardened.

The *receiver* in all modern and semimodern handguns and shoulder guns firing metallic cartridges made with built-in primers is the steel frame to which the breech end of the barrel is screwed. Depending upon the design of the weapon, it receives the bolt, block, or other device having the same purpose; it holds the ejector which throws out the fired cartridge case; and it functions as part of the loading and firing subassembly.

The receiver of this pistol is marked on the left "REMINGTONS ILION N.Y. U.S.A. PAT. MAY 3d NOV. 15th 1864, APRIL 17, 1866" without any commas except the two quoted. In addition, it is marked on the right side with initials, probably those of an inspector.

The grips are made of walnut. The left grip is stamped with initials within a medallion design.

No Trigger Guard on Normal Specimen

The true, normal specimen has no trigger guard. The trigger is variously described as a "spur-type trigger," "sheath trigger," or "stud trigger," but all these mean the same thing.

When the pistol is cocked and carried in a holster, or even held in the hand, an accidental discharge is an ever-present danger, hence later models or modifications were designed and manufactured with trigger guards. It is possible that a trigger guard could have been added legitimately by members of the armed forces to which the pistol was issued, but the presence of a trigger guard raises a doubt and is a clue which should cause any prospective buyer to examine other features of this particular pistol to be sure that it is not a fake.

The presence of the spur-, stud-, or sheath-type trigger, and the absence of a trigger guard, characterize the U. S. Navy, Model 1866, Remington Pistol, as indicated above, but there are records which seem to indicate that the Remington factory sometimes installed this type of trigger on later models and omitted the trigger guard, thus adding to the confusion if a person confines his examination of a pistol to these two features.

The Remington factory made 7,500 of this model with sheath-, stud-, or spur-type triggers, but the Navy decided that it did not like this type of trigger and also complained that the barrel was too long. In an effort to please the Navy and get more business, the Remington factory took back at least 6,536 of the Model 1866 and altered them to form the pistol described below as U. S. Navy, Model 1867, Remington Pistol. Many advanced collectors and dealers who are experts in this subject believe that more than 6,536 were returned to the factory out of the original first lot of 7,500, because the Model 1866 in its original form, illustrated in Figure 1, is extremely rare today.

Remington-Rider, Rolling Block Designation

Some collectors and dealers refer to the Model 1866 as a "Remington-Rider, Rolling Block, Single-Shot, Cartridge Pistol," or by some similar designation. The reason for this starts with a U. S. Patent, No. 37,501, issued to Leonard Geiger on January 27, 1863. The Remingtons brought Geiger to Ilion, New York, to work in the factory and obtained from him the legal right to use his patent in the design and production of the Model 1866 Pistol.

Joseph Rider, who owned patents covering a hammer shaped something like a fishhook mounted forward of the axis of the breechblock, developed some improvements on the design covered by the Geiger patent. For some reason, Geiger was overlooked by those who have preferred the "Remington-Rider" phrase, and Rider was given great credit, but actually Joseph Rider, in spite of the fact that he was a great inventor, was only one of several men who made minor improvements on the Geiger design incorporated into the Model 1866 Pistol.

The breechblock of the Model 1866 Pistol is locked and supported by the hammer when it is in the down position. In other words, the basic Geiger patent provided for a hammer mounted back of the axis and supporting the breechblock against the backward force of the explosion of the powder in the metallic cartridge case. This feature is found in all three U. S. Martial Single-Shot Cartridge Pistols made by Remington, and also it is part of all other Remington firearms manufactured according to the rolling-block design.

The so-called "rolling block" inside the receiver is separate from the hammer although it rotates with the hammer, hence the origin of the term "rolling block."

Army and Civilian Versions

The records at the present Remington factory are incomplete because of the several reorganizations which took place both before and after the Remington family lost control. Also the records in the National Archives of the United States and those in the Department of Defense (which includes the old War and Navy Departments) are not complete. It is known that the first lot of pistols of this model went to the Navy and were marked with the anchor, but the Remington Co. also is supposed to have sold some pistols to the Army, and others to civilians. Whether or not pistols marked with the anchor went to the Army and civilians is not known.

U. S. Navy, Model 1867, Remington Pistol

Historical Background

Although all available records on these Remington pistols are incomplete, it is believed that this U. S. Navy, Model 1867, Remington Pistol, illustrated in Figure 2, was manufactured at the Remington plant by modifying the U. S. Navy, Model 1866, Remington Pistol. This belief is supported by the supposition that a Navy contract dated January 10, 1870, was signed which provided that the Remington factory should convert 3,000 pistols of the type we call Model 1866. For this reason, some collectors, dealers and historians refer to the Model 1866 Pistol as "U. S. Navy, 1870 Modification, Remington, Single-Shot Pistol." However, equally experienced experts argue that the Navy contract for modification was dated November 14, 1866.

Disregarding the argument about the date the contract was signed and what model year should be given this pistol, it is generally accepted that at least 6,536 of these pistols were completed to form the pistol designated here as U. S. Navy, Model 1867, Remington Pistol, on or before November 11,

1876. Apparently one contract called for altering 3,000 from Model 1866 to Model 1867, and a later contract, or an extension on the previous contract, required the modification of 3,536 more pistols, thus adding up to the total of 6,536 mentioned above.

Technical Description

The U. S. Navy, Model 1867, Remington Pistol, illustrated in Figure 2, is cal. .50, center-fire. It has a 7-inch, round barrel, rifled with three grooves, marked with an anchor and initials. When it left the factory, it was blued. When the barrel is 7 inches long, the total length is 11.75 inches and the weight is 2 lbs. The blade-type front sight has a round base. An open, V-shaped notch is cut out of the upper portion of the breechblock to form the rear sight.

This model has a reasonably conventional trigger instead of the stud-, spur-, or sheath-type trigger characteristic of what experts regard as the original or true Model 1866 Pistol. Also, this model has an oval trigger guard. The receiver, trigger, trigger guard, hammer, and breechblock are case-hardened. Walnut grips are fastened to the butt frame.

The receiver is marked "REMINGTONS ILION N.Y. U.S.A. PAT. MAY 3d NOV 15th 1864. APRIL 17th 1866", with the punctuation exactly as given here, on the left side. In addition the initials of an inspector are found on the left side of the receiver and also on the left side of the frame to which the grips are attached.

This Model 1867 Pistol is fundamentally an alteration, improvement, or modification of the Model 1866 Pistol. The barrel is 1.5 inches shorter; the breechblock is made for center-fire instead of rim-fire cartridges; the trigger has a different shape; and there is a trigger guard.

Variations

Some specimens vary from the above description of the Model 1867 Pistol by having a barrel of a different length, such as a barrel 8.5 inches long, like that on the Model 1866 Pistol. Other specimens have the sheath-, spur-, or stud-type trigger, even though there is a trigger guard.

Basis for Arguments

The collectors who specialize in Remington single-shot, martial, cartridge pistols argue among themselves about many details. You can get as many expert opinions as there are men who claim to be experts on Remington firearms.

This is not surprising. Experts on the early Smith & Wesson revolvers do not agree as to how the models should be designated, how many were made, when they were made, whether serial numbers run consecutively or run parallel in batches, and other details which are important to specialists, but only bore beginners.

The author is well aware of the difficulty in settling such arguments because many years ago he obtained a vast amount of information from three of the executives at the Smith & Wesson factory, one of whom was Frank H. Wesson, a descendant of the founders. Another was David Murray, Sales Manager, and the third was Fred Miller, Service and Repair Manager. Their reports were examined and verified as correct by Harmon L. Remmel, of Little Rock, Arkansas, in 1947. Mr. Remmel at that time was generally regarded as one of the foremost collectors specializing in early Smith & Wesson revolvers.

The advice and information from Harmon L. Remmel and the three Smith & Wesson executives were followed in revising the descriptions of Smith & Wesson revolvers in *The Gun Collector's Handbook of Values*. In spite of the exhaustive study of their own records by the Smith & Wesson factory experts, and the work of Harmon L. Remmel, collectors and dealers are still arguing about the details mentioned above. Since this situation exists with regard to Smith & Wesson revolvers, which are of comparatively recent origin, it is easy to understand how the experts on Remington pistols fail to agree.

U. S. ARMY, MODEL 1871, REMINGTON PISTOL

Technical Description

The U. S. Army, Model 1871, Remington Pistol (Figure 3) is cal. .50, center-fire, and has an 8-inch, round barrel, rifled with three grooves and blued at the factory. There is a knife-blade-type front sight on the barrel and a V-shaped rear sight formed by cutting a notch out of the top of the breechblock. The trigger was blued at the factory. The breechblock and the hammer were finished bright. The frame was casehardened in mottled colors. Walnut grips are attached to the butt frame. The total length is 12 inches and the weight is 2 lbs.

The receiver is marked on the left side "REMINGTONS ILION N.Y. U.S.A. PAT. MAY 3d NOV. 15th 1864. APRIL 17th 1866", with the punctuation exactly as stated here. In addition the receiver is marked with initials, probably those of an inspector. The frame to which the walnut grips are fastened is stamped with a serial number inside one of the grips. The left grip has an inspector's initials stamped in script inside a medallion design.

Differences Between Model 1871 and Model 1867

U. S. Army, Model 1871, Remington Pistol differs from U. S. Navy, Model 1867, Remington Pistol as follows: (1) The Model 1871 has an 8-inch barrel whereas the Model 1867 has a 7-inch barrel; (2) the Model 1871 has a front sight having a better design than that of the Model 1867; (3) the walnut butt is rounded and has what collectors call a "fishtail shape" to fit the shooter's hand; (4) the balance of the Model 1871 is far better than that of the Model 1867; and (5) the accuracy of the Model 1871 is greater than that of the Model 1867. Even today, the Model 1871 is extremely popular with those who specialize in target marksmanship. This is true whether the pistol is fired in its original condition or when fitted with a barrel having a caliber less than the caliber .50 of the original.

This Model 1871 was the last of the United States Martial,

Single-Shot, Cartridge Pistols, and the third of the three Remington pistols recognized by experts as U. S. Martial Single-Shot Cartridge Pistols. Five thousand Model 1871 Remington Single-Shot Pistols of the above description were manufactured by Remington and delivered to the U. S. Army in 1870, five years after the close of the Civil War in 1865, which was supposed to mark the end of the martial, single-shot, cartridge pistol era and the beginning of the use of cartridge revolvers by the armed forces of the United States.

The So-called U. S. Army, Experimental Model 1869, Springfield Pistol

Colonel B. R. Lewis, U. S. Army, Retired, is authority for the statement that the so-called U. S. Army, Experimental Model 1869, Springfield Pistol was never standardized, although it was officially authorized and tested, 25 being tested by the U. S. Cavalry. He reports that it was not made over from a rifle, "but had parts reduced in scale, the mountings resembled the Model 1842 Pistol; the breech was marked '1869'; and it fired a Special Cadet cartridge, cal. .50, with a short cartridge case, 1.312 inches long, although it was tested with the standard cartridge with no complications. Rumors to the contrary are false. Both Springfield and Rock Island Museums have samples."

Samuel E. Smith, Markesan, Wisconsin, reports that he examined a genuine pistol of this model at the Museum of the U. S. Armory, Springfield, Massachusetts, in 1961, and that it had been there since 1869. He adds: "About all we know of or see today are either fakes or stage pistols made in Philadelphia years ago." This refers to those offered for sale by collectors and dealers and not to the specimens at the National Armories.

Figure 4 is a line drawing of the so-called Model 1869, Springfield Pistol, prepared by Charles Winthrop Sawyer and presented to the author of this book in 1939 with the warning that he did not know whether it was a true representation

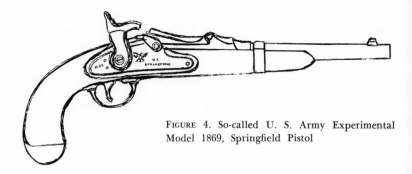

FIGURE 4. So-called U. S. Army Experimental
Model 1869, Springfield Pistol

of one of those made at the Springfield Armory, or one of
the fakes. Furthermore, Mr. Sawyer admitted that in his
various books on firearms he had done the best he could with
the information available to him, but that undoubtedly his
books contained several errors which would be corrected in
the future when other arms historians gained access to the
original records on arms production.

Charles Winthrop Sawyer was not only an advanced collector but also an author of several books on firearms in
American history listed in the Bibliography of this text.

When he presented the drawing, he said that at one time
he called the pistol "Model 1868, Army, Pistol," but at no
time did he regard it as anything more than an experimental
model made at Springfield, and that it could be called "Experimental Model 1869" with as much accuracy as designating
it "Model 1868."

Sawyer described it as cal. .50, center-fire, with an 8.5-inch,
rifled barrel; a total length of 18.5 inches; and weighing about
5 lbs. He said that the lock and the breech were the same
as for the U. S. Rifle, Model 1868. His opinion was that the
pistol was too heavy and the recoil excessive for service issue
and he emphasized that his investigation indicated that few
were made and that if any were issued to the Army, they
were issued for testing only and not for martial use.

Since cartridge revolvers were being issued to the armed forces of the United States and the only U. S. Martial, Single-Shot, Cartridge Pistols in service after the Civil War were the three Remington models described previously, there was no justification for experimenting with a single-shot cartridge pistol assembled from musket and rifle parts. The only reason for giving this monstrosity the dignity of mention in this book is to warn all collectors and dealers against being swindled.

THE U. S. ARMY AFTER THE CIVIL WAR

Before, during, and after the Civil War, the regular United States Army had to protect the thousands of people moving to the West and guard the men building the railroads reaching toward the Pacific. The last armed conflict between soldiers and Indians did not take place until September, 1898, when a detachment from the Third Regiment of Infantry, consisting of two officers and 100 enlisted men, engaged in a skirmish with Indians at Leech Lake, Minnesota. During this engagement, which lasted two days, several were killed and wounded. Reinforcements from the Regiment joined in the fight and peace was restored. Curiously enough, the organization which was the military ancestor of the Third Infantry, under the command of Colonel Josiah Harmar, U.S.A., took part in the first campaign against Indians in the United States in 1790.

The author is particularly interested in the fact that the Third Infantry opened and closed our wars and campaigns against the Indians because for a short time he served as a Reserve Second Lieutenant on active duty with the Third Infantry, at Fort Des Moines, Iowa, before being sworn into the regular United States Marine Corps as a Second Lieutenant, in 1926.

The U. S. Army, Model 1871, Remington Pistol, although only a single-shot pistol, was carried by the soldiers to whom it was issued as late as 1880, and used by them in battles with the Indians. The year when it was withdrawn from service is not known, but it may have been long after 1880.

THE U. S. NAVY AFTER THE CIVIL WAR

At the end of the Civil War in 1865, the United States Navy was the strongest navy in the world. It had grown from 69 serviceable vessels of all types in 1861 to 626 vessels in 1865, of which 65 were ironclads of great power in that era, and 160 other vessels were steam-driven men-of-war. The enlisted strength had expanded from 7,600 bluejackets in 1861 to 51,500 in 1865, with a corresponding increase in commissioned officers.

After the capture of Richmond, Virginia, the Congress of the United States ordered a rapid demobilization. Almost all of the sailing vessels and ironclads were sold, the gunboats being sold for junk. In addition, hundreds of merchant vessels that had been converted to ships of war were sold for what they would bring on a suddenly depressed market.

The United States Navy almost reached the bottom by 1881, when there was not one vessel fully armed, manned, and equipped for battle; and only a very few were fit for normal cruising, which in plain English means they could move from one port to another, fire salutes and avoid battle. Strangely enough, the best vessels of what had once been the greatest navy in the world were principally ships with wooden hulls, built before 1861, and armed with pre-Civil War smoothbore broadside guns.

It is not surprising that a nation that would let its Navy deteriorate in vessels also economized in small arms by continuing the use of the U. S. Navy, Model 1866, Remington Pistol to some extent, although most pistols of the Model 1866 were converted, as explained before, to the U. S. Navy, Model 1867, Remington Pistol, which was one of the few handguns issued to enlisted men and officers during an era when cartridge revolvers were universally accepted as martial arms.

Fortunately for the Navy, William H. Hunt, Secretary of the Navy in 1881, reported to the Congress of the United States that it was no longer possible to protect American merchant vessels against attack in foreign waters. Wealthy shipowners began to lobby Congress to protect their investments. This led gradually to appropriations in 1883 for building four small steel cruisers. From then on, the United States Navy expanded until it was able to defeat the Spanish Navy in the war which began in 1898. Along with the increase in the number of war vessels and the personnel strength, went the slow, gradual adoption of cartridge revolvers for officers and enlisted men. We do not know when the last U. S. Navy, Model 1867, Remington Pistol was recalled from service, but it probably was not before 1883.

THE U. S. MARINE CORPS AFTER THE CIVIL WAR

The United States Marine Corps, as a semiautonomous branch of the Navy, suffered along with the Navy after the Civil War. However, it is startling when anyone learns for the first time that the United States Marine Corps did not suffer greatly from demobilization immediately after 1865 for the simple reason that all during the Civil War its number of officers and enlisted men remained almost the same as it was in 1861. Within a few years after the end of the Civil War the strength of the Corps was cut to less than it had been at any time since the beginning of the Mexican War.

Although the records are inconclusive, it is believed that the Navy generously issued a few of the U. S. Navy, Model 1867, Remington Pistols to the Marine Corps. Knowing the Marine Corps as the author does, and relying upon its emphasis on rapid but accurate marksmanship with handguns and shoulder arms from 1775 to the present, it is safe to prophesy that future research will show that the United States Marine Corps in some manner, whether by hook or by crook, obtained cartridge revolvers while the Navy and the Army were still carrying the Remington single-shot cartridge pistols, although the production records of all small arms after the Civil War show that the Remington single-shots were far outnumbered by cartridge revolvers for all branches of the armed forces.

THE ROAD AHEAD

In the previous chapters we have described and illustrated all the U. S. Martial and U. S. Secondary Martial Single-Shot Pistols. In the next two chapters, we shall examine Kentucky (Pennsylvania) Pistols and Confederate Pistols. These, too, were "Guns of Glory." The book will close with a chapter on Dueling Pistols, the "Guns of Sorrow," although a few were used in battle.

CHAPTER 9

Kentucky Pistols

DEFINITION AND CHARACTERISTICS

Definition

THE true *Kentucky Pistol* is a single-shot pistol, either flintlock or percussion, that was made by the same men who made the well-known Kentucky rifle. These pistols are really miniature Kentucky rifles, with their slender stocks and "furniture" like that of the rifles. The "furniture" means the trigger, trigger guard, ramrod thimbles, muzzle cap, and other parts which are usually of the same metal and with the same finish. Kentucky pistols are normally full-stocked, that is, the stock, which is made of wood, extends to the muzzle, or almost to the muzzle. A half-stocked or three-quarter-stock pistol is regarded as a hybrid or freak type, not representative of the Kentucky pistol in its pure form.

Kentucky pistols, like Kentucky rifles, were handmade. No two are alike. They are as individual as the men who made them, all of whom were pioneer Americans who took orders from no person, not even cash customers. Each maker scorned the work of his competitors and associates. If he ever made two Kentucky pistols which were approximately identical, it was because he was making a matched pair, whether it was for a man who wanted the pistols for personal protection, or for an officer who carried them into combat.

Figure 1 represents a typical Kentucky flintlock rifle. Figure 2 is a simplified line drawing of a Kentucky flintlock pistol of the American colonial period from the collection of Herman P. Dean. Figure 3 is a composite drawing representing a typical Kentucky flintlock pistol near the close of the flintlock era and the beginning of percussion ignition. The flint is not shown in this picture.

Unmarked Pistols

One of the striking features of the Kentucky pistol is that it is frequently found unmarked, especially if it was made during the Revolutionary War. The probable explanation is that during the Revolution gunmakers feared reprisals would come from the British if they were known to be making arms for the American forces. Since it is well known that matched pairs of Kentucky pistols were made for and carried into combat by officers of the Revolutionary Army, and also the Navy, this is a reasonable explanation.

Another reason for unmarked Kentucky pistols is that the makers could only produce a limited number and were not anxious to advertise their business because they had more orders than they could fill.

A third reason for the lack of marks is that few of the gunsmiths made more than ten pistols in their entire lives. Some made three, others made six, and it was rare for a manufacturer of Kentucky rifles to produce more than ten Kentucky pistols. Even if we reject the theory that the makers were afraid of British reprisals, and the idea that they did not want to solicit business, we are faced with the fact that the Kentucky pistol was made only on special order, hence the maker did not have the same incentive to mark the pistol that he had to mark the Kentucky rifles, because making rifles was his main business and making pistols was only a sideline.

Where They Were Made

Most Kentucky pistols were made in eastern Pennsylvania, although others were made in the present states of New

FIGURE 1. A typical Kentucky Flintlock Rifle

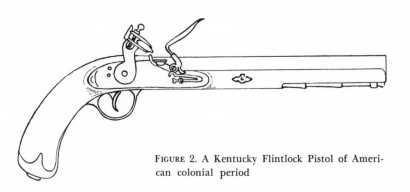

FIGURE 2. A Kentucky Flintlock Pistol of American colonial period

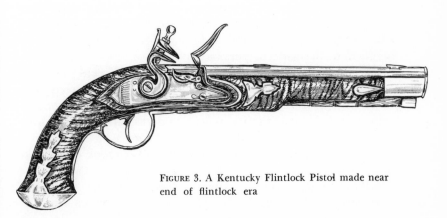

FIGURE 3. A Kentucky Flintlock Pistol made near end of flintlock era

York, New Jersey, Tennessee, and Ohio, with a few being made in South Carolina, Virginia, and other states. However, we must remember that the map of the United States has changed greatly since pioneer days and when we mention a state we must also give the year or period we are talking about. For example, West Virginia was carved out of Virginia during the Civil War.

Total Number Made

It is impossible to estimate the total number of Kentucky pistols made, either as flintlock or percussion, or converted from flintlock to percussion. For some reason, the number of genuine Kentucky pistols in the original flintlock condition is greater than the number of pistols originally made as percussion pistols or converted from flintlock to percussion. This percentage also reflects on Kentucky rifles. Proportionately more Kentucky pistols are found in the original flintlock condition than Kentucky rifles, taking into consideration the number of pistols made and also the number of rifles manufactured. For example, in the collection of Calvin Hetrick, of New Enterprise, Pennsylvania, 50 percent of the pistols were in the original flintlock condition, 37.5 percent were converted from flintlock to percussion, and 12.5 percent were made originally as percussion pistols.

This distribution of percentages in the Hetrick collection is in almost inverse proportion to the number of Kentucky rifles made originally as flintlocks, converted from flintlock to percussion, or made as percussion arms.

We mention the Calvin Hetrick collection because Hetrick was the first collector of antique arms to publicly recognize the Kentucky pistol as a distinct type, the first to acquire a collection of representative pieces, and the first to announce his discovery to the world of gun collectors, which he did in the first edition of *The Gun Collector's Handbook of Values,* published in 1940.

Following the announcement of Calvin Hetrick came the statements of Joe Kindig, Jr., of York, Pennsylvania, an outstanding authority on Kentucky rifles; and that of Richard D. Steuart, of Baltimore, Maryland, who is famous as one of the pioneers in the field of Confederate firearms. Both of these gentlemen confirmed Hetrick's classification of the Kentucky pistol as a unique type. Later, all of the original Hetrick specimens, plus many more important pieces, were acquired by Herman P. Dean, President, Standard Printing & Publishing Co., Huntington, West Virginia, who was for many years the publisher of a wide range of books on ancient and modern arms.

HISTORICAL BACKGROUND

The Slow Development of Rifled Arms

In order to understand Kentucky pistols, we must know the origin and development of Kentucky rifles. First, however, we should survey the history of rifled shoulder arms.

When a round lead ball the same size as the bore (internal diameter) of the barrel was driven down the barrel with repeated blows from the ramrod, it was eventually "seated"; that is, it fitted the bore tightly and would be guided by the rifling to give it a spin to insure range and accuracy when it left the muzzle.

Another method was to use a lead ball slightly smaller than the bore, wrap it with a greased patch of paper, leather, or cloth, which would make it fit the bore tightly and still be guided by the rifling when it left the muzzle. Both methods were used in loading muzzle-loading, rifled arms as early as 1575.

Regardless of which loading method was used, a rifled arm was much slower to load than a smoothbore in which the ball was simply dropped down the barrel. The armed forces of the world did not like the slow loading of rifled arms, although sportsmen, who had plenty of time to load before firing at game, preferred rifled arms when they could afford the additional expense.

Throughout the world, for several centuries accuracy of fire was not regarded as important. As late as World War I, soldiers were trained to fire by volleys from formations in which they stood shoulder to shoulder. Of course, there were exceptions in all wars, but even today there are generals who do not appreciate the importance of each shot being an aimed shot.

Hickory ramrods were common in the early days of shoulder arms and also pistols. The soldier had to exert so much force on the ramrod that it often broke while he was trying desperately to ram a lead ball down the bore. When the ramrod broke, the soldier was helpless unless he had a bayonet on his weapon, but many of the early shoulder arms were not made with bayonets. This is especially true of the Kentucky rifles.

It required skill and training to fire a rifled arm accurately. A smoothbore could be fired quickly in the general direction of a closely massed enemy without much training or skill, hence raw levies of recruits or drafted men could be thrown into battle with smoothbores and accomplish more than they could with rifled weapons.

Furthermore, it did not require much brains, skill, or experience for a man to make a smoothbore, hence smoothbores could be made faster and cheaper than rifled arms. Governments have always been economical in providing arms for their soldiers, sailors, and marines, until dire necessity convinced politicians that they were, themselves, in danger if they did not give their troops adequate weapons.

King Christian IV of Denmark was one of the first rulers to equip his soldiers with rifled arms, which he did early in the seventeenth century. Other rulers copied his example gradually. About 1750, the states and kingdoms that later formed the present Germany, Sweden, Norway, and Denmark were all providing rifles for special light infantry organizations, snipers, and others we know as "sharpshooters," but the majority of European soldiers were issued smoothbore weapons.

Before the development of the Kentucky rifle, the European rifle which was its ancestor was comparatively short with a large bore. Some were equipped with both front and rear sights, some had front sights only, and others had no sights. Early immigrants who settled in Pennsylvania, Kentucky, Tennessee, and adjacent states, came from the kingdoms and states which later became Germany. Others came from Switzerland and Austria. They brought their rifles with them to America. Since some of them were gunsmiths in Europe, they began making weapons like those they used at home. For logical reasons, they slowly changed the design to meet the conditions they found in the New World.

Transition from European to American Designs

Lead was hard to obtain in the frontier settlements and it cost money, hence the rifle makers drilled the bore smaller in diameter to use smaller bullets. They increased the length of the barrel to give it what we called increased "sighting radius," which produced more accuracy in aiming. They used available wood, often curly maple, for the stock. Rifles using greased patches for loading were provided with a hinged, brass patch-box cover over the recess that held the patches. The ornamentation met the desires of the purchasers, hence there might be any kind of symbol or design etched, stamped or engraved on the furniture of the rifle.

Origin of the True Kentucky Rifle

The Kentucky rifle originated as a distinct type in the vicinity of Lancaster, Pennsylvania, and many of the early makers of this important American shoulder arm lived in various parts of Pennsylvania. The name Kentucky was not applied until long after this weapon evolved as an arm entirely different from anything previously made in any other part of the world. The whole weight of history supports the statement that we should cease calling it the Kentucky rifle and rightfully refer to it as the *Pennsylvania rifle.* For the same reason, the Kentucky pistol should be called the *Pennsylvania pistol,* but historians, novelists, collectors, dealers, and museum curators have been using the word "Kentucky" for so many years that it is doubtful that a change can be made now.

The Kentucky rifle became a fully developed type sometime between 1725 and 1728. The oldest specimen of which the author has knowledge is marked 1728. Flintlock shoulder arms somewhat resembling the true Kentucky type were made before 1728, but they retain characteristics of the European weapons from which they evolved.

Characteristics of Early Kentucky Rifles

An examination of more than 200 early Kentucky rifles shows that the average bore diameter is 0.45 inch, the average weight is 9 pounds, and the average barrel length is 40 inches, although many of the rifles may have been shortened. Of this large group of early specimens, one-third were rifled with seven grooves, one-fourth were rifled with eight grooves, 5 percent were rifled with six grooves, 2 percent were cut with octagonal grooves, 2.5 percent were cut with straight grooves, and 30 percent were smoothbores, although a number of these obviously had been rebored to remove the rifling. The average stock of these early rifles has a drop at the heel of 4 inches, is made of curly maple, and has a butt of the shotgun type. The butt plate, trigger guard, patch box, and other fittings (furniture) are almost always made of brass.

The only European influence on the early Kentucky rifles is found in the incised carving and the raised carving sometimes executed in panels, often for the full length of the stock in the better-grade pieces. Those made after 1820 generally lack the beautiful carving, but have metal inlays, usually silver, if they were made for wealthy men, although those carried by frontiersmen for hunting or warfare were often decorated with brass.

The decorations, whether executed on silver or brass, include an 8-pointed star, which is one of the oldest decorations found on the Kentucky rifle; a crescent moon with or without a star; a crooked heart with the point turned to one side to "hex" an enemy; the Chinese ying-yang symbol which represents the male and female characteristics, including darkness and light, strength and weakness, etc.; various fraternal emblems, such as the square and compass of Ancient, Free and Accepted Masonry; animals, birds, fish, leaves, acorns, etc. The barrel is sometimes found with "X" marks, usually on the underside, to protect the owner from evil spirits, witches, and demons.

Kentucky rifles made after 1820 usually have a thinner buttstock, the butt plate is more crescent-shaped, carving is rarely found, and there are usually more inlays. These changes took place because the Kentucky rifle after 1820 became more of a sporting arm than an absolute necessity for the frontiersman in shooting game for food and protecting his family. Nevertheless, the Kentucky rifle was used in the War of 1812; against the Indians in many campaigns after 1800; by some of the Texans in their fight with Mexico; to some extent in the Mexican War; and even at the beginning of the Civil War.

Caliber and Balls of Lead to the Pound

In addition to the examination of more than 200 early Kentucky rifles already mentioned, which were collected by William K. Knepp, of San Fernando, California, the author of this text once examined a collection of 43 Kentucky rifles which were authentic flintlock pieces in their original condition, probably made before 1800. The average caliber was .439, the average barrel length was 58.14 inches, and the average weight was 9.546 pounds.

A rifle of caliber .439 would fire round lead bullets whose weight was such that about 57 balls could be made from one pound of lead, depending upon how tightly the shooter wanted the ball to fit the rifling, and whether or not he used a greased patch.

These are only average figures. In reality, of the 43 rifles, 16 used 60 balls to the pound, 4 used 80 balls to the pound, 4 used 52 balls to the pound, and 6 used 120 balls to the pound. The number of balls to the pound for the remainder of the group varied greatly, hence an average figure gives only an approximate idea of the caliber and the number of balls to the pound.

Accuracy

In flintlock days, a soldier armed with a musket, which was a smoothbore, usually did well to hit a man at 100 yards, but men armed with the Kentucky rifle could hit a man easily at 300 yards, even without much training. Experienced soldiers in the American Army during the Revolution, when armed with the Kentucky rifle, could place aimed shots inside a circular target having a diameter of 6 inches at 250 yards, and a few could do that well at 300 yards. All this means that almost all Kentucky riflemen could hit an enemy somewhere on his body at 300 yards. Those with experience could hit a vital area at 250 yards, and some at 300 yards.

Kentucky Rifle and Pistol Classifications

Kentucky Rifles Were Not United States Martial Shoulder Arms

Although the Kentucky rifle was accurate and was used during several wars and campaigns fought by the armed forces of the United States, it was never made at either of the two U. S. National Armories, and it was not made under contract between the United States and private manufacturers, hence it is not classified as a United States Martial Shoulder Arm. There were several reasons why the Kentucky rifle was never officially adopted by the United States, as follows:

1. It was essentially a handmade, individually designed and manufactured rifle, produced by individualists who were proud of their craftsmanship, considered the quality of their products more important than the profits that could be made through mass production, and refused to be hurried by anyone, even in time of war.

2. Since it was a rifle, it required more time to load, especially when a patch was used with the lead ball.

3. The Kentucky rifle was never made with a bayonet or with any device for fixing a bayonet to the barrel and stock, even temporarily.

4. As a rifle, it required more training to make use of its superior qualities than a smoothbore musket, hence soldiers with little or no instruction in marksmanship could not be rushed into battle with this type of weapon.

5. The admirals and generals of the armed forces of the United States, like their counterparts in Europe, were hesitant to adopt any new weapon. This military and naval attitude has existed in all armies and navies since the beginning of the world and prevails even today among a surprisingly large number of high-ranking officers.

Classification of Kentucky Rifles and Pistols

The Kentucky pistol, like the Kentucky rifle, was never made at either the U. S. Armory, Springfield, Massachusetts, or the U. S. Armory, Harpers Ferry, Virginia. Also, the Kentucky pistol, *as such,* was not made under contract between the United States and private contractors.

There are some exceptions to this statement. For example, Henry Deringer, Senior (the father of Henry Deringer, Jr., who produced the derringer), produced pistols which meet the requirements of a Kentucky pistol according to any practical definition that can be written. One of these was the U. S. Pistol, Contract Model 1807 (1806) Henry Deringer, Senior, which is classified as a United States Martial Flintlock Pistol.

Another example is U. S. Pistol, Contract Model 1807–1808, I. Guest, which is more properly referred to as U. S. Pistol, Contract Model 1807–1808, John Guest, because the capital letter "J" is often mistaken for the letter "I." This, too, is classified as a United States Martial Flintlock Pistol.

Despite the fact that Henry Deringer, Senior, John Guest, and others made both Kentucky pistols and U. S. Martial Pistols, there is a sharp distinction. When such pistols were not made under contract with the United States, they were not United States Martial Pistols. In a similar manner, if they were not made under contract with one of the several states, and did not meet any of the other requirements we have set forth in previous chapters for placing pistols in the U. S. Secondary Martial Pistol ·classification, then they are simply Kentucky pistols.

Kentucky rifles can never be classified as U. S. Martial Shoulder Arms. Depending upon various circumstances, similar to the conditions set forth in previous chapters for distinguishing between U. S. Martial and U. S. Secondary Martial Pistols, Kentucky rifles sometimes can be treated as U. S. Secondary Martial Shoulder Arms. When they do not fall into that group they can be regarded as U. S. Semi-Martial Shoulder Arms.

Following the logic of all that has been said before in this book, a Kentucky pistol can fall into any one of three categories: (1) It can be a U. S. Martial Pistol if it meets requirements repeatedly set forth; (2) it can be a U. S. Secondary Martial Pistol; and (3) it can be regarded as a U. S. Semi-Martial Pistol if it fails to fall into the first two groups.

Returning to the beginning of this chapter, it is absolutely true that when Kentucky pistols were not made to specifications promulgated by the government of the United States, that is, when no two were made alike, and they were not made under a federal contract, they cannot be referred to as U. S. Martial Pistols. Federal markings, inspectors' initials, and other indications of manufacture for and acceptance by the United States are important criteria.

Finally, most Kentucky pistols were not marked to show who made them. When unmarked, and with no two made alike, we have a typical Kentucky pistol that can be proudly displayed by its owner as a type all its own.

Kentucky Pistols Classified as Dueling Pistols

Kentucky pistols made in matched pairs, conforming to the requirements for dueling pistols explained in the chapter on that subject, can be classified as dueling pistols. Since dueling pistols were often taken into campaigns and wars by officers, and sometimes used in action, Kentucky-type dueling pistols can be placed in the U. S. Secondary Martial classification.

The Erroneous Classification of Kentucky Pistols Before 1940

Before 1940, large Kentucky pistols were often classified by collectors, dealers, historians, and authors as "horsemen's pistols," especially when they were made in *martial calibers and sizes.* By this phrase we mean flintlock pistols ranging from cal. .54 to cal. .69; with a barrel length anywhere between 8.5 inches and 11 inches; and other parts in proportion. These were the usual ranges of calibers and barrel lengths, but a large collection of Kentucky flintlock pistols of martial type would show many with barrels averaging cal. .44 or cal. .45. These are the approximate average calibers for the overwhelming majority of all Kentucky rifles examined by the author.

The barrel length of Kentucky pistols classified as "horsemen's pistols" before 1940 ranged from 8.5 inches to 12 inches, although a very large collection would include a comparatively large number with barrels averaging 9.5 inches long. Nevertheless, one expert in Kentucky pistols reports genuine specimens made caliber .70 with a 10-inch barrel.

These so-called "horsemen's pistols" were single-shot pistols, hence they generally were made in pairs so that the horseman would have two shots at an enemy before reloading. Kentucky pistols are rare as individual pieces, and almost impossible to find in pairs.

During the percussion era, the usual caliber of pistols for martial or semi-martial use was .54, but some semi-martial pistols were made caliber .38 and a few were made caliber .75.

In measuring specimens today, it must be understood that the barrel may have been rebored after it was made, it may have been worn by long use, or the barrel may not be the original. This explains confusion in caliber designations when a collector is trying to recognize a newly purchased flintlock or percussion pistol from the facts in a book.

The Recognition of the Kentucky Pistol as a Distinct Type

Between September 1, 1937, when the author retired from the United States Marine Corps, and the publication of the first edition of *The Gun Collector's Handbook of Values,* he was in constant communication with collectors, dealers, museum curators, historians, and arms authors whom he had met previously in various parts of the world. In addition, he wrote to everyone who he thought might offer good ideas for what should be included in the new book and how the values should be determined.

Shortly before the book went to press, Calvin Hetrick, of New Enterprise, Pennsylvania, wrote that he thought Kentucky pistols belonged in a classification and chapter of their own, even though they overlap some other classifications. He further said that the reason that Kentucky pistols had not been recognized as a distinct type (as miniature Kentucky rifles) before was that the experts had somehow failed to observe the characteristics of design, workmanship, and ornamentation common to both Kentucky rifles and what Hetrick now designated as Kentucky pistols. His discovery was confirmed by experts who had not thought of the Kentucky pistol classification before, but now saw the logic of it. Therefore, the publication of the first edition of *The Gun Collector's Handbook of Values* in 1940 marked the beginning of the use of "Kentucky pistol" in referring to a distinct type of firearm. To the best of our knowledge and belief, all publications before 1940 did not use this term.

In the next few pages, we shall describe specimens from the original Hetrick collection. Although not illustrated in this text, photographs of these important Kentucky pistols are found in *The Gun Collector's Handbook of Values.*

KENTUCKY PISTOLS FROM ORIGINAL HETRICK COLLECTION

KENTUCKY FLINTLOCK PISTOL, *Revolutionary War period,* cal. .36, rifled, with eight deep grooves; 9.5-inch octagon barrel; 14.875 inches over all. Kentucky-rifle-type front and rear sights. Engraved lock plate, 4.125 inches long. Iron pan with fence. High-quality, full burl maple stock fastened to barrel with dart-shaped silver pins. Silver butt cap, finely engraved silver inlays on each side of grip, silver barrel pin escutcheons and name plate. Brass trigger guard, engraved brass lock-pin escutcheons, ramrod thimbles, and muzzle cap. Silver-tipped hickory ramrod. Weight 2 lbs. This is the only early rifled Kentucky flintlock pistol from the Hetrick collection. It is extremely rare. It is unsigned, but it is known that this particular piece was the personal arm of Captain William Cowan, of Chester County, Pennsylvania, who carried it at the Battle of Yorktown, in the Revolutionary War.

KENTUCKY FLINTLOCK PISTOL, *Colonial period, early type, about 1740,* cal. .48, smoothbore; 7.5-inch, brass, half-octagon, half-round barrel; 13.375 inches total length. No sights. Engraved lock plate, 4.875 inches long; iron pan with fence; no bridle over tumbler or frizzen pin; pan and plate separately forged and pinned together. Full stock, curly maple, round-pin-fastened; engraved brass butt cap and trigger guard, brass ramrod thimbles. No fore-end cap. Very early type butt design. Ramrod and trigger on this specimen not original, but probably either replacements taken from another early pistol, or good reproductions. This pistol is regarded by many experts as probably one of the first flintlock pistols of the pure Kentucky type made in America. Weight 1 lb., 12 oz.

KENTUCKY FLINTLOCK PISTOL, *probably pre-Revolutionary period,* cal. .44, smoothbore; 9.125-inch, part-octagon, part-round barrel; 13.625 inches total length. No sights. Lock plate 4.25 inches long, severely plain with single vertical slash across the "tail," that is, the rear of the lock plate. Marked on inside of lock plate "H V F". No frizzen spring. Iron pan and lock plate separately forged and fastened together with screws, and this assembly is fastened to the stock with round pins. Full-length, walnut stock with bird's-head-shaped butt. Brass butt cap extends toward tang. Brass trigger guard, side plate, ramrod thimbles, and fore-end cap. Simple, neat engraving on butt cap, trigger guard, and side plate. Ramrod not original, but probably either a replacement from another pistol or an excellent reproduction. Early-type, wide trigger with curl to rear. The stock is exceptionally slender for a pistol of this size. Weight 1 lb., 11 oz. This pistol is unsigned except for the initials inside the lock plate, mentioned above.

KENTUCKY FLINTLOCK PISTOL, *Revolutionary period,* cal. .44, smoothbore; 10-inch octagon barrel; 15.5 inches total length. Kentucky-rifle-type sights. Lock plate 5 inches long, severely plain with slash across the tail of the lock plate. No roller on frizzen. Pan and lock plate separately forged. Iron pan with fence. Fastened with round pins. Full-length, curly maple stock with attractive red violin finish. Brass butt cap with extension toward tang. Brass trigger guard, thimbles, barrel-pin escutcheons, and muzzle cap. Early-type trigger with curl to rear. Silver name plate. Not signed on lock or barrel, but has peculiar lock-pin escutcheons exactly like the Kentucky Flintlock Pistol, Revolutionary period originally, converted from flintlock to percussion, cal. .38, described below, and has the same red violin finish. The striped hickory ramrod with a worm (threaded, screwlike tip for removing a bullet or holding a cleaning patch) is original. Weight 2 lbs. This was one of a pair carried by Captain Samuel Russell, of Pennsylvania, in the Revolutionary War, when he served with Sullivan's expedition. Not illustrated.

KENTUCKY FLINTLOCK PISTOL, *Revolutionary period,* cal. .44, smoothbore; 8.75-inch, brass, part-octagon, part-round barrel. Total length 14.25 inches. No sights. Plain lock plate, 4.25 inches long, with curved slash across tail of lock plate. There is a roller on the frizzen. The pan is separately forged. Iron pan with high fence. Full-length maple stock with dark finish. Silver butt cap with extensions toward tang. Silver trigger guard. Silver name plate with monogram. Silver ramrod thimbles, fore-end cap, and side plate. Butt cap, trigger guard, side plate, barrel, and tang are simply but tastefully engraved. Fine relief carving on stock at rear of tang. Incised carving on fore stock. Excellent workmanship. Ramrod not original. Not signed on barrel or lock, but inside of lock plate is marked with large, curiously curved "H". The trigger guard is of the early type.

KENTUCKY FLINTLOCK PISTOL, *period of 1812 or later,* cal. .48, smoothbore; 9-inch octagon barrel. Total length 14.5 inches. Barrel is fastened with round pins. Kentucky-rifle-type front sight. No rear sight. Plain lock plate, 4.25 inches long, with vertical slash across tail. Iron pan with fence. Lock plate marked "J.J. HENRY BOULTON". Full-length maple stock with red violin finish. Heavy brass furniture including butt cap, trigger guard, ramrod thimbles, side plate, and fore-end cap. Butt cap extends upward toward tang at rear. Hickory ramrod. Barrel not marked. Weight 2 lbs., 1 oz. This pistol shows many of the characteristics of the Kentucky rifles of the same period.

Details of Typical Kentucky Percussion Pistols

KENTUCKY PISTOL, *converted from flintlock to percussion,* originally made during Revolutionary War period. Cal. .38, smoothbore, 10-inch octagon barrel. Total length 15.5 inches. Original browning still on barrel, equivalent in quality to the browning on the Hall rifles. Barrel marked in script "S.M.", which may stand for Simon Miller, Hamburg, Pennsylvania, who was probably the maker of this pistol. Lock plate, 4.5 inches long, marked "T. Ketland & Co." Full-length, curly maple stock, with red violin finish and incised carving around the tang. Silver inlays around barrel muzzle. Silver butt cap, name plate, and escutcheons for dart-shaped barrel pins. Brass trigger guard, ramrod thimbles, and fore-end cap. Early-type trigger. Hickory ramrod. Weight 1 lb.,

6 oz. This was one of a pair of pistols carried, when in the original flintlock condition, by Colonel Nathan Dennison, a Pennsylvania officer, at the Battle of Wyoming, July 3, 1778.

KENTUCKY PISTOL, *converted from flintlock to percussion, period about 1800*, cal. .34, smoothbore; 9.75-inch octagon barrel. Total length 15.375 inches. Plain, handmade lock plate, originally made for flintlock ignition, with vertical slash across tail of lock plate, and marked in script "A.J." Full-length, dark-finished, curly maple stock with brass butt cap, trigger guard with spur, ramrod thimbles, and long fore-end cap. Barrel fastened with flat pins. Silver name plate. Kentucky-rifle-type front and rear sights. Very slender and graceful in design. Barrel not marked. Kentucky-type hickory ramrod. Weight 2 lbs.

KENTUCKY PERCUSSION POCKET PISTOL, *probably pre-Civil War period*. This is not a martial or semi-martial pistol, but according to tradition a few of this type were made for captains of steamboats cruising between Pittsburgh and New Orleans, to keep order among the passengers and crew. Caliber about .32, 4.875-inch octagon barrel, rifled with seven grooves. Total length 8.75 inches. Front and rear sights. Lock plate 3.25 inches long, marked "T. Howell Philadelphia". Barrel marked "J.Fleeger, Allegheny". This was the John Fleeger who was proprietor of the Allegheny Iron Works, Pittsburgh, Pennsylvania. The tang extends toward the butt, but there is no butt cap. Full-length, fine quality, naturally striped, curly maple stock. Brass trigger guard and ramrod thimbles. Silver fore-end cap. Barrel fastened with flat pins. Weight 1 lb., 3 oz.

ILLUSTRATIONS OF SPECIFIC PISTOLS

The remainder of this chapter will be devoted to Kentucky pistols found in the collection of Samuel E. Smith and other specialists. Some of these can be classified only as Kentucky pistols, while others belong in overlapping classifications.

HENRY DERINGER, SENIOR, KENTUCKY FLINTLOCK PISTOL

Technical Description

The Henry Deringer, Senior, Kentucky Flintlock Pistol (Figure 4) is identical with the U. S. Pistol, Contract Model 1807 (1806) Henry Deringer, Senior, illustrated in Figure 6, Chapter 3, "United States Martial Flintlock Pistols," except for minor details which definitely indicate that this specimen, when classified as a Kentucky Flintlock Pistol, does not have the proofmark "P" within a circle on the barrel. Also, it does not have any initials of an inspector on any part, and lacks any other martial markings.

This Kentucky pistol is cal. .52. It has a 10-inch, round, smoothbore barrel, which is pin-fastened to the full-length, walnut stock that extends to 0.25 inch from the muzzle. It has a small, rounded front sight, although some collectors describe the shape of the front sight as "pyramidal." There is no rear sight. The total length is 16.5 inches and the weight is 2 lbs., 9.5 oz.

It is brass-mounted. It has a brass trigger guard, a brass butt cap, and brass thimbles. The rounded butt has a brass butt cap made with short, rounded extensions, often called "spurs," that extend upward and into the stock, flush with the surface on each side of the butt portion of the stock.

There is a horizontal iron pan with a fence, and a flat, double-necked hammer with a beveled edge. The trigger guard is pin-fastened to the stock and the two brass thimbles also are fastened by means of pins. The hickory ramrod has the enlarged front end commonly called a "swell tip," but it is not as enlarged as the front end on some ramrods.

The trigger guard forks at the rear of the trigger guard loop to extend along the under surface of the stock, but the fork is so small that it is barely visible in any illustration and can be recognized only as a very small, Y-shaped portion of the trigger guard forming two sides of a triangle, the under surface of the butt being the other side of the triangle.

The lock plate is marked "H. DERINGER PHILA" between the hammer and the frizzen spring and has a beveled edge. The rear end of the lock plate comes to a small rounded point which collectors describe as "teat-shaped." The lock-plate marking was too faint on the specimen illustrated to show it accurately in Figure 4.

Approximate Date of Manufacture

In addition to being identical with the U. S. Pistol, Contract Model 1807 (1806) Henry Deringer, Senior, described and illustrated in the chapter on United States Martial Flintlock Pistols, except for martial markings this pistol also closely resembles U. S. Pistol, Contract Model 1808, S. North, Navy, illustrated in Figure 13 of Chapter 3 as a U. S. Martial Flintlock Pistol. These resemblances to two early U. S. Martial Flintlock Pistols, one made by Henry Deringer, Senior, and the other by Simeon North, lead collectors and historians to believe that the pistol was made by Henry Deringer, Senior, at his Philadelphia plant after he moved to Philadelphia from Richmond, Virginia, in 1806, and at about the same time as the two U. S. Martial Flintlock Pistols which it resembles were manufactured.

Arguments About Classification

Since this pistol so closely resembles one U. S. Martial Flintlock Pistol, and is identical with another except for martial marking, some authorities want to classify it as a U. S. Secondary Martial Flintlock Pistol, while others are just as determined to identify it as a Kentucky Flintlock Pistol because it has the characteristics of that type.

JOHN GUEST KENTUCKY FLINTLOCK PISTOL

Historical Background

John Guest is often listed as I. Guest because the firearms bearing his name are often found marked either J. GUEST or I. GUEST; but the capital letter "I" was intended to be a "J" when it was put on the guns made by John Guest. Throughout the history of American flintlock and percussion arms there have been many examples of weapons marked with a "J" that looks like an "I," when the maker used only the initial letter of his first name, whether it was John, Joseph, or some other first name beginning with "J."

This is repeatedly mentioned in several chapters of this book because some collectors, dealers, and authors seem to think that they are describing weapons made by two different men because of the letter "J" resembling the letter "I." Another reason for repeating this explanation is that gun collectors often buy, borrow, or steal a book on antique arms merely to look for the description of one particular weapon in their collections. When they fail to read through a single chapter, as they sometimes do, and when they do not read a book from beginning to end, which is a common practice, they are puzzled if the description and illustration seem to vary from the gun in which they are interested.

John Guest was employed by the Warwick Iron Works for the casting of cannon for the American forces during the Revolutionary War. In association with Abraham Henry and Peter Brong, he signed a contract with Tench Coxe, U. S. Purveyor of Public Supplies, to manufacture pistols and rifles for the United States. These weapons probably were used during the War of 1812 from 1812 to 1815.

John Guest made the U. S. Pistol, Contract Model 1807–1808, described and illustrated in Chapter 3. The same pistol in the past has been classified as a U. S. Secondary Martial Pistol. Actually, its manufacture and use probably entitles it to be placed in either category, depending upon the marking and other details.

Technical Details

The John Guest Kentucky Flintlock Pistol (Figure 5) is identical with the U. S. Pistol, Contract Model 1807–1808, described and illustrated in Chapter 3 as a U. S. Martial Flintlock Pistol, except for the absence of markings indicating federal inspection, purchase and use. John Guest is known to have made Kentucky rifles and pistols. This fact, together with the design features of the pistol illustrated in Figure 5, which meet the fundamental requirements for a pistol of the Kentucky type, qualify it for consideration in this chapter.

The John Guest Kentucky Flintlock Pistol is cal. .54. It has a 10.25-inch, round, smoothbore barrel. There is a brass, blade-type front sight, but no rear sight. The barrel on this specimen does not have the eagle head and the proofmark found on the top surface of the barrel of the U. S. Pistol, Contract Model 1807–1808, made by John Guest, but it is marked in script with what appears to be "I. GUEST", although this is really intended to be read as "J. GUEST". The total length is 16 inches.

The pistol is brass-mounted. The full-length walnut stock extends to within 0.0625 inch from the muzzle. The barrel and two thimbles are pin-fastened. The hammer has a beveled edge and is of the design habitually described as "flat, double-necked." The iron pan has a fence. There is no back strap. The hickory ramrod has an enlarged front end, as it appears mounted on the pistol. This end is generally described as being "flared," "bell-shaped," or having a "swell tip," but all these terms mean the same thing in describing this pistol ramrod as they do in referring to other hickory ramrods.

The brass butt cap has extensions (spurs) on each side of the butt, which is rounded.

The flat, bevel-edged lock plate is marked "DREPERT" in all-capital letters between the hammer and the frizzen spring, in the same style and manner as it is marked on U. S. Pistol, Contract Model 1807–1808, made by John Guest. The lock plate is not marked "U S" behind the hammer as it is on the U. S. Pistol, Contract Model 1807–1808, which is one of the major reasons for classifying this specimen either as a U. S. Secondary Martial Flintlock Pistol, or as a Kentucky Flintlock Pistol. Actually, it can be placed in either category.

The name DREPERT on the lock plate on both this

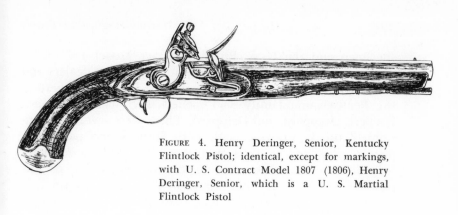

FIGURE 4. Henry Deringer, Senior, Kentucky Flintlock Pistol; identical, except for markings, with U. S. Contract Model 1807 (1806), Henry Deringer, Senior, which is a U. S. Martial Flintlock Pistol

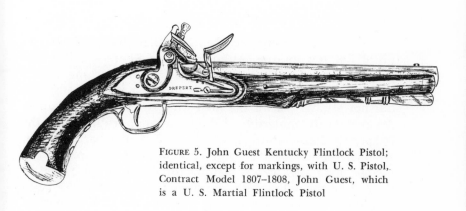

FIGURE 5. John Guest Kentucky Flintlock Pistol; identical, except for markings, with U. S. Pistol, Contract Model 1807–1808, John Guest, which is a U. S. Martial Flintlock Pistol

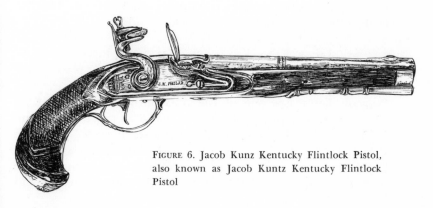

FIGURE 6. Jacob Kunz Kentucky Flintlock Pistol, also known as Jacob Kuntz Kentucky Flintlock Pistol

specimen and the U. S. Pistol, Contract Model 1807–1808, made by John Guest, has caused some collectors, dealers and authors to attribute the manufacture to Henry Dreppert of the Pennsylvania family who spelled their name Dreppert, Drepert, Dreppard, and Drippard. There were several generations of this family who made both flintlock and percussion pistols, rifles and muskets, but they also made lock plates for sale to other gunmakers, hence the designation of this pistol as a product of John Guest should not be thrown into doubt by the presence of a lock plate bought from another arms maker.

Variations in Markings

The use of a Drepert-marked lock plate on a John Guest pistol was not unique. Although many Kentucky rifles and pistols were not marked at all, when there is marking, it may be misleading. The name on the top of a barrel is usually, but not always, that of the man who assembled the weapon. A name on the underside of the barrel, not visible unless the weapon is disassembled, is usually that of the barrel maker, although it may be the name of someone who repaired the weapon long after it was manufactured. As we have seen in the case of the John Guest pistol, and other pistols described and illustrated in this book, the name on the lock plate often is not that of the man who made or assembled the pistol because buying lock plates from other gunsmiths in America or Europe was a common practice.

JACOB KUNZ KENTUCKY FLINTLOCK PISTOL

Historical Background

Jacob Kunz was one of the outstanding makers of Kentucky rifles and pistols, both flintlock and percussion, from 1795 to 1839. His products are sometimes marked "J. KUNZ PHILAD" on the barrel and the lock plate is marked "J. K. PHILAD". On other specimens of his craftsmanship the barrel is marked "J. KUNTZ PHILAD" on the barrel and the lock plate of the same weapon is marked "J.K. PHILAD". The capital letter "J" is sometimes made so that it looks like the capital letter "I."

This has led to the erroneous assumption on the part of some people that Kunz and Kuntz were different men. Furthermore, some otherwise experienced collectors, dealers and authors have thought that there were four gunsmiths of a similar name, that is: I. Kuntz, J. Kuntz, I. Kunz, and J. Kunz, but all these variations of spelling and marking pertain to only one man, Jacob Kunz, or Jacob Kuntz if you prefer, who spent his entire gunmaking life in and around Philadelphia, Pennsylvania.

If you search the old City of Philadelphia directories, you will find that he had a shop on Germantown Road, from 1819 to 1829, and the spelling varies from Kunz to Kuntz, but old city directories, and even modern city directories, are not always reliable sources of information.

The same man made the Kuntz Pistol, described and illustrated in Chapter 4, "U. S. Secondary Martial Flintlock Pistols." On that pistol the barrel is marked "KUNTZ PHILADEL", and the lock plate is marked "J.K. PHILADEL".

Technical Description

The Jacob Kunz Kentucky Flintlock Pistol (Figure 6) is cal. .44. It has a 9-inch, smoothbore, iron barrel, part round and part octagonal in cross section. The barrel is marked on top "J. KUNZ PHILAD". The lock plate is marked "J.K. PHILAD". The total length is 14.5 inches.

The pistol is brass-mounted with high-quality engraving on the butt cap, trigger guard, and lock plate. The lock plate, sometimes referred to as the "side plate," is more elaborately engraved than the other parts which are decorated. Unfortunately, the engraving is so indistinct that it is almost impossible to portray accurately either in a photograph or a drawing.

The full-length walnut stock extends to the muzzle. There

is a brass cap at the end of the stock, variously referred to as a "fore-end cap," "nose cap," etc. The butt has a shape known to collectors as a "bird's-head" design and is typical of the few authentic Kentucky flintlock pistols made by Kunz (alias Kuntz). The butt is finely checkered in the "grip" portion. The specimen illustrated is from the Samuel E. Smith collection and has a silver shield bearing the initials of the original owner. This shield is on the upper surface of the grip portion of the butt and not visible in a side-view drawing. The presence of a shield of this type is not necessarily typical of Kunz (alias Kuntz) Kentucky Flintlock Pistols.

Joseph Golcher Kentucky Flintlock Pistol

Identification

The only means of identifying the maker of the Joseph Golcher Kentucky Pistol (Figure 7) is the marking on the lock plate which consists of "JOS^H GOLCHER" over "WARRANTED", in two horizontal, parallel lines between the hammer and the frizzen spring. The words are in capital letters. The "H" in the abbreviation for "JOSEPH" is raised above the line and is slightly smaller than the letters "JOS." Some authors, collectors, and dealers have erroneously referred to this marking as that of "Josh Golcher," but there was no such man known to have made either Kentucky rifles or Kentucky pistols.

However, there was a Joseph Golcher who made Kentucky rifles, Kentucky pistols, and other firearms, both flintlock and percussion, first in Philadelphia, Pennsylvania, where he made Kentucky rifles and Kentucky pistols near the end of the flintlock era; and then in San Francisco, California, where he made percussion firearms.

During the flintlock period, specimens having the workmanship of Joseph Golcher were sometimes marked "GOULCHER", and others were marked with his first name spelled out in full, or with it abbreviated "JOS" or "JOS^H" as on the specimen illustrated.

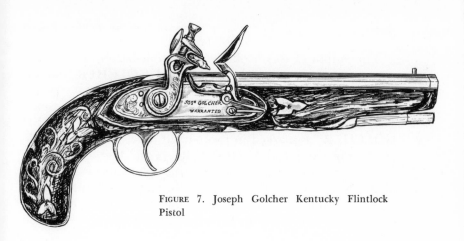

FIGURE 7. Joseph Golcher Kentucky Flintlock Pistol

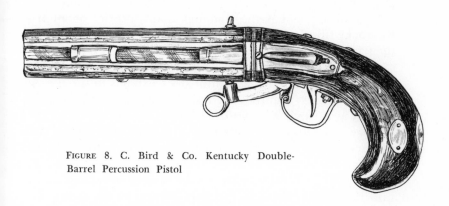

FIGURE 8. C. Bird & Co. Kentucky Double-Barrel Percussion Pistol

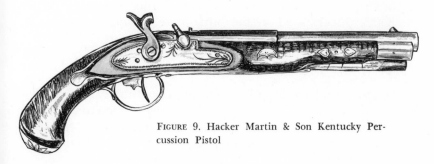

FIGURE 9. Hacker Martin & Son Kentucky Percussion Pistol

The author of this book owns a double-barrel, side-by-side, percussion shotgun, marked "JOSEPH GOLCHER" on the right lock plate and marked "SAN FRANCISCO" on the left lock plate. This shotgun has two lock plates, one on each side of the stock to hold the hammer. Although "JOSEPH GOLCHER" is marked in two curved lines, with "JOSEPH" in the top curve and "GOLCHER" in the bottom curve on the shotgun lock plate, the lettering is identical with that of the Joseph Golcher Kentucky Flintlock Pistol and the engraved ornamentation is of the same style and type. In addition, the craftsmanship of both weapons shows a common origin.

The specimen illustrated meets all the requirements for classifying it as a Kentucky Flintlock Pistol of the later part of the flintlock era, including a *roller* to relieve tension.

In addition, it has the common characteristics of all true Kentucky flintlock pistols. The "furniture," which means the trigger, the trigger guard, the ramrod thimbles, the muzzle cap, and many other parts, are made of brass. It is full-stocked, meaning that the walnut stock extends to the muzzle. It has a hickory ramrod, mounted as shown in the illustration. It is a single-shot muzzle-loader.

Since this pistol was made later in the flintlock period than the majority of specimens usually found in collections, the stock at the butt is thinner, there is little carving in the wood, and it is elaborately inlaid with silver countersunk into the stock, including the butt portion of the stock. The hammer and the portion of the lock plate behind the hammer are engraved with a scroll design. Earlier Kentucky pistols had a thicker stock at the butt, more carving in the wood, and less inlay work and engraving.

Technical Description

This pistol has a 6-inch, octagon, smoothbore, steel barrel. There is a small front sight of the shape sometimes called "pyramidal," although it is actually a simple post-type sight with a shape that requires considerable imagination to describe as that of a pyramid. The total length is 11 inches. The caliber is .44 at present, but the original bore diameter was probably 0.439 inch, which means that it could fire lead balls whose weight was such that about 57 balls could be made from one pound of lead, depending upon how tightly the shooter wanted the ball to fit.

The stock is cut away near the front to make it easier to insert the hickory ramrod, as the illustration clearly shows.

The hammer is of the double-neck design. There is a *comb,* which is that part of the hammer which is behind the hammer screw. The *roller,* which is difficult to recognize in any illustration, is a separate round piece of steel fastened on the end of the frizzen spring by means of a pin to relieve the friction on the end of the pan cover so that the pan cover can fly forward when the pistol is fired without encountering too much friction. As stated before, this is one of the identifying characteristics of a weapon made late in the flintlock period, shortly before the general adoption of percussion locks.

The frizzen (battery) and the pan cover are forged integral, that is, they are made as one part, which is a common characteristic of all true flintlock pistols.

C. BIRD & CO. KENTUCKY DOUBLE-BARREL PERCUSSION PISTOL

Historical Background

The "C Bird & Co. Pistol" is described in Chapter 4, "U. S. Secondary Martial Flintlock Pistols." The lock plate is marked "C. BIRD & CO.", "PHILADa", and "WARRANTED", in three horizontal, parallel lines between the hammer and the frizzen spring. The last letter in the abbreviation for Philadelphia is in lower case and is dropped below the base line for the other letters. Some pistols with this marking on the lock plate also are marked "Philadelphia" on the barrel.

C. Bird & Co. were gun manufacturers, gun dealers, or lock plate manufacturers in Philadelphia, Pennsylvania, from 1812 to about 1820. Many experts believe that they specialized in making lock plates, did not make any other gun parts, and did not assemble parts into complete firearms. However, the experts do not agree among themselves, principally because there is very little definite information about the Bird family's production of firearms or firearm parts.

Before C. Bird & Co. operated their plant in Philadelphia, a Mark Bird was employed with other men to cast cannon for the American forces during the Revolutionary War. On May 28, 1776, he contracted to manufacture 100 smoothbore muskets for Pennsylvania. It is believed that he started working in the gun trade before 1775 and was active until about 1790. His father was William Bird, the founder of Birdsboro, Pennsylvania. Double-barrel, over-and-under, percussion rifles attributed to him were made between about 1858 and 1860. Also, we know definitely that the locks of some Kentucky percussion rifles are marked "W. BIRD".

The above statements are generally accepted among experts on Kentucky pistols and rifles, both flintlock and percussion. However, in the author's book, *The Gun Collector's Handbook of Values,* there is a list of "Gunmakers of the Flintlock Period" which has been included in several editions over a very long period of time. In the list appear the following entries:

> Bird, C.; Pa.; K
> Bird, C. & Co.; Chap. 4

In the explanation that goes with the list, the letter "K" means that the individual or organization is known to have made Kentucky rifles. Since many of those who made Kentucky rifles also made Kentucky pistols, it is possible that C. Bird actually made Kentucky pistols. The code phrase "Chap. 4" refers to the "Bird & Co. Pistol," classified as a U. S. Secondary Martial Flintlock Pistol.

The above entries in *The Gun Collector's Handbook of Values* have not been challenged or disputed by anyone for about twenty years.

Technical Description

The C. Bird & Co. Kentucky Double-Barrel Percussion Pistol (Figure 8) is cal. .36. It has two 6.5-inch, octagon barrels, one mounted above the other. The illustration is a side-view drawing because it shows the mechanism better. Depressing a lever on the left side of the pistol permits the barrels to be rotated manually. Each barrel has its own nipple (cone, teat, or tit). The hammer strikes the primer in the nipple upward because it is what the collectors call an "under hammer," that is, instead of being located so that it can fall on the primer in the nipple like most percussion firearms, it is under the barrel being fired and must come upward to hit the primer.

This pistol has a swivel breech. The mainspring functions not only as a mainspring but also as a trigger guard. There are two lock plates, one for each barrel. These have the design characteristic of Kentucky percussion rifles. The total length is 11.25 inches.

Calvin Hetrick, of New Enterprise, Pennsylvania, in a letter to the author dated November 13, 1945, said that although there is no maker's name on this pistol, he believed it was made to special order by "the Bird Brothers." It was part of his collection at that time. Since he was the first to recognize the Kentucky pistol as a separate type, the first to acquire a collection of representative pieces, and the first to announce his discovery to the world (which he did in the first edition of *The Gun Collector's Handbook of Values,* published in 1940), his reference to it as being made by "the Bird Brothers" can mean only one thing, that it was made by C. Bird & Co., or at least by the Bird Brothers either before or during the existence of their firm of that name.

HACKER MARTIN & SON KENTUCKY PERCUSSION PISTOL

Technical Description

The Hacker Martin & Son Kentucky Percussion Pistol (Figure 9) is cal. .38, and has an 8-inch, smoothbore barrel.

The top of the breech is marked "H. MARTIN & SON". The stock is made of maple and tiger-striped. All furniture is brass except for the silver inlays countersunk into the stock. In other words, this can be described as a "brass-mounted pistol."

In the right-side view of Figure 9, slightly forward of the front end of the lock plate there is a silver ornament which looks like a half-moon with the horns of the crescent pointing downward, except that there is an additional "horn" or point pointing downward from the middle of the otherwise crescent-shaped, silver inlay. Between that ornament and the portion of the stock behind the brass fore-end cap, there are two heart-shaped ornaments. The heart near the front has its point toward the front, and the heart behind has the point toward the rear. These, too, are silver inlays.

The lock plate is beautifully etched or engraved but the ornamentation is mostly at the front and rear of the lock plate with a small about at the upper surface of the lock plate, between the hammer and the nipple.

Most experts would call the stock a "full stock," but the stock, even with its brass fore-end cap, does not quite extend as far forward as the muzzle. The hickory ramrod has a very slightly enlarged front end, but it is not large enough to be called a "swell tip."

The maple stock is cut away along the forward, bottom portion to make it easier to remove and replace the hickory ramrod.

The front sight is a modified blade type. The rear sight is a small, open, notch-type sight, mounted on the barrel.

The hammer is of the gooseneck type and offset on the right so that it will not be in the way of the shooter's aim when he is using the sights. There is no etching or engraving on the hammer.

The brass trigger guard is superficially of the conventional type of the flintlock and early percussion period, which means that it forms the loop for the trigger guard proper and then forks before extending along the forward, lower surface of the buttstock for reinforcement. There is one departure from the conventional design and that is a slight thickening of the trigger guard at the rear part of the oval loop, just before it forks.

The stock is rounded at the rear to form a graceful butt and there is a brass butt cap that has simple but beautiful etching or engraving of the same modest pattern as that on the lock plate.

The design of the nipple mounting suggests that this pistol may have been made originally as a flintlock and converted to percussion, but the relationship between the nipple mounting and the lock plate is such a harmonious design, both artistically and mechanically, that it is not difficult to accept this as made originally for percussion fire. The suggestion of conversion in the appearance of the nipple mounting can be explained by the fact that some of the early weapons made as percussion firearms had nipple seats similar to those used on conversions.

Tiger Striping

The tiger-striped maple of which the stock is made is naturally striped, instead of being given this decorative appearance by the artificial method described for early pistol stocks in a previous chapter of this book. As mentioned before, maple which is naturally tiger-striped is difficult to find, hence a pistol made with a stock of this wood is rare.

Historical Background

The technical description and the tiger striping of this pistol were given first in order to prepare for the historical background because about ten years ago the author discovered that a gunsmith named Hacker Martin, who was born in 1895, lived near Johnson City, Tennessee, and had two occupations. On the first floor of a gristmill, he ground grain into flour with machinery driven by a water wheel. On the second floor of the gristmill, Hacker Martin had a gunsmith shop and was making both flintlock and percussion rifles and pistols of the Kentucky type.

These Kentucky rifles and pistols were not manufactured to be sold as ancient arms to collectors and dealers, but were made for a surprisingly large number of modern marksmen who enjoy firing the Kentucky-type firearms. Obviously, it is possible for someone to have bought one of the Kentucky firearms from the modern-day Martin Hacker and removed his marks in order to substitute marks which would give the weapon the appearance of those made during the flintlock and percussion eras, but any such "faking" was above and beyond the control of the modern-day Hacker Martin and not made by him with an intention to deceive.

Experts on wood and metallurgists can determine the approximate age of the parts of weapons when there is any doubt about authenticity. Also, many advanced collectors and dealers can recognize a contemporary product without much effort. Regardless of when it was made, the specimen illustrated does represent a typical Kentucky pistol of the percussion era. Incidentally, the tiger striping does not show in a photograph and is difficult to portray accurately in a drawing.

The modern-day Hacker Martin we found in Tennessee was the great-grandson of a gunsmith; his grandfather was a gunsmith; and so was his father. They, in turn, were related to the Bean family, all of whom were Tennessee gunsmiths. The Martins inherited tools and equipment for making firearms from the Bean family, which included a gunsmith who was the father of the first white child known to have been born west of the Allegheny Mountains.

This is merely one example of the fact that generations of men, starting with the American colonial period and extending into the modern metallic cartridge era, have been gunsmiths, passing on their skills and equipment from father to son. The principal reason for this is that a good master gunsmith who can work in both wood and metal must spend many years as an apprentice and a journeyman before he can operate his own plant successfully. The only exceptions have been men born with an exceptionally great aptitude for this very exacting occupation.

KENTUCKY PISTOLS IN THEIR LAST WAR

In the next chapter, we shall find that Kentucky pistols, both flintlock and percussion, were used by Confederates at the opening of the Civil War, but soon they were able to acquire revolvers. The end of the Civil War definitely marked the last use of Kentucky pistols and it almost sounded the death knell for all single-shot pistols.

CHAPTER 10

Confederate Pistols

CLASSIFICATION

IT is obvious that the single-shot martial pistols used during the Civil War by the Confederate States of America cannot be classified either as U. S. Martial Pistols or U. S. Secondary Martial Pistols because they were not used by the armed forces of the United States.

The importance of Confederate pistols in the military and naval history of the United States justifies their inclusion in this text. The same thing applies to Kentucky pistols and dueling pistols. Since it is not possible to classify any Confederate pistols as United States pistols, and since only a limited number of Kentucky pistols and dueling pistols can be classified in the strict sense as either U. S. Martial Pistols or U. S. Secondary Martial Pistols, these three great groups of single-shot pistols are treated as an exceptional family of martial pistols.

In preparing the title for this book, the first thought was to call it *U. S. Martial, U. S. Secondary Martial, Confederate, and Semi-Martial Single-Shot Pistols,* but this would be too cumbersome, hence the title was shortened to *U. S. Martial and Semi-Martial Single-Shot Pistols.* This does not mean that there is any doubt about the strictly martial classification of Confederate pistols.

DEFINITION OF CONFEDERATE PISTOLS

It is extremely difficult to define a Confederate firearm. There are several approaches to the subject, as follows:

1. Firearms manufactured during the Civil War within the borders of the Confederate States of America, when properly marked and accurately identified (with or without conclusive markings), are certainly Confederate arms. These are the ones in the greatest demand by collectors who specialize in this field.

2. Firearms which can be classified as U. S. Martial weapons, made either by one of the U. S. Armories or by private manufacturers who had contracts with the United States which they fulfilled, were in U. S. forts as federal property. Others were in the arsenals of the several Southern states, issued to the states by the United States for use by state troops. Almost all of these United States Martial weapons, including, of course, U. S. Martial Single-Shot Pistols, were seized either by individual Southern states or by the Confederate States of America at the outbreak of the Civil War. However, unless such firearms can be identified as having been used by the Confederates, either by markings on the weapons or otherwise, they must be classified as U. S. Martial firearms and not as Confederate arms.

3. Firearms which are normally classified as U. S. Secondary Martial weapons were in the possession of the state forces of the Southern states at the outbreak of the Civil War, hence it was not necessary for them to be taken from the federal government, simply because they were state property already. Other weapons in the U. S. Secondary Martial classification were owned by individuals, officers and crews of merchant vessels, and semiofficial military and naval organizations. Like U. S. Martial weapons, these cannot be classified as Confederate arms without proper identification.

4. Firearms made in Europe were imported in great quantities shortly after the outbreak of the Civil War. Some were imported before the U. S. Navy effectively established a blockade of Southern ports and others were brought past the

Union blockade by vessels outfitted and manned especially for that purpose by the Confederates. Like the U. S. Martial and U. S. Secondary Martial weapons, these, too, cannot be classified as Confederate without adequate identification.

5. Firearms of martial caliber and size, which cannot be classified either as U. S. Martial or U. S. Secondary Martial arms, manufactured in the North, were imported by Southerners even after the Civil War formally began with the shelling of Fort Sumter, in the harbor of Charleston, South Carolina. Importation of such arms lasted only a short time before the United States discovered what was going on and took legal action against the disloyal Northern arms dealers. Since all weapons in this group were essentially civilian firearms, they cannot be classified as Confederate arms any more than other weapons lacking an accurate indication of Confederate use.

6. Firearms were captured on the field of battle from the United States forces by the Confederates in great quantities. Some historians believe that more than one-half of all weapons used by the Confederates were in this category. Again, there must be some way to identify them as having been used by the Confederates or they cannot be given the Confederate classification.

7. Finally, the source of supply is immaterial by itself. *A Confederate weapon is Confederate according to its use by the Confederates during the Civil War (1861 to 1865) and not where it was made or how it was obtained.*

CONFEDERATE TYPES, MAKES AND MODELS

The Confederates used any and all types, makes, models, modifications, and variations of firearms, including flintlock, percussion, and cartridge weapons. They used single-shot pistols, muskets, musketoons, rifles, carbines, and shotguns. They carried into battle revolvers and repeating shoulder arms. Even pikes and spears were issued officially.

The reason for the multiplicity of firearms was that the Southern states had many small shops that could turn out weapons slowly and in small quantities, but there were very few factories of the "heavy industry" type and even these were not equipped or manned for mass production of inter-changeable parts. The Confederates attempted to set up arms factories for large-scale production but they found it difficult to obtain raw materials and trained men to process the raw materials when they got them. Furthermore, a man-power shortage developed as the Civil War progressed. Em-ployees of arms factories were organized and trained as com-panies and battalions even though this meant taking time off their jobs. In a few cases, the employees of arms factories were ordered into battle. Throughout the war, the officers responsible for arms production were constantly quarreling with those who wanted to draft the workmen into line regi-ments.

Confederate Single-Shot Pistols Are Rare

Genuine Confederate single-shot martial or semi-martial pistols are extremely rare for the same reason that single-shot martial, single-shot secondary martial, and single-shot semi-martial pistols used by the Union forces are rare.

Percussion revolvers were in common use at the outbreak of the Civil War by both civilians and armed forces, hence the Confederates as well as the Union forces preferred re-volvers to single-shot pistols. Near the end of the Civil War, some percussion revolvers were converted to fire metallic cartridges, and there were many revolvers used on both sides of the conflict which were manufactured as cartridge arms.

Nevertheless, Claude E. Fuller, one of the great authori-ties on United States Martial and United States Secondary Martial Firearms, and one of the comparatively few experts on Confederate weapons, repeatedly stated in his published writings, and in his letters to the author of this book, that thousands of Confederates went into battle in 1861 armed with single-shot flintlock pistols, and throughout the entire war many of them used either single-shot flintlock pistols or single-shot percussion pistols, even though 1861 marked

A. W. SPIES & CO.,

IMPORTERS OF

GUNS, PISTOLS, RIFLES,

GUN MATERIALS,

FOR MANUFACTURING

GUNS, GUNSMITHS' TOOLS, POWDER FLASKS,

Belt Pouches, Sporting Implements,

And every article needful for Sportsmen.

RODGERS' MOSTENHOLMS,

AND OTHER

FINE CUTLERY.

GENERAL HARDWARE.

91 MAIDEN-LANE, New-York.

SHIP'S ARMS, CUTLASSES, BOARDING PIKES, &c.

FIGURE 1. Advertisement run by A. W. Spies & Co. in a New York City directory, about 1853. The single-shot percussion pistol at the upper left is opposite a pepper-box pistol. Below the crossed shoulder arms is a drawing of a Colt percussion revolver, showing that as early as 1853, revolvers were beginning to drive single-shot pistols off the market.

311

the beginning of the use of repeating weapons and metallic cartridges. In addition, Claude E. Fuller said many times that there were more muzzle-loading arms used on both sides than breechloaders, even though breech-loading was already widely accepted in Europe and the United States as better than muzzle-loading.

Although there is no question about the accuracy of Fuller's statements about the use of single-shot pistols by Confederates during the Civil War, such arms are rare today if we insist upon finding some means of identifying these single-shot pistols as Confederate weapons instead of relying upon family tradition, or other vague and unreliable collateral evidence. In other words, *the pistol itself must speak for itself as Confederate or it is not Confederate.*

Figure 1 is an advertisement run by A. W. Spies & Co. in a New York City directory, about 1853. The single-shot percussion pistol at the upper left is opposite a pepper-box pistol. Below the crossed shoulder arms is a drawing of a Colt percussion revolver, showing that as early as 1853 revolvers were beginning to drive single-shot pistols off the market.

False Marks

It is comparatively easy to make a die or stamp for marking metal parts of a firearm. It also is easy to etch or engrave metal parts. It is slightly more difficult to remove the original marks from the metal parts of a firearm before substituting false marks, but it can be done by a skilled gunsmith. The original marks on the wooden parts of a gun can be removed and new ones made in their place.

Marking metal or wooden parts with the letters "C.S.A.", or the designation of a Confederate organization, such as "2nd. Va. Inf.", has been a common practice among dishonest gunsmiths, collectors and dealers since about 1940, and it existed as long ago as 1900, when people began specializing in Confederate arms.

A beginner may think it unlikely that anyone would go to the trouble of faking Confederate arms, but there are several gunsmiths in the United States who reproduce rare and valuable Colt percussion revolvers so skillfully that only an expert can recognize them as counterfeits. The same gunsmiths manufacture all types, models and makes of fake Confederate weapons and mark them so cleverly that occasionally one is bought by a collector or dealer who should know better.

The motive is profit. All genuine Confederate weapons are valuable. Single-shot Confederate pistols are in such great demand that their values are much higher than almost all other martial, secondary martial, or semi-martial single-shot pistols. Therefore, a dishonest person can make a very good living by devoting himself entirely to the production of Confederate arms, whether he makes them entirely from raw material, or re-marks other guns.

Claud E. Fuller's Comments on Handguns of the Confederacy

Fuller's Place in Firearms History

The late Claud E. Fuller was a collector, historian and successful author in two major fields of gun collecting. He was not only one of the greatest authorities we have had in America on United States Martial and United States Secondary Martial Firearms, but he was the co-author, along with Richard D. Steuart, another outstanding arms expert, of *Firearms of the Confederacy,* published in 1944 by Standard Publications, Inc., Huntington, West Virginia. The president of the publishing corporation was and is Herman P. Dean, who is another arms expert of national standing.

Fuller's Explanation of the Limited Use of Single-Shot Pistols

When the author of this present book was preparing the first edition of *The Gun Collector's Handbook of Values,* Fuller sent extensive notes, photographs, and suggestions regarding both U. S. Martial Arms and Confederate Arms. Then, when revised editions were brought out, he continued to give generously of his time, but the one thing we were

troubled about was the accurate identification and classification of Confederate handguns, especially single-shot pistols of
definite Confederate manufacture or use.

About 1942, Claud E. Fuller wrote the following letter
to the author, explaining why genuine Confederate single-
shot pistols are so rare. Later, he included the same ideas in
Firearms of the Confederacy. Although there is some variation
in phraseology between the personal letter and the comments
in that book, the owner of the copyright of *Firearms of the
Confederacy*, Herman P. Dean, has kindly granted permission
to quote the personal letter in order to avoid any doubt
about copyright violation. Here is what Fuller said in 1942:

The War Between the States was the first major war in which
revolvers were widely used. Previously, the War with Mexico
had demonstrated the efficiency of the Colt percussion revolver
and the superiority of that type of weapon over the old, single-
shot pistols. During the fifteen years which intervened between
the Mexican War and the War Between the States, percussion
revolvers had been invented, patented, and manufactured in
an infinite variety of designs but most of them were either in-
fringements on the patents of Samuel Colt or cleverly designed
to avoid patent-infringement and still embody the basic features
of the Colt revolver.

The young soldier who volunteered for duty in one of the
state organizations, or later in the Army of the Confederate
States of America, first wanted a horse to ride into battle.
Second, he wanted a pair of what he called "Navy sixes," which
is what you prefer to designate as the Colt Model 1861 Navy
Revolver; also listed by you and others as the Colt New Model
Belt Pistol; New Model Navy Pistol; Model of 1861 Navy
Pistol; and Round-Barreled Navy Colt Pistol. He did not
know or care about all these titles you and others have given
the Colt revolver he liked.

Of course, you are correct in saying that it was cal. .36,
6-shot, single-action, with a 7.5-inch, round barrel marked
"Address Col. Sam'l Colt, New York, U.S. America", but the
young Confederate volunteer was not interested in technical
details. He did know that the total length was 13 inches and he

probably suspected that it weighed 3 lbs., as you have carefully stated, but again he wanted results and was not concerned with what he regarded as petty details.

The young Southern volunteer may have glanced at the straight, round cylinder with rectangular slots because his officers and non-commissioned officers probably explained to him what the slots were for. He could not miss the fact that the cylinder was engraved with a naval engagement scene, but he paid little attention to the brass back strap and the brass, oval trigger guard. He did not know that many years later collectors would describe his revolver as having a creeping loader-lever and a Navy-type latch.

The youngster serving under the Stars and Bars of the Confederacy soon found that the Colt revolver cost more than he could afford because the demand for either genuine or imitation Colt Model 1861 revolvers, or any other revolvers, was so great that in 1861 many of them sold for as much as $500 apiece in Confederate currency.

The Confederate recruit often owned a derringer, either one made by Henry Deringer, Jr., or one of the many imitations which were beginning to come on the market in quantities. He did not care for a pepper-box pistol, even though it was a multi-shot weapon, because Southerners wanted a real revolver, not a transitionary type.

With this background, I again urge you to be very careful in listing Confederate single-shot martial pistols, either flintlock or percussion, because it is extremely difficult to accurately identify most of these pistols as made by Southerners or carried by them during the War Between the States.

When the Southern states seceded from the Union, they took over federal arsenals in the South, where they acquired a few hundred "horse pistols." These were single-shot pistols used by the United States up to and including the Mexican War. Some were flintlocks, but most of them were awkward, large-bore pistols converted from flintlock to percussion.

Where they got the pistols we do not know, but thousands of Confederates went to the front in 1861 carrying single-shot, flintlock pistols. The State of Virginia issued both flintlock pistols and flintlock pistols converted to percussion. These are what you refer to as Virginia Manufactory (Virginia Armory) pistols, but I do not mean to suggest that all flintlock pistols carried by Virginia soldiers in 1861 came from the Virginia Armory.

Here is one example. In 1864 or possibly in 1865, a Union soldier of the Fifth Ohio Cavalry captured a Confederate cavalryman who was armed with a Morse breech-loading carbine and an English-made, single-shot, flintlock pistol, having a 9-inch, brass barrel, silver mountings, rosewood stock, and "H. NOCK, LONDON" marked on both the barrel and the lock plate. The Confederates entered the War armed with anything they could get, but as hostilities continued, a remarkably high percentage of their better arms were captured in battle from the Union Army.

There are many more things that I could say, but I believe the collector should be suspicious of single-shot pistols with lock plates marked with the names of Southern rifle makers and bearing the year 1863 or later dates. From 1863 on, the Confederacy had neither the mechanics nor the material to waste on the manufacture of single-shot pistols, when their few revolver factories were short of both.

BIRD & CO. CONFEDERATE FLINTLOCK PISTOL

(Figure 2). This pistol is exactly like the Bird & Co. Pistol described in Chapter 4, "U. S. Secondary Martial Flintlock Pistols," except that it is marked on the left side of the barrel "C.S.A".

As stated previously, a Confederate marking in itself means very little in identifying or classifying a firearm as a Confederate weapon. The specimen illustrated was examined by the author of this book when it was in the collection of an expert on Confederate arms who also was an authority on U. S. Martial Flintlock Pistols and U. S. Secondary Martial Flintlock Pistols. We both compared the "C.S.A" marking on the Bird & Co. Pistol with the "C.S.A" marking on pistols in his collection which were beyond any doubt authentic Confederate pistols and reached the conclusion that it was actually marked "C.S.A." during the Civil War by a Confederate.

Nevertheless, anyone who buys a so-called Confederate

weapon merely because it has Confederate marks on it should have the advice of an expert in this field, and even then he may be swindled.

RAPPAHANNOCK FORGE CONFEDERATE FLINT-LOCK PISTOL, identical with the Rappahannock Forge Pistol, described and illustrated in Chapter 3, "U. S. Martial Flintlock Pistols," of this text. This pistol is described in Chapter 4, "U. S. Secondary Martial Flintlock Pistols," in *The Gun Collector's Handbook of Values,* Fifth Revised Edition, copyright 1960, but since the publication of the latter book, research has indicated that it belongs in the U. S. Martial classification, where we have it in the present text. The pistol is illustrated in Figure 3, but Figure 1, Chapter 3, is a more accurate drawing.

The Confederate version has the same caliber, barrel length and markings, and sometimes the barrel is marked "J. Hunter". This is by no means conclusive evidence of Confederate use because James Hunter owned and managed the Hunter Iron Works, also called Rappahannock Forge, at Falmouth, Virginia, where he made flintlock muskets, pistols, carbines, sabers, and wall rifles (also called rampart rifles) during the American colonial period and also during the Revolutionary War.

Since the same pistol is sometimes marked "J. Hunter" when classified as a U. S. Martial Flintlock Pistol, we fail to find any distinguishing Confederate marks in the descriptions of the so-called Confederate version. However, most experts on Confederate arms are careful to include the Rappahannock Forge Pistol when they list the arms of the Confederacy, even though they do not give any convincing methods for distinguishing between one that is rightfully classified as a U. S. Martial Flintlock Pistol and one that should be listed as a Confederate Flintlock Pistol.

RAPPAHANNOCK FORGE CONFEDERATE PERCUS-SION PISTOL. This pistol is simply a Rappahannock Forge Flintlock Pistol, as described above, converted to percussion by any of several methods accepted during the Civil War for converting flintlocks to percussion ignition for martial use.

This percussion version, like the original flintlock pistol, must be classified as a U. S. Martial Flintlock Pistol unless there is some authentic Confederate marking somewhere on the pistol. However, the writers on Confederate arms all list this as one of the pistols in that group and we present this information for whatever it may be worth to the reader.

ELGIN-TYPE, CONFEDERATE PERCUSSION CUTLASS PISTOL. The so-called "Elgin-Type, Confederate Percussion Cutlass Pistol" is not identical with the U. S. Pistol, Navy Contract Model 1837, C. B. Allen, Elgin Cutlass Pistol, described and illustrated in Chapter 6, "U. S. Martial Percussion Pistols." Also, it is not identical with the Morrill, Mosman & Blair Cutlass Pistol (also called Morrill, Mosman & Blair Bowie-Knife Pistol, etc.) described and illustrated in Chapter 7, "U. S. Secondary Martial Percussion Pistols."

The Confederate version was manufactured in England. The barrel is engraved on top "J. Gerald, Alabama, C.S.A." Although we have repeatedly cautioned the reader about accepting Confederate marks without corroborating evidence of authenticity, it should be stated that at least one specimen with this marking has been accepted as a genuine Confederate pistol since before 1900 by the leading authorities on Confederate arms.

FAYETTEVILLE, CONFEDERATE, PERCUSSION PISTOL-CARBINE

Historical Background

The Fayetteville Arsenal, sometimes called the Fayetteville Arsenal and Armory, at Fayetteville, North Carolina, was a United States arsenal and armory until the soldiers of the State of North Carolina took possession of it on April 22, 1861.

The machinery seized by soldiers of the State of Virginia when the U. S. National Armory, Harpers Ferry, Virginia, was captured in April, 1861, was first claimed as State of Vir-

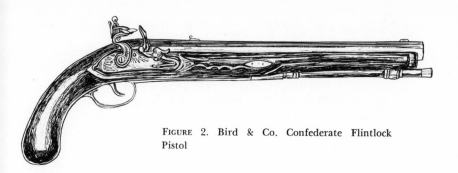

FIGURE 2. Bird & Co. Confederate Flintlock Pistol

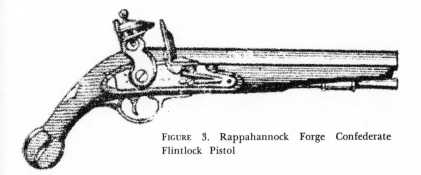

FIGURE 3. Rappahannock Forge Confederate Flintlock Pistol

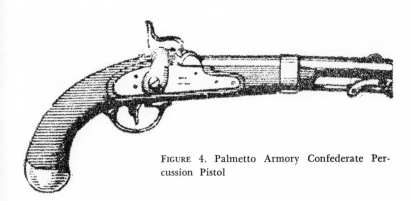

FIGURE 4. Palmetto Armory Confederate Percussion Pistol

ginia property, but turned over to the Confederate States of America and shipped to Fayetteville. Along with the most important machinery of the Harpers Ferry Armory, there were shipped numerous unassembled parts of various types of firearms. Among these were parts for the U. S. Pistol-Carbine, Model 1855, Harpers Ferry, described and illustrated in Chapter 6, along with the U. S. Pistol-Carbine, Model 1855, Springfield. Both the Springfield and the Harpers Ferry versions of the Model 1855 Pistol-Carbine should be considered in order to understand the design and assembly of the Fayetteville, Confederate, Percussion Pistol-Carbine.

When the supply of parts needed to assemble the pistol-carbine was exhausted, no attempt was made to manufacture new parts or continue production of this weapon in any manner.

General Sherman's army was approaching Fayetteville in March, 1865. The machinery was sent by train to the small town of Egypt, in Chatham County, North Carolina, and there hidden in an abandoned mine. Sherman's men learned where the machinery was hidden, probably from escaped slaves who had helped load and transport the machinery. In May, 1865, the Union Army moved the machinery to Raleigh, North Carolina.

Technical Description

The Fayetteville, Confederate, Percussion Pistol-Carbine is fundamentally the same as the U. S. Pistol-Carbine, Model 1855, Harpers Ferry. The lock plate has what collectors call a "humpback shape" and is not milled to receive the Maynard tape-priming mechanism. The lock plate is stamped forward of the hammer "Fayetteville", with an eagle, and "C.S.A." underneath the eagle. The lock plate is stamped "1862" behind the hammer. This is the year that the assembly of this pistol-carbine began, and the same year that other weapons were manufactured or assembled at Fayetteville. The detachable stock is the same as for the U. S. models.

Experts always have regarded the U. S. Pistol-Carbine,

Model 1855, Harpers Ferry as a pattern or experimental model and not one intended for mass production, hence it is difficult to understand how the soldiers of the State of Virginia were able to find many parts for this pistol-carbine at Harpers Ferry.

Regardless of where the Confederates got the parts for· the very few pistol-carbines assembled at Fayetteville, the Confederate version is an extremely rare weapon and very valuable, hence the author must once more warn the reader against buying what may be a modern reproduction or a genuine U. S. Pistol-Carbine, Model 1855, Springfield, re-marked and reworked to give the appearance of a Fayetteville weapon.

Palmetto Armory Confederate Percussion Pistol

Technical Description

The Palmetto Armory Confederate Percussion Pistol is identical with U. S. Pistol, Model 1842, Palmetto Armory, described and illustrated in Chapter 6. Figure 4 is a drawing of this pistol, but Figure 7, Chapter 6, is more accurate as to details.

Authors of magazine articles and books on Confederate arms classify it as having the same description as the U. S. Pistol, Model 1842, Palmetto Armory. It is true that this percussion pistol was manufactured by William Glaze & Co., operating the Palmetto Armory, Columbia, South Carolina, for the primary benefit of the State of South Carolina. It is logical to assume that this pistol, having been made expressly for the state forces of South Carolina, and issued to them for service over a long period of time, was carried into battle by South Carolina troops during the Civil War, hence there is no argument about classifying this particular pistol as a Confederate arm.

Soldiers from the State of South Carolina called into federal service before the Civil War used this pistol, hence it can be unequivocally classified either as a U. S. Martial Percussion Pistol, or as a Confederate Percussion Pistol, regardless of the presence or absence of any Confederate markings.

Nevertheless, some experts argue that if there are no U. S. proofmarks, and no marks of a U. S. inspector, the pistol is "more Confederate" than if it has such United States marks.

Figure 5 is a drawing of a portion of a Palmetto Armory musket, altered to the breech-loading system invented by Merrill, presented here to show the Palmetto Armory marking on the lock plate. "PALMETTO ARMORY" is in a curve over a palmetto tree. Under the tree is "S.C." Behind the hammer, the lock plate is marked in two lines "COLUMBIA" over "S.C. 1852".

Radcliffe & Guignard Confederate Percussion Pocket Pistol

Technical Description

The Radcliffe & Guignard Confederate Percussion Pocket Pistol (Figure 6) is not a martial pistol in the strict sense of the term, but it is typical of percussion pocket pistols sold in the Southern states during the Civil War, both to civilians and to members of the Confederate forces. Confederate officers and enlisted men who could afford to buy a pocket pistol out of their own funds often did so in order to have a pistol in their pocket to be used in case they took off their pistol belt temporarily, or lost their martial pistol in combat.

Union officers and enlisted men also carried pocket pistols. This custom was not unique with Union and Confederate forces during the Civil War. The carrying of pocket or "hideaway" handguns, sometimes called "sneak guns," was a common practice in America long before the Revolutionary War, and has existed during all wars and campaigns fought by the United States of America up to and including World War II and the Korean "Action."

At various times U. S. armed forces have issued orders forbidding this practice, with special application to enlisted men, but as is often the case with orders and regulations, the individual disregarded the official mandate and carried a pocket

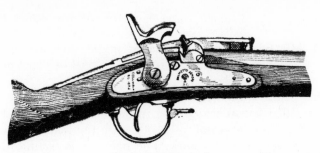

FIGURE 5. Palmetto Armory marking on the lock plate of a musket

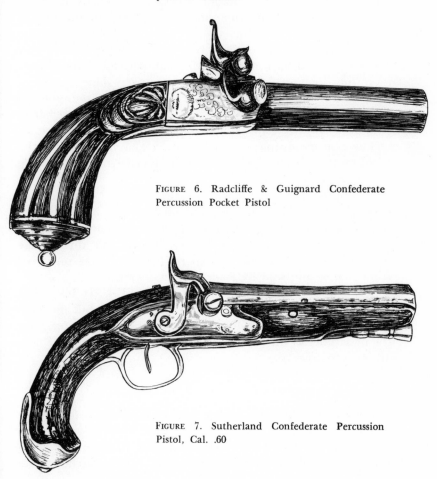

FIGURE 6. Radcliffe & Guignard Confederate Percussion Pocket Pistol

FIGURE 7. Sutherland Confederate Percussion Pistol, Cal. .60

pistol. His justification was that it might save his life, and this outweighed the danger of receiving a trial by court-martial if caught by his superiors.

This pistol is cal. .44, which is a martial caliber. It has a round, rifled barrel which is 3 inches long, hence the barrel is too short for the pistol to be placed in the martial category. The total length is 7 inches. The hammer is technically described as "center-hung." There are no sights, hence the center-hung hammer does not obstruct aiming as it might do if there were sights and the hammer were in the line of aim.

There is a folding trigger. In the illustration, the trigger has been folded back. Cocking the hammer causes the trigger to spring downward into position for firing. The reason for the folding trigger is to prevent accidental discharge. Folding triggers are found on many single-barrel and double-barrel percussion pistols, especially those of European manufacture.

The iron mountings on this pistol are elaborately decorated with scrollwork and floral designs produced either by etching or engraving, probably by engraving.

The buttstock, sometimes called the "handle" by collectors, is deeply fluted. This feature and other design and construction aspects of this single-shot pistol are characteristic of percussion pistols made in France before and during the American Civil War, hence experts believe it was imported from France and sold by Radcliffe & Guignard.

The barrel is marked on top "RADLIFFE & GUIGNARD COLUMBIA S.C.", usually in all-capital letters, but on some specimens the name of the firm is in all-capital letters and the remainder of the barrel marking is "Columbia S.C." There are no proofmarks.

Historical Background

Thomas W. Radcliffe, of the firm of Radcliffe & Guignard, operated a business in Columbia, South Carolina, both before and after the Civil War. He imported merchandise from Europe and sold firearms, military equipment, watches and a general line of jewelry. In addition, he sold civilian sporting goods. He employed gunsmiths. We do not know who Guignard was and we do not know whether Radcliffe was a gunsmith or gun manufacturer himself. Historical records indicate that he was an importer and dealer and not a manufacturer.

For example, Radcliffe imported from England the Tranter Percussion Revolver, cal. .31, 5-shot, double-action, with a 3-inch octagon barrel on which he stamped or engraved his name, and sometimes the name of his firm, although the same pocket revolver is also marked "Tranter's Patent".

Shortly before the firing on Fort Sumter, Radcliffe organized a company of volunteers called the Chicora Rifles, and became its captain. He took his men to Charleston, South Carolina, but was shortly promoted to the rank of Major and ordered to command a Confederate training depot at the town of Lightwood Knox Spring, where he served with credit.

At the end of the Civil War, he reopened his business at Columbia, South Carolina, and again sold the merchandise he retailed before the war, although now he emphasized civilian goods because the Federal troops discouraged the sale of firearms of military value. The whole period of his activity extends from about 1850 to about 1870, but these years are not verified by reliable records.

SAMUEL SUTHERLAND CONFEDERATE PERCUSSION PISTOLS

Historical Background

Samuel Sutherland was an importer and dealer in cutlery, pistols, powder flasks, revolvers, rifles, shot pouches, shotguns, and sporting goods of all kinds. He operated his business under a trade name, Southern Importing House, in Richmond, Virginia, as early as 1859, and possibly before.

During the Civil War, he was known to many Confederates as "The Armorer of the South," because of his extensive and successful work in the modification, alteration and repair of firearms of all types, makes, and models both for the State of Virginia and for the Confederate States of America.

Under the direct supervision of Samuel Sutherland, many of the flintlock arms produced at the Virginia Armory, known to collectors as Virginia Manufactory weapons, were converted to percussion ignition for use during the Civil War. In addition, he supervised the conversion of sporting handguns and shoulder arms from flintlock to percussion. Those which were made originally as percussion arms of civilian caliber either were rebored to martial calibers, or fitted with new barrels of martial caliber and length.

At the end of the Civil War in 1865, Sutherland gave up his business in Richmond, Virginia, and moved to Baltimore, Maryland, where he took over the Merrill Firearms Co., which produced shoulder arms from 1864 until it closed down in 1869. Actually, the Merrill Firearms Co. was formed to promote the use of the James H. Merrill breech-loading system, and only part of the arms bearing their name were their own products, the remainder being made for them by Remington.

SUTHERLAND CONFEDERATE PERCUSSION PISTOL, cal. .60 (Figure 7), single-shot, with a 6.25-inch, octagonal, brass barrel. The lock plate of the specimen illustrated is marked "Sutherland, Richmond" forward of the hammer, but the lettering is too faint to reproduce accurately in the drawing.

It is brass-mounted. The full-length walnut stock extends to the muzzle. There is a hickory ramrod. The brass trigger guard forks at the rear to form the conventional trigger-guard oval and then continues along the forward surface of the butt for reinforcement. There is a brass butt cap.

Originally, this was a French, martial-type, flintlock pistol. Sutherland converted it to percussion ignition during the Civil War.

SUTHERLAND CONFEDERATE PERCUSSION PISTOL, cal. .45 (Figure 8), single-shot, with a 6-inch octagonal steel barrel. The left side of this pistol has a belt hook, 2.5 inches long, which may or may not indicate that it was intended for use by the Confederate Navy or by Confederate blockade-runners, who generally were not in the Confederate Navy but independent operators. The lock is of the "back-action" type and is engraved in two parallel, horizontal lines "S.Sutherland" over "Richmond, Va." but this marking is too faint on the specimen illustrated to reproduce accurately in a drawing. Incidentally, the back-action lock came into limited use about 1830 in Europe, but it was never popular either there or in the United States. The steel ramrod on this pistol is of the swivel design. The lock plate is etched or engraved with floral and scroll work and the butt is checkered.

Virginia Manufactory Percussion Pistol, First Model

Technical Description

The Virginia Manufactory Percussion Pistol, First Model, which is recognized as a genuine Confederate percussion, single-shot pistol, is very similar to the Virginia Manufactory Flintlock Pistol, First Model, described in Chapter 4, "U. S. Secondary Martial Flintlock Pistols," and illustrated with a specimen dated 1807, except that the one in Figure 9 of this chapter has been converted to percussion.

The Confederate version is cal. .70, and has a 12.5-inch barrel. The total length is 18.5 inches. It is iron-mounted. The lock plate is flat with a beveled edge and is marked in capital letters "VIRGINIA" and "MANUFACTORY" in curved script between the hammer and the front of the lock plate, but on the specimen illustrated this marking is too faint for accurate reproduction in the drawing. However, this specimen is marked on the lock plate behind the hammer with "RICHMOND" in a curved line. Beneath "RICHMOND" is the year, 1808.

The hammer is "straight"; that is, it is neither the goose-neck nor the double-neck type. The nipple mounting is the bolster type used in converting martial arms from flintlock to percussion. Whether the conversion was accomplished before or at the beginning of the Civil War is not important. Other details follow the description of the Virginia Manufactory Flintlock Pistol, First Model, except as they relate to percussion fire. Variations from the one illustrated also follow the comments on variations given in Chapter 4.

Identification as Confederate Pistol

Since this pistol was made at the Virginia Manufactory in Richmond, which was established in 1797 by the State of Virginia to manufacture firearms exclusively for the armed forces of Virginia, it falls into one or more of the requirements set forth at the beginning of this chapter.

In addition to using the percussion modification, the Confederates went into battle with a few in their original, unconverted flintlock condition. These follow the description in Chapter 4, "U. S. Secondary Martial Flintlock Pistols."

VIRGINIA MANUFACTORY PERCUSSION PISTOL, SECOND MODEL

The Virginia Manufactory Percussion Pistol, Second Model was designed and manufactured at Richmond according to the pattern of U. S. Pistol, Model 1805 (1806), Harpers Ferry, described and illustrated in Chapter 3, "U. S. Martial Flintlock Pistols," except that the Confederate percussion pistol deviated from the flintlock version to provide for percussion ignition, and incorporated other minor changes.

Like the first model, this second model was used by Confederates both in the original flintlock and the percussion version. The second model, whether flintlock or percussion, is Confederate for the same reason as the first model.

VIRGINIA MANUFACTORY PERCUSSION PISTOL MARKED "C.S. RICHMOND"

Figure 10 illustrates a Virginia Manufactory Pistol originally made as a flintlock, but converted to percussion. It is cal. .54. The 10-inch, round, smoothbore, key-fastened barrel has a front sight near the muzzle. There is no rear sight. The total length is 16.625 inches. It resembles U. S. Pistol, Model 1805 (1806), Harpers Ferry, described and illustrated in

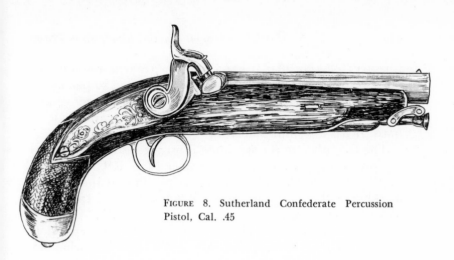

FIGURE 8. Sutherland Confederate Percussion Pistol, Cal. .45

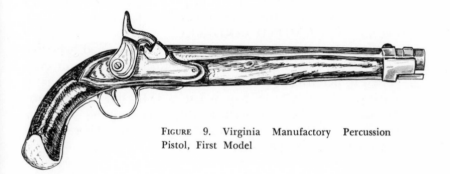

FIGURE 9. Virginia Manufactory Percussion Pistol, First Model

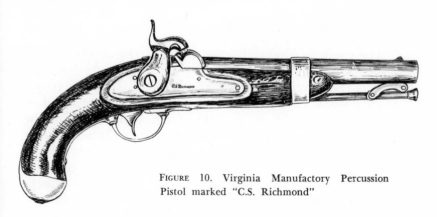

FIGURE 10. Virginia Manufactory Percussion Pistol marked "C.S. Richmond"

Chapter 3, except that it has a steel, swivel-type ramrod, and other features consistent with a pistol converted to percussion ignition. It is brass-mounted. The butt cap, trigger guard, ramrod thimble, and barrel reinforcing band are made of brass. It has a walnut half stock.

The lock plate of the specimen illustrated is marked in one horizontal line, forward of the hammer, "C.S. RICHMOND", in all capital letters, executed in script. This is the original marking of the lock plate before it was converted from flintlock to percussion.

Virginia Manufactory pistols, both flintlock and percussion, of this general description are often called Richmond-Virginia Pistols when not marked "Virginia Manufactory," providing that the lock plate is marked "C.S. RICHMOND", like the specimen illustrated; marked "RICHMOND"; or marked "RICHMOND VIRGINIA".

When the original flintlock lock plate is retained, whether the pistol is found in its original flintlock condition or converted to percussion, it may have a year marked on it, usually some year as early as 1812 or as late as 1816, but the presence or absence of the year mark is not a determining factor in classifying this pistol as a Confederate arm. There is no year mark on the specimen illustrated.

THE SO-CALLED COOK & BROTHER CARTRIDGE PISTOL

Technical Description

The Cook & Brother Cartridge Pistol (Figure 11) is cal. .50, rim-fire. The round barrel tapers slightly in diameter toward the muzzle and is 8.625 inches long. The total length of the pistol is 12.75 inches. In the illustration, there is a small projection near the upper edge of the walnut grip of the buttstock. This is called a stud or a spur. It serves as a handle for pulling backward the back strap, which is pivoted at the lower end, at the approximate spot where the buttstock screw (shown in the illustration) holds the walnut grip to the butt frame.

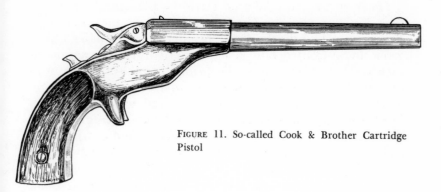

FIGURE 11. So-called Cook & Brother Cartridge Pistol

When the back strap is pulled all the way back, it opens the breech. After the breech is opened, a rim-fire cartridge is inserted, the back strap is returned to the position shown in the illustration, and the pistol is ready to fire.

After the pistol has been fired, the back strap is pulled back again to open the breech. A hook at the top of the breechblock extracts the brass case of the fired cartridge.

The pistol is marked on top, where it is not visible in a side-view drawing, "COOK C.S.A. 1863". All letters are capital letters but the first "C" is more than twice the size of the other letters. There is a comparatively large, blade-type front sight near the muzzle, and a small rear sight.

Experts regard this as a fake for reasons given at the end of the discussion of the historical background, below.

Historical Background

Cook & Brother was a company or partnership organized in June, 1861, by Ferdinand W. C. Cook and his brother, Francis L. Cook, both of whom were British subjects. They manufactured musketoons, rifles, carbines and edged weapons (swords and bayonets) at their factory located at No. 1 Canal Street, New Orleans, Louisiana, and it is known that they stamped their name on the barrels of firearms made there.

On April 24, 1862, Admiral David G. Farragut, U. S. Navy, took his fleet past the Confederate forts on the Mississippi River. On April 25 the Cook Brothers, acting under orders given by a Confederate general, started the evacuation of their factory. They loaded the principal machinery for making firearms on schooners and went to Vicksburg, Mississippi. There they unloaded the machinery and took it overland, first to Selma, Alabama, and then to Athens, Georgia, where they put into operation a new arms factory and continued to make musketoons, rifles, carbines, and two types of bayonets, beginning early in 1863.

Shoulder arms made at Athens, Georgia, are stamped "Cook & Bro., Athens, Ga." with the year, a serial number and a simplified drawing of the Confederate flag.

Near the end of the Civil War, the Cooks organized their workmen into a battalion. Ferdinand W. C. Cook, while serving as a Major of the Confederate Army, took his battalion into action, opposing the soldiers under Union General William T. Sherman, at the Battle of Griswoldville. In December, 1864, Major Cook was killed while leading his men in an engagement near Savannah, Georgia.

Francis L. Cook, the surviving brother, continued to operate the factory, which is referred to as the Athens Armory in official records. When fully manned, it could produce 10,000 rifles per year.

Although the Cooks had been making arms for the Confederacy, they had certain privileges as British subjects; hence on August 20, 1868, about three years after the close of the Civil War, the United States Army officially turned over to Francis L. Cook the Athens Armory and all the property in it.

There are voluminous records, both Union and Confederate, regarding the Cook brothers and the firearms and edged weapons they manufactured for the Confederates, but nowhere has anyone found any official reference to the single-shot cartridge pistol described and illustrated here.

Following the policy previously given for judging a pistol on its own merits, the principal justification for classifying this cartridge pistol as a Confederate weapon is that the marking on the top of the barrel coincides in the style of lettering with that used on undisputed Confederate arms made by the Cook brothers, and the workmanship throughout is of the same quality as the Cook shoulder arms.

Since there are no reliable records that this pistol was made by the Cooks, the workmanship and the marking "COOK C.S.A. 1863" do not constitute sufficient evidence to identify this pistol as genuine. Instead, it is regarded by experts as a very clever fake. It is discussed in detail in this text as an example of what to avoid.

CONFEDERATE PERCUSSION DERRINGERS

Why Confederates Carried Derringers

Confederates, like soldiers of all armies of the world since pocket firearms were developed, liked to carry a small handgun that they could use if they suddenly came under enemy fire when they did not have their regular-issue firearms in their possession. Also, it was a good idea in the minds of those who had no regard for the more formal rules of warfare to have a "hideaway" pistol or revolver that could be used when they were captured; assuming, of course, that the Union soldiers did not search them thoroughly.

Derringers, whether made by Henry Deringer, Jr., or one of the many gun manufacturers who imitated his single-shot pistol, were common in the South before the Civil War and were sold in many retail stores.

Henry Deringer, Jr., described his own invention in these words:

> It is a single-barrel pistol with a back-action percussion lock, patent breech, wide bore, and a walnut stock. It varies in length from 1½ to 6 inches for the ordinary pistol, and from 6 to 9 inches for the dueling pistol. It is commonly mounted with German silver. The barrels used are all rifled. The locks vary in proportion to the length of the barrels. On the lock

plates and breech of such pistol the words DERINGER PHILADEL^A are stamped, the stamps being the same which have been used from the first manufacture of these pistols and by which they are known everywhere.

Notice that Deringer said that "PHILADEL^A" was stamped with the last "A" raised above the other letters in the abbreviation for Philadelphia. His description is reasonably accurate but he used several abbreviations for Philadelphia and sometimes spelled it out in full on his unique pistols.

Popularity of Derringers in South

Henry Deringer, Jr., began manufacturing the short-barrel, large-caliber, single-shot percussion pistols that eventually became known as "derringers" in 1825, in Philadelphia, Pennsylvania. Almost immediately there was a great demand for his pistols throughout the Southern states, and the sale of his pistols, and those which were imitations made by his competitors, continued until after the close of the Civil War.

Figure 12 is a reproduction of an advertisement in the Memphis, Tennessee, directory, published in 1855 by F. H. Clark & Co., in which they state that they sell "Pistols in great variety including colts of all sizes and the genuine Derringer."

The use of the lower-case "c" in "colts" and the two "r's" in "Derringer" was characteristic of the disregard for accuracy in describing firearms which has been common throughout the history of the United States.

Figure 13 is a picture of a genuine derringer made by Henry Deringer, Jr., from a catalog issued in 1864 by Schuyler, Hartley & Graham, New York City dealers in firearms and military goods, in which they advertised Deringer pistols in four different barrel lengths.

Derringers with Southern Markings

Henry Deringer, Jr., manufactured his percussion derringers for anyone who would buy them, but dealers who

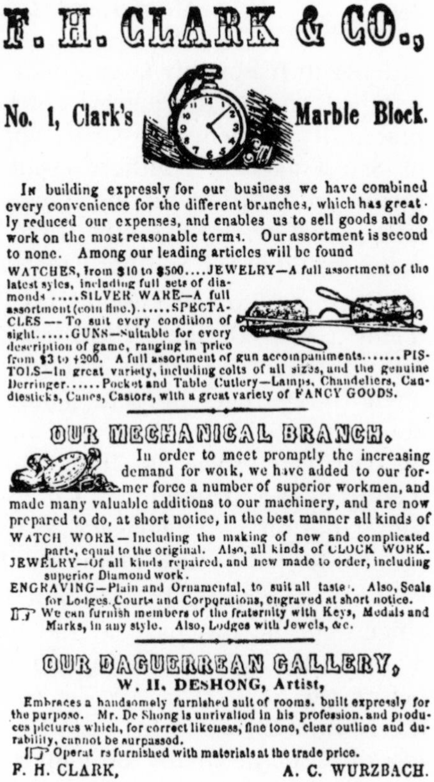

F. H. CLARK & CO.,

No. 1, Clark's Marble Block.

In building expressly for our business we have combined every convenience for the different branches, which has greatly reduced our expenses, and enables us to sell goods and do work on the most reasonable terms. Our assortment is second to none. Among our leading articles will be found

WATCHES, from $10 to $500....JEWELRY—A full assortment of the latest sylcs, including full sets of diamonds .....SILVER WARE—A full assortment (coin fine.)......SPECTACLES — To suit every condition of sight......GUNS—Suitable for every description of game, ranging in price from $3 to +200. A full assortment of gun accompaniments.......PISTOLS—In great variety, including colts of all sizes, and the genuine Derringer......Pocket and Table Cutlery—Lamps, Chandeliers, Candlesticks, Canes, Castors, with a great variety of FANCY GOODS.

OUR MECHANICAL BRANCH.

In order to meet promptly the increasing demand for wotk, we have added to our former force a number of superior workmen, and made many valuable additions to our machinery, and are now prepared to do, at short notice, in the best manner all kinds of

WATCH WORK—Including the making of new and complicated parts, equal to the original. Also, all kinds of CLOCK WORK.

JEWELRY—Of all kinds repaired, and new made to order, including superior Diamond work.

ENGRAVING—Plain and Ornamental, to suit all tastes. Also, Seals for Lodges, Courts and Corporations, engraved at short notice.

☞ We can furnish members of the fraternity with Keys, Medals and Marks, in any style. Also, Lodges with Jewels, &c.

OUR DAGUERREAN GALLERY,

W. H. DESHONG, Artist,

Embraces a handsomely furnished suit of rooms, built expressly for the purpose. Mr. De Shong is unrivallod in his profession, and produces pictures which, for correct likeness, fine tone, clear outline and durability, cannot be surpassed.

☞ Operat rs furnished with materials at the trade price.

F. H. CLARK, A. C. WURZBACH.

FIGURE 12. Advertisement of F. H. Clark, Memphis, Tennessee, in which the firm says it sells the "genuine Derringer"

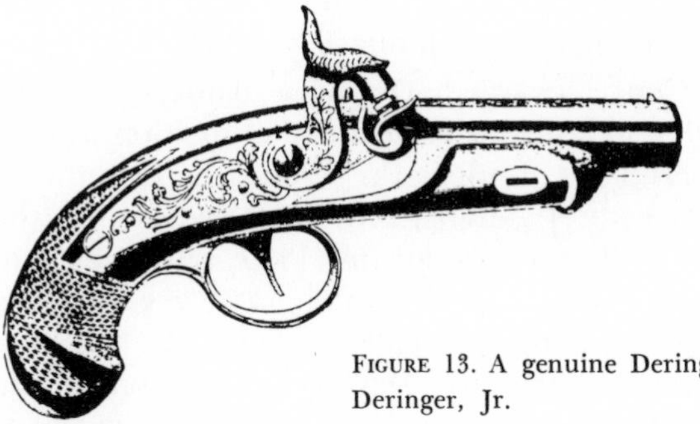

FIGURE 13. A genuine Deringer made by Henry Deringer, Jr.

ordered in reasonably large quantities could have their names stamped on the derringers. Long before derringers became practically an item of wearing apparel in the gold rush days of San Francisco, Southern dealers in many cities ordered these deadly little weapons. This subject is discussed at great length in *Guns of the Old West,* but here are a few of the many examples of Southern markings:

"Deringer Philadela. Mand. for F.H. Clark & Co., Memphis, Tenn."; and "Deringer Philadela. Manud. for Hyde & Goodrich Agents N. Orleans". These were genuine derringers made by Deringer himself. There are other derringers with Southern markings which may or may not have been made by Deringer, such as "F.R. Bitterlich & Co., Nashville, Tenn."; "H.E. Dimmick & Co., St. Louis, Mo."; "G. Erichson, Houston"; "F. Glassick & Co., Memphis, Tenn." and "Schneider & Glassick, Memphis, Tenn."

Henry Deringer, Jr., did not have a patent on his derringer but he did have a trademark issued by the United States. Although his derringer was extensively counterfeited before the Civil War, and he could not do anything about the counterfeiting of his peculiar pistol by Southerners during the war, he finally brought suit for trademark infringement against Adolphus Joseph Plate of San Francisco. The suit was filed on November 10, 1863, and in it Deringer asked for fifteen thousand dollars for damages suffered through trademark infringement. The case came to trial in the District Court of San Francisco on January 8, 1868.

The District Court awarded Deringer damages to the amount of $1,770, and issued a permanent injunction against Plate's using Deringer's trademark. Plate thereupon appealed. Henry Deringer, Jr., lived until 1868 and died at the age of eighty-one, while the case against Plate was still pending in the form of Plate's appeal. Finally, a few years after Deringer died, the Supreme Court of the State of California rejected Plate's appeal, held for Deringer, and upheld the lower court. This California Supreme Court decision, cited as *Deringer v. Plate,* was to become a landmark in trademark infringement cases, just as Deringer's name, changed to "derringer" and spelled with a lower-case "d" in all dictionaries, was to become one of the most famous names in all gun history.

The Deringer Used by Booth to Murder Lincoln

The most famous of all firearms associated with Confederate history and the history of the United States was a genuine Deringer made by Henry Deringer, Jr., in Philadelphia. It is cal. .44, with a 2.5-inch barrel marked "Deringer, Philadelphia". The total length is 6 inches. It has a polished hardwood stock and forearm and a bird's-head-shaped butt. The wood is checkered. This is the weapon John Wilkes Booth used to murder President Abraham Lincoln. It is the property of the United States, it is safely guarded in Washington, D. C., and despite the advertisements some dealers have published in the past, it has never been for sale and never will be.

The Deringer Family Also Made Dueling Pistols

Henry Deringer, Senior, and Henry Deringer, Jr., both made dueling pistols which were among the most popular and accurate dueling pistols used all over the United States, especially in the South. In addition to being used in duels, these pistols often were carried in wars and campaigns by officers who sometimes used them in battle.

CHAPTER 11

Dueling Pistols

DUELS AND DUELING PISTOLS DEFINED AND CLASSIFIED

Definition of Duel

A *duel,* in the broad sense of the term, is a combat between two persons fought with deadly weapons. Duels have been fought with clubs, battle-axes, spears, and swords of various types. Gun duels have been fought in the United States of America with shotguns, rifles, muskets, musketoons, carbines, revolvers, and single-shot pistols. Many of the firearms used in duels have been muzzle-loaders. Guns used in duels have been flintlock, percussion and cartridge weapons.

Formal Duels

In this chapter we are primarily interested in duels fought under formal agreements, with single-shot pistols especially designed for duels, with witnesses (called "seconds") present, and often with surgeons in attendance.

The cause of formal duels usually was some injury or insult, real or imagined, although the person who was the challenger often merely wanted an excuse to murder another man. Some challengers were simply homicidal maniacs. Others wanted to eliminate a man whom they regarded as a rival in business, politics or love.

Duels Forbidden by State Constitutions and Laws

The Constitution of the State of California adopted in 1849, Article XI, Section 2, which is still in effect, says:

> Any citizen of this State who shall, after the adoption of this Constitution, fight a duel with deadly weapons, or send or accept a challenge to fight a duel with deadly weapons, either within this State or out of it, or who shall act as second, or knowingly aid or assist in any manner those thus offending, shall not be allowed to hold any office of profit, or to enjoy the right of suffrage under this Constitution.

The constitutions of other states and the statutes of the various states forbid duels. Many of these constitutions and statutes existed long before California wrote the above-quoted provision into its Constitution of 1849.

However, the courts have interpreted duels to mean "formal duels," that is, combat between two persons, fought with deadly weapons, by agreement. Anyone who has access to a large law library will find this interpretation of a duel upheld in the following cases, cited as they are found in the court decisions of the states mentioned:

State v. Fritz, 133 North Carolina 725, 45 S.E. 957; State v. Mc Mull, South Carolina 126; Bassett v. State, 44 Florida 2, 33 South 262, 265; Davis v. Modern Woodmen of America, 98 Missouri App. 713, 73 S.W. 923; and People v. Morales, (1926), 77 California App. 483, 247 Pacific 221.

Duels Forbidden by Army and Navy

The Articles of War and the Articles for Governing the Navy (called "Rocks and Shoals" unofficially by the Navy) both forbid duels and provide that officers who engage in duels or act as what the lawyers call "accessories before, during, and after the event" shall not only lose their commissions but also be tried by a general court-martial, serve any prison sentence awarded by the court, reduced to the lowest enlisted rank and dishonorably discharged. The author knows this to be true because he had to hear the Navy Articles read once each month during the entire time that he served in the Naval Academy and the U. S. Marine Corps.

Constitutions and Statutes Ignored

In spite of the fact that most of the civilized nations of the world, including the United States, have long forbidden duels, and regardless of the very definite provisions in state constitutions and statutes against duels in the United States, the constitutions, laws, and military and naval regulations have been ignored so much that when someone is brought to trial for a duel it becomes front-page news.

Until recently, men who engaged in duels were rarely brought to trial if they were regarded as "gentlemen" of rank, title, position, wealth, or influence. Men lacking the above "qualifications" who engaged in duels were treated differently. If only one survived, he was brought to trial either on a manslaughter or a murder count. If both escaped death, both were brought to trial.

Women have fought duels, both formal duels and informal duels, but they have never been given the same consideration as the "gentlemen" who fought formal duels, probably because law enforcement almost always has been a male prerogative and men regard it as a gross affront to civilization for females to indulge in such unladylike practices.

A California Duel

Hubert Howe Bancroft, author of *History of California* which was published in at least seven volumes in San Francisco, California, from 1884 to 1890, described a duel between Colonel John Bankhead Magruder and Doctor William B. Osborn, fought in San Diego, California, in 1852. Bancroft repeated the same account in his *California Inter Pocula*, published in San Francisco in 1888, hence Bancroft, who ranks as one of the great American historians, must have considered this duel of great interest.

Colonel John Bankhead Magruder was challenged to a duel

by Doctor William B. Osborn. The customs existing in California at that time provided that the person challenged had the right to name the time, place, and weapons for the duel. Magruder specified that the duel must be fought with "Derringer pistols across the dining-room table."

There is no record that either of the men was even wounded as a result of a duel, hence we must assume one of two things. Either the duel did not take place, or the dining-room table must have been of an unusually great diameter, because two men firing "Derringer pistols," regardless of the caliber and size of the pistols, across an ordinary dining-room table could not fail to wound one another. This is merely one example of the nonsense connected with all aspects of dueling.

The Classification of Dueling Pistols

An authentic dueling pistol, constructed to be used in a formal duel, is commonly defined as a single-shot pistol with a long barrel. Dueling pistols for formal duels were customarily made in matched pairs and placed in a box, usually called a "case," together with accessories, as explained below.

During both flintlock and percussion days, officers often carried dueling pistols with them on campaigns and during wars, primarily to be ready to engage in duels with other officers or with civilian "gentlemen" meeting the "qualifications" already explained.

However, when their regular martial pistols were not immediately available, or when additional pistols were needed during combat, dueling pistols were fired at the enemy. This happened often enough to classify these pistols as semi-martial weapons.

Confederate pistols designed as dueling pistols can be classified correctly either as dueling pistols or Confederate pistols.

Some collectors and dealers have described pistols as dueling pistols when they do not belong in that classification, merely to add prestige to their weapons or to obtain a higher price when sold. In case of doubt, honest experts can decide how a pistol should be classified.

Cased Sets of Dueling Pistols

Men of limited income could not afford to own a pair of dueling pistols and even if they could, the peculiar attitude of law-enforcement officials, including judges, during the dueling era was such that poor people, or what we might now call lower-middle-class people, were treated as criminals if they engaged in duels, as we have said before. For this reason, dueling pistols were made without regard to expense, in pairs, and in cases or boxes of elaborate construction consistent with the quality of the pistols themselves. Together with the pair of pistols, the case or box contained accessories, such as loading and cleaning tools, cleaning patches, a powder flask, bullets, extra flints for flintlock pistols, and a box of primers if the pistols were of the percussion type. These cases or boxes were divided into rectangular compartments in some specimens and in others, notably those of French construction, into compartments contoured to fit the accessories.

Some cases carried labels, or even engraved plates, stating the name of the manufacturer, but when there was fear of the enforcement of the laws against dueling, the cases were often made without identifying labels or plates.

STANDARDIZATION OF DUELING PISTOLS

European Attempts at Standardization

With the development of firearms Englishmen of rank, title and position gradually quit wearing swords and fighting sword duels. Their duels, which they often referred to as "affairs of honour," were fought with single-shot pistols after they abandoned swords. Of course, when the challenged man had the right to choose the type of weapon, he could select pistols, swords, or any other deadly weapon.

The records are incomplete, but it has been estimated that in France about eight thousand noblemen were killed in duels from about 1600 to about 1640. This caused the French nobility to draw up an elaborate set of rules which the English translated to mean a Code of Honour. Although the original rules applied to sword duels, they were modified to meet the requirements of formal duels with single-shot pistols and the rules for pistol duels came into use as swords were discarded by the French.

The English, Irish, and Scotsmen took the French rules for pistol duels and rewrote them to suit their own personalities and customs. For example, the Irish prepared what they called the Clonmel Rules, which were similar to the French Code of Honor. Under the Irish rules, the challenger sent a written challenge to a duel, which was delivered by his second. The man challenged could choose the time, place and type of weapons, although the management of the duel was left to the seconds appointed by both the challenger and the man challenged.

Under the Irish Clonmel Rules, if the challenged man chose pistols as the weapons, each must have a smoothbore barrel, caliber .50, nine inches long, made without sights.

From about 1775 to about 1800, the dueling pistol used in France, England, Ireland and Scotland had a full-length stock and an octagonal barrel, although sometimes the barrel was part round and part octagonal. There is no special significance to the shape of the barrel. Furthermore, some authentic Scottish dueling pistols did not have wooden stocks, but were of "all-metal" construction, to use a gun collector's term.

During the same period, the barrel of the dueling pistol was treated with acid to produce what we call a "browned finish." The purpose of browning is to reduce glare from sunlight and also reduce rusting.

From time to time, the rules were modified regarding the design and construction of the pistols and the method of managing the duels, but the facts presented here are sufficient to give a general idea of the European background for the development of American dueling pistols.

Flintlock and percussion pistols were all "handmade."

Some gunmakers manufactured a supply of dueling pistols, but all of those who made dueling pistols also made them to special order. Therefore, between the individualism of the pistol manufacturers and the whimsical desires of the purchasers, there never was any high degree of standardization, in spite of what some authors have said.

American Attempts at Standardization

In North America, both before and after the American Revolution, there were many attempts to standardize the design and construction of dueling pistols, especially flintlock pistols made from about 1750 to about 1815. In Canada, the Frenchmen in the Province of Quebec tended to follow the French rules existing at that time, but the British subjects in Canada tended to follow English, Scottish or Irish rules. In what is now the United States, during American colonial days and after the Revolution until about 1815, there was a characteristic "Yankee" effort to be at least slightly different from the British and French.

The so-called American flintlock dueling pistols from about 1750 to about 1800, and to some extent up to 1815, were single-barrel, smoothbore pistols, caliber .50. The barrel was not supposed to be longer than 10.5 inches or shorter than 9 inches. The sights had to be fixed; that is, they could not be made adjustable for elevation or deflection. The butt (often called the grip), the safety device, the firing mechanism, the trigger, and the trigger guard could be of any design or construction.

Generally, flintlock dueling pistols were stocked to the muzzle, although from about 1740 until the end of the flintlock dueling pistol era, many were made with half-length, walnut stocks. The barrel was almost always octagonal in cross section, although round barrels were permitted and used. During target practice in preparation for a duel, the sights were used, but the arbitrary Dueling Code made it unethical for the contestants to take deliberate aim by using the sights. They were supposed to aim and fire on signal or on command, according to the agreement reached by the seconds, and this did not allow time for lining up the sights with the opponent.

Trigger Pull and Hair Triggers

An American attempt at standardization which copied to a great extent European rules of the same era limited the trigger pull of the flintlock dueling pistol to three pounds. This was tested by cocking an unloaded pistol and suspending a weight from the trigger. If it required a weight of more than three pounds to pull the trigger and cause the cock (hammer) to fall, the pistol had to be adjusted by a gunsmith or discarded.

So-called "hair triggers" were invented and developed in Europe and America. This meant that the lock mechanism was either originally manufactured or later altered so that the pistol could be fired by an extremely slight pressure on the trigger. This pressure had to be so very light that the shooter did not have to apply enough pressure on the trigger to throw the pistol out of alignment with the target and thereby disturb the aim.

The hair-trigger mechanism depended upon a small, powerful spring which was first compressed. To use the language of that period, the spring was *set*. Originally, this was done by pushing the trigger forward a short distance, but some pistols were made with two triggers, one for setting the hair-trigger mechanism and the other for actually firing the pistol. Eventually, pistols were made so that the setting was accomplished by pressing a small button.

Variations from American "Standards"

When anyone says that flintlock dueling pistols were standardized as to design or construction in America, he is making a broad, general statement to which there are numerous exceptions. A "typical specimen" is merely one which does not deviate too much from others made for the same purpose during the same era and in the same country.

For example, there are in existence today, in museums and private collections, many beautifully engraved, inlaid, and otherwise elaborately ornamented dueling pistols, usually in matched pairs, in cases as ornamental as the pistols. These were, in most instances, made as "presentation pieces" or "presentation sets," given to individuals by personal friends, the American colonies, states, and cities, sometimes simply as gestures of friendship and other times in recognition of distinguished public service in peace or in war.

These highly decorated pistols allegedly were seldom used in duels because the gold, silver, or ivory ornamentation, and even the engraving would reflect the light and disturb the aim. This is the traditional concept, but it is not consistent with the facts.

Since all dueling codes ruled out as unethical taking a deliberate aim, and the pistol was merely pointed quickly at the adversary on command or signal, it is not reasonable to believe that the reflection of sunlight from a decorated pistol would affect the aim enough to change the outcome of the duel, especially in view of the fact that pistol duels were conducted at a very short distance between the shooters. Actually, both decorated and plain dueling pistols were used throughout the whole, long, sordid history of dueling.

Percussion Dueling Pistols

Many of the above comments on flintlock dueling pistols apply in principle to percussion dueling pistols, keeping in mind that the adoption of the percussion ignition system changed the mechanical operation of pistols and remembering that new social customs developed as the years rolled along.

There was no year or place when flintlock dueling pistols were discarded in favor of percussion pistols. Both were used for many years because the ignition systems for firearms overlapped each other chronologically. The same thing applies to all types of firearms throughout history. Dueling pistols as a class did not constitute an exception to firearms evolution.

FRENCH FLINTLOCK DUELING PISTOL

Pistol Description

Figure 1 is a drawing of a French flintlock dueling pistol made by Le Faure Sons, in Paris, France. This is one of a matched pair originally boxed in a beautifully decorated, green Morocco leather case, with gold trimming.

The pistol is cal. 56. The round, rifled barrel is 12 inches long with gold-inlay decorations and three countersunk, gold-inlay manufacturer's marks. The cock (hammer) is of the gooseneck type, offset to the right to permit the use of a small rear sight near the rear end of the barrel which could be lined up with a small, low, blade-type front sight mounted near the front of the barrel. The stock extends to the muzzle and its butt portion is exquisitely checkered to provide a good grip for the shooter. The ramrod under the barrel has a metal front end (at the end which is forward when the ramrod is mounted).

At the portion of the stock where it begins to curve downward to form the butt, sometimes called the "wrist" of a pistol, there is a silver band. Superficially, this appears to be merely one more of the many elaborate decorative features of the pistol, but it marks the location where the butt itself can be removed by twisting it 90 degrees to the left. After

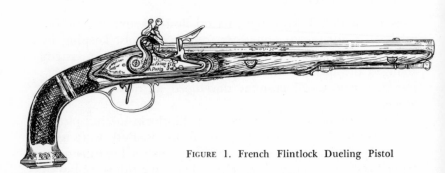

FIGURE 1. French Flintlock Dueling Pistol

removing the butt, a shoulder stock (Figure 2) can be mounted, thus forming a weapon that could be classified as a flintlock pistol-carbine.

All metal parts of the pistol, including not only the barrel but the lock plate, the hammer, the frizzen (battery), the trigger guard, the trigger, and even each visible screwhead, are elaborately decorated with the highest quality of engraving, much of it so minute that it cannot be adequately portrayed in either a drawing or a photograph.

The lock plate is engraved in two parallel, horizontal lines between the cock (hammer) and the frizzen spring "Le FAURE fils" over "A PARIS". The French word for sons, *fils,* is in lower-case letters. All other letters are capital letters. The lettering is executed with fancy flourishes.

Accessories

Figure 2 is a drawing by Herschel Logan of the accessories for the Le Faure Sons flintlock dueling pistol. Illustrated are the shoulder stock (labeled "extension stock" in the drawing), a bullet mold, the extractor screw attached to the ramrod to remove a lead ball stuck in the barrel, the bullet-seating "point" for the ramrod, the vent cleaner for cleaning out the vent (touchhole), a powder measurer, an oilcan, a screwdriver, an ornamented power flask with a device for measuring the amount of powder released, a mallet for forcing the ramrod down the barrel when necessary for a tight fit in loading, and the combination loading and cleaning rod.

A typical cased set of flintlock dueling pistols included many of these accessories except the extension stock (shoulder stock). Some cased sets did not have all these items and others included lead balls.

The presence of the shoulder stock (extension stock) takes this specimen out of the usual "typical" group of flintlock dueling pistols because it was extremely unusual for anyone to fight a duel with a flintlock pistol having a shoulder stock mounted as the above. The use of a shoulder stock is inconsistent with all that has been stated previously about the vari-

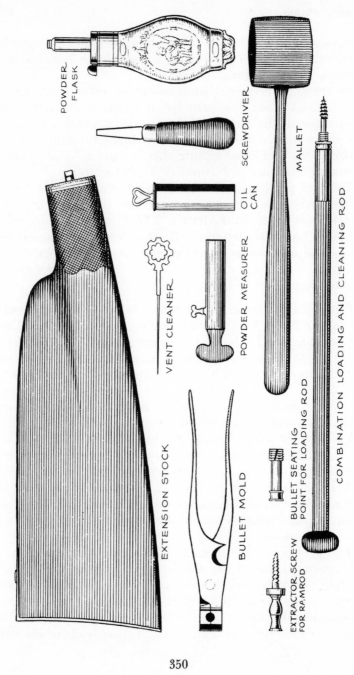

POWDER FLASK

SCREWDRIVER

MALLET

OIL CAN

POWDER MEASURER

VENT CLEANER

EXTENSION STOCK

BULLET MOLD

BULLET SEATING POINT FOR LOADING ROD

COMBINATION LOADING AND CLEANING ROD

EXTRACTOR SCREW FOR RAMROD

FIGURE 2. Accessories for French Flintlock Dueling Pistol

ous "codes" and "rules" of dueling. The presence of the shoulder stock raises a presumption that the man who ordered this set may have intended to provide himself with a pair of dueling pistols, either one of which could be used in warfare as a pistol-carbine with the extension stock mounted.

CALDERWOOD FLINTLOCK DUELING PISTOL

Historical Background

William Calderwood, of Philadelphia, Pennsylvania, is the same Calderwood who made the Calderwood Contract Pistol, Model 1807, described in Chapter 3, "United States Martial Flintlock Pistols." In addition to making U. S. Martial Flintlock Pistols under contract with the United States, he also made other types of firearms, including rifles. It is believed that his period of activity as a firearms manufacturer extended from about 1807 to about 1820, but the records are not complete or conclusive.

Technical Details of Calderwood Dueling Pistol

The Calderwood Flintlock Dueling Pistol (Figure 3) is cal. .52. It has a 9-inch, octagonal, smoothbore barrel, stamped "CALDERWOOD PHILA", together with two Calderwood proofmarks, on top of the barrel. The lock plate is stamped in all-capital letters "CALDERWOOD".

This pistol is brass-mounted except for the iron ramrod thimble. It has a late-type flintlock mechanism with a roller on the frizzen. The purpose of the roller and the fact that its presence indicates that a flintlock pistol was made late in the flintlock period have been discussed in connection with other pistols in previous chapters.

There is a half-length walnut stock and there is an iron rib under the barrel. The wooden ramrod has an ivory tip at the end visible in the drawing. There is a small front sight. The total length is 14 inches and the weight is 2 lbs. This pistol probably was made by William Calderwood at his shop on Germantown Road, Philadelphia, about 1815.

It is one of the rarest of all authentic American flintlock dueling pistols and is from the collection of Samuel E. Smith, Markesan, Wisconsin.

DERINGER DUELING PISTOLS

Historical Background

Henry Deringer, Senior, and his son, Henry Deringer, Jr., made dueling pistols during both the flintlock and the percussion eras, and there is a remote possibility that Henry Deringer, Jr., even made cartridge-type dueling pistols long after dueling began to decline as an accepted custom for "gentlemen."

It is easy to overlook the widespread ramifications of the arms manufacturing conducted by the Deringers, especially because of Henry Deringer, Jr.'s fame as the inventor of the large-caliber, single-shot pistol with a short barrel that is now called a derringer.

In both the flintlock and percussion periods, the Deringer dueling pistols generally met the accepted requirements for this type of weapon. Deringer flintlock dueling pistols in the early versions were fully stocked; that is, with stocks extending to the muzzle. The barrels were made in 9-inch and 10-inch lengths.

Late-model Deringer flintlock dueling pistols were available with either a half-length or a three-quarter-length stock.

The maximum allowable trigger pull was 3 pounds for the Deringer dueling pistols, both flintlock and percussion. The barrel on most specimens found today is octagonal in cross section and smoothbore, cal. .50, with fixed sights for target-practice dueling pistols, and either no sights, or only a front sight on those intended for duels.

Technical Details of Deringer Flintlock Dueling Pistol

The Deringer Flintlock Dueling Pistol illustrated in Figure 4 is one of the rarest of all flintlock pistols made by the Deringers. It is cal. .55, with an 11.25-inch, octagonal, smooth-

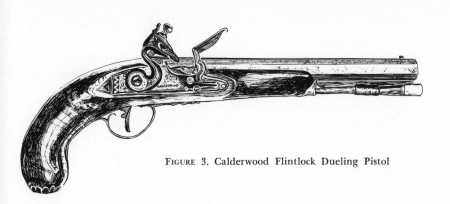

FIGURE 3. Calderwood Flintlock Dueling Pistol

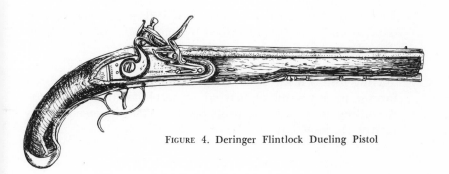

FIGURE 4. Deringer Flintlock Dueling Pistol

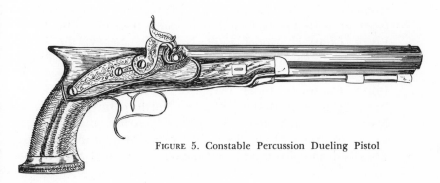

FIGURE 5. Constable Percussion Dueling Pistol

bore barrel. The barrel is marked on top in capital letters "H. DERINGER PHILᴬ", with the last capital letter "A" raised above the base line for the other letters. There is a knife-blade front sight and a V-notch rear sight. There is a full-length walnut stock, extending almost to the muzzle. The stock curves gracefully at the rear to form the butt. The total length is 16.25 inches and the weight is 2 lbs., 11 oz.

The lock plate is stamped "H. DERINGER" between the hammer and the frizzen spring. This marking is entirely visible when the pistol is cocked, but after firing, the forward movement of the cock (hammer) partially covers the marking on the specimen illustrated.

The lock is of an early type and has a gooseneck hammer. The horizontal pan has a fence. The lock plate is pointed at the rear end, which is described by some collectors as a "teat-shaped" or "tit-shaped" rear tip.

The specimen illustrated is one of the rare, early, flintlock dueling pistols made by Deringer strictly for dueling and not for use as any kind of martial or secondary martial pistol. According to experts, it probably was made about 1810 by Henry Deringer, Jr.

SIMEON NORTH FLINTLOCK DUELING PISTOLS

Historical Background

Simeon North, of Middletown, Connecticut, was active from about 1799 to about 1852 as the manufacturer of various types of both flintlock and percussion firearms. The U. S. Pistol, Contract Model 1799, North & Cheney; the U. S. Pistol, Contract Model 1808, S. North, Navy; the U. S. Pistol, Contract Model 1811 (1810), S. North, Army; the U. S. Pistol, Contract Model 1813, S. North, Army; the U. S. Pistol, Contract Model 1816, S. North, Army; the U. S. Pistol, Contract Model 1819, S. North, Army; and the U. S. Pistol, Contract Model 1826, S. North, Army and Navy are described and illustrated in Chapter 3, "United States Martial Flintlock Pistols." These are only a few of the many weapons he made.

Simeon North flintlock pistols of all types are rare and valuable, hence they are reproduced and the reproductions sold as genuine by dishonest gunsmiths, collectors and dealers. Several flintlock dueling pistols supposedly made by Simeon North have been manufactured within recent years and they are such excellent reproductions that they are frequently bought and sold innocently by collectors and dealers.

For example, one beautifully made pair of so-called "greatcoat" pistols engraved "S. NORTH Middletown, Conn." were made in England during the present century. The faker took a pair of good English flintlock pistols, removed the name of the English maker, removed the British proofmarks, and then engraved the Simeon North markings on the pistols. In order to make the pistols worth even more, the faker set cleverly made, small, genuine gold North proofmarks into the barrel.

Simeon North Flintlock Dueling Pistol Details

An authentic Simeon North flintlock dueling pistol, not illustrated here but examined by the author and several experts, is cal. .50, smoothbore. It has a 10.25-inch, octagonal barrel. The barrel was originally browned. It has a countersunk gold seal with "S. NORTH MIDDLETOWN CONN" in raised letters, and the word "CONNECTICUT" engraved in Old English script on the barrel.

There is a single set-trigger. There are two iron thimbles; an engraved, doubleneck hammer; and a safety lock. The vent (touchhole) is gold-lined. The tang is engraved. The half-length walnut stock has a horn tip. The butt is checkered and has a shape described by collectors as "square type." There is a rib under the barrel to facilitate the mounting of the horn-tipped, hickory ramrod. There are silver wedge escutcheons. All parts except the barrel are casehardened.

This specimen is one of a matched pair. Each pistol of the pair has the serial number 11.

Although it is difficult to describe any flintlock dueling pistol as "typical," the details of craftsmanship found on the specimen described, especially the high-quality engraving and the gold work, are characteristic of Simeon North flintlock dueling pistols.

CONSTABLE DUELING PISTOLS

Richard Constable, who made the Constable Dueling Pistol illustrated in Figure 5, is the same Constable who made the Constable Pistol described in Chapter 4, "U. S. Secondary Martial Flintlock Pistols" (but not illustrated there) ; and the Constable, Philadelphia, Pistol described and illustrated in Chapter 7, "U. S. Secondary Martial Percussion Pistols."

Richard Constable had a gun business in Philadelphia, Pennsylvania, from 1816 to 1851. He imported parts from England and assembled them into arms in his shop. It is known that he had a shop at 88 South 2nd Street, Philadelphia, from 1817 to 1851.

Constable either made or assembled both flintlock and percussion firearms of various types, including the U. S. Martial Flintlock Pistol and the U. S. Secondary Martial Percussion Pistol referred to above. In addition, he made dueling pistols, both flintlock and percussion. Furthermore, he made or assembled a percussion derringer described and illustrated in *Guns of the Old West*.

It is not fair to Richard Constable to infer that all his weapons were assembled from parts made by others, because we do not know this to be a fact. We do know that a few were merely assembled by him, but there is evidence that some of his firearms consisted of parts made both by himself and others. This being true, it is easy to believe that he was capable of making an entire firearm, assembled entirely from parts made in his own plant.

This business of using parts made by others was a very common practice during the flintlock and percussion eras and continued into the cartridge era for the simple reason that some men specialized in lock plates, others were barrel experts, and still others were stock makers.

CONSTABLE PERCUSSION DUELING PISTOL (Figure 5), cal. .45. It has a 10-inch, octagonal, smoothbore barrel. The words "CONSTABLE PHILADELPHIA" are engraved on the lower portion of the barrel, together with two British proofmarks, indicating that at least the barrel was made in England. These marks are not visible in any side-view illustration.

The lock plate is engraved "CONSTABLE", but this does not mean that Richard Constable made the lock plate, because it was possible to import lock plates with any engraving or other means of marking which the importer ordered.

The weight of the specimen illustrated is 2 lbs., 6 oz. The illustration clearly shows the gooseneck hammer, the engraving on the hammer and lock plate, the checkered butt, the trigger guard with a unique shape, the ramrod, and the very small front sight. The butt has a shape described by collectors as a "saw-handle butt."

The specimen illustrated is one of a pair of dueling pistols, cased with all accessories, obtained directly from a family in Virginia which can trace its ancestors back to Colonial America. The pair of pistols was used in a duel in the 1850's by an ancestor of the family from which the cased set was purchased by Samuel E. Smith. Design and construction details indicate that the pair of pistols was made about 1845. This estimated date of manufacture has been confirmed by several experts.

THE BEGINNING AND THE END OF THE STORY

No Pistol Is on an Island of Its Own

No single-shot pistol is on an island of its own. We have presented the highlights and the landmarks of the development of the flintlock pistol and we have explained its firing mechanism. Following that, we have described and illustrated U. S. Martial Flintlock Pistols, U. S. Secondary Martial Flintlock Pistols, percussion lock development and cartridge design, U. S. Martial Percussion Pistols, U. S. Secondary Martial Percussion Pistols, and U. S. Martial Single-Shot Cartridge Pistols. There are no U. S. Secondary Martial Single-Shot Cartridge Pistols in the strict sense of the term.

Following the development of U. S. Martial and U. S. Secondary Martial Single-Shot Pistols, we have discussed and illustrated Kentucky Pistols (which ought to be called Pennsylvania Pistols), Confederate Pistols, and Dueling Pistols. None of the pistols in these last three chapters can be regarded as United States Pistols, and yet they are very much American pistols. They form an important part of our United States history, and many of them were used in battle, either by U. S. armed forces or by Confederates who fought for what they sincerely believed to be their rights under the American system of government.

Anyone who reads the entirety of this book will be convinced that no pistol is on an island of its own. Each pistol embodies features which were developed or invented long before that particular pistol was even an idea in the mind of its inventor or manufacturer. Many of the pistols in this book were made by the same man, or at least by members of the same family. All of them are American pistols. All are "Guns of Glory" except the dueling pistols, and even some of those were used in battle enough to remove part of the infamy connected with the vicious custom of dueling.

The Road Ahead

There are many gaps in the history of American single-shot pistols. Some pistols were not marked by the manufacturers. Some were marked with the names of those who made only one or more parts of the assembled pistol. Through the ages, the markings on many pistols have become indistinct.

Many manufacturers kept no records. Others kept accurate records which have been mislaid, lost, or destroyed. The records of the United States Government and the records of the several states are often incomplete and inconclusive regarding U. S. Martial Pistols and U. S. Secondary Martial Pistols.

Although very few Kentucky pistols were made, and many of them have been lost, the principal problem is identifying a pistol as an authentic Kentucky specimen. As explained earlier, the Kentucky pistol was not recognized as a distinct type before 1940, hence there may be many genuine specimens in existence which are classified by their owners under some other name.

Genuine Confederate single-shot pistols are even more difficult to identify accurately, for reasons given before. This is another field for further research.

Although the author of this book has read every available account of a duel fought in this country, whether found in newspapers, magazines, books, court reports, or unpublished manuscripts, he has been amazed at the lack of precise descriptions of the pistols used in formal or informal duels. This is another realm for additional research by arms historians.

Suggestions Invited

Any reader of this book is cordially invited to mail detailed descriptions, drawings, and photographs of single-shot pistols not described or illustrated in this text to the author, at his permanent mailing address, Post Office Box 327, Redondo Beach, California, but the author offers no compensation for such service and cannot be responsible for material lost in the mail, especially if it is not sent by registered, first-class mail, or by insured parcel post. Furthermore, the author cannot guarantee the immediate return of such material or information.

No Appraisals or Identifications by Mail

The author must refuse to appraise the value or supply the correct identification of firearms he has not examined personally. Also, he refuses to be responsible for firearms sent to him for examination, either for purposes of appraisal or identification.

The reader is referred to the author's book, *The Gun Collector's Handbook of Values*, for descriptions, illustrations, and values of guns for collectors.

General Salute

Finally, the author acknowledges with thanks the help of hundreds of collectors, dealers, museum curators, and authors who have made this text possible. It is impossible to list more than a few of these people and organizations in the Acknowledgments sections and the Bibliography.

Bibliography

Albaugh, William A., III, and Edward N. Simmons, *Confederate Arms.* Harrisburg, Pa.: The Stackpole Co., 1957.

Baker, Ezekiel, *Remarks on Rifle Guns,* also titled *Baker's Remarks on the Rifle.* London: Joseph Mallet, 1835.

Bancroft, Hubert Howe, *History of California,* Vols. I to VII. San Francisco: A. L. Bancroft & Co., 1884–1890.

Bannerman, David B., *Military Goods Catalogue.* New York: Francis Bannerman Sons, 1913, *et seq.*

Bosworth, N. A., *Treatise on the Rifle, Musket, Pistol and Fowling Piece.* New York: J. S. Redfield, 1846.

Botkin, B. A., *A Treasury of American Folklore.* New York: Crown Publishers, 1944.

Brown, F. R. ("Bob"), *Encyclopedia of Modern Firearms—Parts & Assembly,* Vol. I. Montezuma, Iowa: F. R. ("Bob") Brownell, 1959.

Burrard, Gerald, *The Modern Shotgun* (in two volumes). New York: Charles Scribner's Sons, 1931.

Casey, Brigadier General Silas, *Infantry Tactics* (in three volumes). D. Van Nostrand, 1865.

Chapel, Charles Edward, *The Art of Shooting.* New York: A. S. Barnes & Co., Inc., 1960.

———, *The Boy's Book of Rifles.* New York: Coward-McCann, Inc., 1948.

———, *The Complete Book of Gun Collecting.* New York: Coward-McCann, Inc., 1961.

———, *The Complete Guide to Gunsmithing: Gun Care and Repair.* New York: A. S. Barnes & Co., Inc., 1962.

———, *Field, Skeet, and Trap Shooting.* New York: A. S. Barnes & Co., Inc., 1962.

———, *Forensic Ballistics.* Chicago: Institute of Applied Science, 1933.

———, *Gun Care and Repair—A Manual of Gunsmithing.* New York: Coward-McCann, Inc., 1943.

———, *Gun Collecting.* New York: Coward-McCann, Inc., Revised Edition, 1947.

———, *The Gun Collector's Handbook of Values.* New York: Coward-McCann, Inc., Revised Edition, 1960.

————, *Guns of the Old West*. New York: Coward-McCann, Inc., 1961.

————, *Simplified Pistol and Revolver Shooting*. New York: Coward-McCann, Inc. 1950.

————, *Simplified Rifle Shooting*. New York: Coward-McCann, Inc., 1950.

Clemens, Samuel Langhorne (Mark Twain), *Roughing It*. New York: Harper & Brothers, 1903.

Cline, Walter M., *The Muzzle-Loading Rifle, Then and Now*. Huntington, W. Va.: Standard Printing and Publishing Co., 1942.

Connecticut Historical Society, *Samuel Colt's Own Record of Transactions with Captain Walker and Eli Whitney, Jr., in 1847*. Hartford, Conn.: The Connecticut Historical Society, 1949.

Damon, G. E., *Gun Fun With Safety*. Huntington, W. Va.: Standard Publications, Inc., 1947.

Deane, *Deane's Manual of the History and Science of Fire-Arms*. London: Longman, Brown, Green, Longman's & Roberts, 1858.

Dillin, John G. W., *The Kentucky Rifle*. Wilmington, Del.: George N. Hyatt, 1959.

Dougall, James Dalziel, *Shooting: Its Appliances, Practice, and Purpose*. London: Sampson Low, Marston, Searle & Rivington, 1881.

Edwards, William B., *The Story of Colt's Revolver*. Harrisburg, Pa.: The Stackpole Co., 1957.

Foertsch, Hermann, *The Art of Modern Warfare*. New York: Oscar Priest, 1940.

Frémont, John C., *The Exploring Expedition to the Rocky Mountains, Oregon and California*. Buffalo: Derby, Orton & Mulligan, 1854.

Frith, James, and Ronald Andrews, *Antique Pistol Collecting*. New York: Arco Publishing Co., Inc., 1960.

Fuller, Claud E., *The Breech-Loader in the Service*, Topeka, Kan.: F. Theodore Dexter, 1933.

————, *The Rifled Musket*. Harrisburg, Pa.: The Stackpole Co., 1958.

————, *Springfield Muzzle-Loading Shoulder Arms*. New York: Francis Bannerman Sons, 1930.

————, *The Whitney Firearms*. Huntington, W. Va.: Standard Publications, Inc., 1946.

Fuller, Claude E., and Richard D. Steuart. *Firearms of the Confederacy*. Huntington, W. Va.: Standard Publications, Inc., 1944.

Gardner, Robert E., *American Arms and Arms Makers*. Columbus, Ohio: The F. J. Heer Printing Co., 1938.

————, *Five Centuries of Gunsmiths, Swordsmiths and Armourers 1400–1900*. Columbus, Ohio: Walter F. Heer, 1948.

George, J. N., *English Guns and Rifles*. Plantersville, S.C.: Small-Arms Technical Publishing Co., 1947.

————, *English Pistols and Revolvers*. Onslow County, N.C.: Small-Arms Technical Publishing Co., 1938.

Glass, Herb, *The American Gun,* Vol. I, No. 2. New York: Madison Books, Inc., 1961.

Gluckman, Arcadi, *Catalogue of United States Martial Pistols.* Buffalo: Otto Ulbrich Co., 1939.

———, *United States Martial Pistols and Revolvers.* Harrisburg, Pa.: The Stackpole Co., 1956.

Gluckman, Arcadi, and L. D. Satterlee, *American Gun Makers.* Harrisburg, Pa.: The Stackpole Co., 1953.

Grant, James, *More Single-Shot Rifles.* New York: William Morrow & Co., 1959.

———, *Single-Shot Rifles.* New York: William Morrow & Co., 1947.

Gunther, Jack Disbrow, and Charles O. Gunther, *The Identification of Firearms.* New York: John Wiley & Sons, Inc., 1935.

Hagan, William T., *The Sac and Fox Indians.* Norman, Okla.: University of Oklahoma Press, 1958.

Hardee, W. J., *Rifle and Light Infantry Tactics* (two or more volumes). Philadelphia: Lippincott, Grambo & Co., 1855.

Hartley, Rachel M., *The History of Hamden, Connecticut.* Hamden, Conn.: Published by the Town, 1943.

Hatch, Alden, *Remington Arms in American History.* New York: Rinehart & Co., Inc., 1956.

Hatcher, Julian S., *Hatcher's Notebook.* Harrisburg, Pa.: Military Service Publishing Co., 1947.

———, *Textbook of Firearms Investigation, Identification and Evidence.* Marines, Onslow County, N.C.: Small-Arms Technical Publishing Co., 1935.

Haven, Charles T., and Frank A. Belden, *A History of the Colt Revolver.* New York: William Morrow & Co., 1940.

Held, Robert, *The Age of Firearms.* New York: Harper & Brothers, 1957.

Hicks, James E.: *Notes on United States Ordnance:* Vol. I, *Small Arms,* 1940. *Notes on United States Ordnance:* Vol. II, *Ordnance Correspondence,* 1940. *Notes on German Ordnance,* 1937. *Notes on French Ordnance,* 1937. *Notes on French Ordnance* (Translation of *Mémoires d'Artillerie*), 1939. *U. S. Firearms* (Revision of Vol. I, above), 1946. AUTHOR'S NOTE: The books by James E. Hicks were published by him at Mt. Vernon, N. Y.

Holcomb, Robert N., *Story of Connecticut* (in three volumes). Hartford, Conn.: 1936.

Holloway, Carroll C., *Texas Gun Lore.* San Antonio, Texas: The Naylor Co., 1951.

Johnson, Melvin M., Jr., and Charles T. Haven, *Automatic Weapons of the World.* New York: William Morrow & Co., 1945.

Kalman, James M., and C. Meade Patterson, *Pictorial History of U. S. Single-Shot Martial Pistols.* New York: Charles Scribner's Sons, 1957.

Karr, Charles Lee, Jr., and Carroll Robbins, *Remington Handguns.* Harrisburg, Pa.: The Stackpole Co., 1951.

Kindig, Joe, Jr., *Thoughts of the Kentucky Rifle in Its Golden Age.* Wilmington, Del., 1960.

Knox, Dudley W., *A History of the United States Navy.* New York: G. P. Putnam's Sons, 1936.

Koller, Larry. *The Fireside Book of Guns.* New York: Simon and Schuster, 1959.

Leffingwell, William Bruce, *The Art of Wing Shooting.* Chicago: Rand, McNally & Co., 1894.

Lenz, Ellis Christian, *Muzzle Flashes.* Huntington, W. Va.: Standard Publications, Inc., 1944.

———, *Rifleman's Progress.* Huntington, West Va.: Standard Publications, Inc., 1946.

Logan, Herschel C., *Cartridges—A Pictorial Digest of Small Arms Ammunition.* Harrisburg, Pa.: The Stackpole Co., 1956.

———, *Hand Cannon to Automatic.* Huntington, W. Va.: Standard Publications, Inc., 1944.

McClellan, George B., *Manual of Bayonet Exercises, Prepared for the Use of the United States Army.* Philadelphia: J. B. Lippincott & Co., 1852.

McGivern, Ed, *Ed McGivern's Book on Fact and Fancy Revolver Shooting and Police Training.* Springfield, Mass.: King Richardson Co., 1938.

McHenry, Roy C., and Walter F. Roper, *Smith & Wesson Hand Guns.* Harrisburg, Pa.: The Stackpole Co., 1958.

Mack, Effie Mona, *Mark Twain in Nevada.* New York: Charles Scribner's Sons, 1947.

Mayer, Dr. Joseph R., *Five Centuries of Gunsmiths, Swordsmiths and Armourers, 1400–1900.* Columbus, Ohio: Walter F. Heer, 1948.

Metcalf, Clyde H., *A History of the United States Marine Corps.* New York: G. P. Putnam's Sons, 1939.

Metschl, John, *The Rudolph J. Nunnemacher Collection of Projectile Arms.* Milwaukee: The Milwaukee Public Museum, 1928.

Nevada State Historical Society, *Nevada State Historical Society Papers, 1925–1926.* Reno: Nevada State Historical Society, 1926.

Nichols, Alice, *Bleeding Kansas.* New York: Oxford University Press, 1954.

Nutter, Waldo E., *Manhattan Firearms.* Harrisburg, Pa.: The Stackpole Co., 1958.

Parsons, John E., *Henry Deringer's Pocket Pistol.* New York: William Morrow & Co., 1952.

———, *The Peacemaker and Its Rivals.* New York: William Morrow & Co., 1950.

———, *Smith & Wesson Revolvers: The Pioneer Single-Action Models.* New York: William Morrow & Co., 1957.

Parsons, John E., and John S. du Mont, *Firearms in the Custer Battle,* Harrisburg, Pa.: The Stackpole Co., 1954.

Peterson, Harold L., *A History of Firearms*. New York: Charles Scribner's Sons, 1961.

Pollard, H. B. C., *A History of Firearms*. London: Geoffrey Bles, 1931. Boston: Houghton Mifflin Co., 1931.

Rohan, Jack, *Yankee Arms Maker*. New York: Harper & Brothers, 1948.

Roosevelt, Theodore, *African Game Trails*. New York: Charles Scribner's Sons, 1910.

————, *Hunting Trips of a Ranchman*. New York: G. P. Putnam's Sons, 1900.

————, *The Rough Riders*. New York: G. P. Putnam's Sons, 1899.

Rosebush, Waldo E., *Frontier Steel, Their Men and Their Weapons*. Appleton, Wis.: C. C. Nelson Publishing Co., 1958.

Russell, Carl P., *Guns of the Early Frontiers*. Berkeley, Calif.: University of California Press, 1957.

Rywell, Martin, *Samuel Colt, A Man and an Epoch*. Harriman, Tenn.: Pioneer Press, 1952.

Sandburg, Carl, *Abraham Lincoln, The Prairie Years and The War Years*. New York: Harcourt, Brace & Co., 1954.

Sandoz, Mari, *The Buffalo Hunters*. New York: Hasting House Publishers, 1954.

Satterlee, L. D., *A Catalog of Firearms for the Collector*. Detroit: Published by Author, 1939.

Sawyer, Charles Winthrop, "The Firearms in American History Series." *Firearms in American History, 1600–1800*, 1910. *Firearms in American History, Vol. II, The Revolver, 1800–1911*, 1911. (An authorized reprint edition of 1,000 copies was published in 1939 by Charles Edward Chapel.) *Firearms in American History, Vol. III, Our Rifles*, 1920. *United States Single-Shot Martial Pistols*, 1913.

AUTHOR'S NOTE: All four titles were originally published by Charles Winthrop Sawyer, at Boston, Massachusetts, under the name of The Arms Co., which was really Sawyer, himself.

Schmitt, Martin F., and Dee Brown, *Fighting Indians of the West*. New York: Charles Scribner's Sons, 1948.

Scott, Winfield, *Abstract of Infantry Tactics*. Boston: Hilliard, Gray, Little & Wilkins, 1830.

————, *Infantry Tactics in Three Volumes*. New York: Harper & Brothers, 1858.

Serven, James E., *Colt Firearms*. Santa Ana, Calif.: James E. Serven, 1954.

Sharpe, Philip B., *The Rifle in America*. New York: Funk & Wagnalls Co., 1938.

Sherlock, Herbert Arment, *Black Powder Snapshots*. Huntington, W. Va.: Standard Publications, Inc. 1946.

Shields, Joseph W., *From Flintlock to M-1*. New York: Coward-McCann, Inc., 1954.

Smith, Lawrence B., *Shotgun Psychology.* New York: Charles Scribner's Sons, 1938.

Smith & Wesson, Inc., *Burning Powder.* Springfield, Mass.: Smith & Wesson, Inc., 1921 *et seq.*

Spaulding, Oliver L., *The Story of the United States Army in War and Peace.* New York: G. P. Putnam's Sons, 1937.

Stevens, Captain C. A., *Berdan's United States Sharpshooters in the Army of the Potomac, 1861–65.* St. Paul, Minn.: Price-McGill Co., 1892.

Strickland, W. P., *The Pioneers of the West or Life in the Woods.* New York: Carlton & Phillips, 1856.

Taft, Robert, *Artists and Illustrators of the Old West, 1850–1900.* New York: Charles Scribner's Sons, 1953.

———, *Photography and the American Scene.* New York: The Macmillan Co., 1942.

Tallant, Robert, *The Romantic New Orleanians.* New York: E. P. Dutton & Co., Inc., 1950.

Ulrich, Arthur L. A., *Century of Achievement, 1836–1936, Colt's 100th Anniversary Fire Arms Manual.* Hartford, Conn.: Colt's Patent Fire Arms Manufacturing Co., 1936.

Van Every, Edward, *Sins of America as "Exposed" by the Police Gazette.* New York: Frederick A. Stokes Co., 1931.

———, *Sins of New York as "Exposed" by the Police Gazette.* New York: Frederick A. Stokes Co., 1930.

Van Rensselaer, Stephen, *An Histology of American Gunsmiths, Arms Manufacturers, and Patentees with Detailed Description of Their Arms.* Morristown, N. J.: Mrs. Stephen Van Rensselaer, 1947.

Vestal, Stanley (pen name of Walter Stanley Campbell), *Joe Meek, The Merry Mountain Man.* Caldwell, Idaho: Caxton Printers, Ltd., 1952.

Ward, Fay E., *The Cowboy at Work.* New York: Hastings House Publishers, 1958.

Williamson, Harold F., *Winchester, The Gun That Won the West.* New York: A. S. Barnes & Co., Inc., 1961.

Winant, Lewis, *Early Percussion Firearms.* New York: William Morrow & Co., 1959.

———, *Firearms Curiosa.* London: Arco Publishers Ltd., 1956.

———, *Pepperbox Firearms.* New York: Greenberg, Publisher, 1952.

Acknowledgments

SPECIFIC ACKNOWLEDGMENTS FOR ILLUSTRATIONS

CHAPTER 1. *The Development of the Flintlock Pistol.* All of the illustrations in this chapter were drawn under the supervision of the author by Dick Spencer and Nancy Beale Gantert and are copyrighted by the author, or by A. S. Barnes & Co., Inc., except Figures 20 and 24, which are used by permission of the National Rifle Association of America; and Figure 29, used by permission of Herman P. Dean.

CHAPTER 2. *The Firing Mechanism of a Flintlock.* Figure 1 is reproduced by courtesy of the National Rifle Association of America. Nancy Beale Gantert drew Figures 2 to 5. The author drew Figure 6. Figure 7 was drawn by Herschel Logan. Permission to use this drawing was originally granted by Herman P. Dean, but the present copyright owner is The Stackpole Co.

CHAPTER 3. *U. S. Martial Flintlock Pistols.* All of the illustrations in this chapter are by Nancy Beale Gantert, principally drawn from photographs of arms in the Samuel E. Smith collection.

CHAPTER 4. *U. S. Secondary Martial Flintlock Pistols.* All of the illustrations in this chapter are by Nancy Beale Gantert, principally drawn from photographs of arms in the Samuel E. Smith collection.

CHAPTER 5. *Percussion Lock Development and Cartridge Design.* Figures 1 to 4 were drawn by Nancy Beale Gantert under the author's supervision. Figures 5 to 24 were drawn by Herschel Logan, and used here by permission of Herman P. Dean, although The Stackpole Co. is the present copyright holder. Figures 25 and 26 are used by permission of the National Rifle Association of America.

CHAPTER 6. *U. S. Martial Percussion Pistols.* All of the illustrations in this chapter were drawn by Nancy Beale Gantert, principally from photographs of arms in the Samuel E. Smith collection, except that Figure 11 was drawn by Herschel Logan, and used by permission of Herman P. Dean.

CHAPTER 7. *U. S. Secondary Martial Percussion Pistols.* All of the illustrations in this chapter were drawn by Nancy Beale Gantert, principally from photographs of arms in the Samuel E. Smith collection.

CHAPTER 8. *U. S. Martial Single-Shot Cartridge Pistols.* All of the illustrations in this chapter were drawn by Nancy Beale Gantert, principally from photographs of arms in the Samuel E. Smith collection, except that Figure 4 was drawn by the late Charles Winthrop Sawyer, who was emphatic in stating that he was not certain that it was a true representation of the so-called U. S. Army, Experimental Model 1869, Springfield Pistol.

CHAPTER 9. *Kentucky Pistols.* Figure 1 was drawn by Dick Spencer as a composite picture of several Kentucky rifles owned by the author. Figure 2 is a drawing supplied by Herman P. Dean. Figures 3, 4, 5, 6, and 7 were drawn by Nancy Beale Gantert principally from photographs of arms in the Samuel E. Smith collection. Figures 8 and 9 were drawn by Nancy Beale Gantert from photographs of arms in the collection of Calvin Hetrick and Everett Saggus, respectively.

CHAPTER 10. *Confederate Pistols.* Figures 1, 12, and 13 are from the author's collection of early illustrations from old publications. Figure 11 is a drawing by Nancy Beale Gantert of an imitation Cook & Brother cartridge pistol which the author borrowed from the owner. Figures 3, 4, and 5 are illustrations supplied by Francis Bannerman Sons; more accurate drawings of the same arms are found in earlier chapters. Figures 2, 6, 7, 8, 9, and 10 were drawn by Nancy Beale Gantert from photographs of arms principally found in the Samuel E. Smith collection.

CHAPTER 11. *Dueling Pistols.* Figures 1, 3, 4, and 5 were drawn by Nancy Beale Gantert from photographs of arms in the Samuel E. Smith collection. Figure 2 was drawn by Herschel Logan and used by permission of Herman P. Dean.

GENERAL ACKNOWLEDGMENTS FOR ILLUSTRATIONS

In the Introduction, it was explained that Samuel E. Smith, Markesan, Wisconsin, owns or has owned almost all the firearms illustrated in this text, and that Dr. J. H. Mathews, Firearms Consultant at the University of Wisconsin, Madison, Wisconsin, provided photographs of pistols. These were photographs of arms in the Smith collection. In addition to these two gentlemen, and the others mentioned throughout the text, the author acknowledges his indebtedness to those mentioned below who provided many photographs and information over a long period of time. Furthermore, the author has carefully checked the illustrations from the collections of those mentioned with photographs of pistols in collections which he has owned in the past.

ACKNOWLEDGMENTS FOR EDITORIAL AND TECHNICAL ASSISTANCE

For many years, hundreds of men and several women have devoted long hours of their valuable time in research and correspondence which led to the writing of this book. Many of them have passed on. Among the living experts who have contributed to the writing of this and the many other books on firearms by the author are the following, listed without rank or title, alphabetically, because each contributed according to his ability:

Robert Abels, New York City; Ed Agramonte, Yonkers, New York; Langdon Albright, Jr., Portageville, New York; Donald Bady, Forest Hills, New York; De Witt Bailey II, Stamford, Connecticut; Miller Bedford, New London, Ohio; H. A. Brand, Miami Shores, Florida; Shelley Braverman, Athens, New York; Frank Royce ("Bob") Brownell, Montezuma, Iowa; Marriner Bigelow Browning, Ogden, Utah; Richard H. Chamberlain, Whittier, California; Robert J. Chapel, Pittsburgh, Pennsylvania; Harold W. Cleveland, Redlands, California; Herman P. Dean, Huntington, West Virginia; Cuddy De Marco, Jr., McKeesport, Pennsylvania; Samuel E. Dyke, Allentown, Pennsylvania; William B. Edwards, Chicago, Illinois; Robert Ellithorpe, Encino, California; Norm Flayderman, Greenwich, Connecticut; Charles W. Fritz, Norwood, Ohio; Arcadi Gluckman, Carmel, California; Russell S. Goldstein, Fall River, Massachusetts; J. Garnand Hamilton, Massillon, Ohio; George E. Hancock, Fairmount, Illinois; Julian S. Hatcher, Falls Church, Virginia; Gil Hebard, Knoxville, Illinois; Robert Held, New York City; Calvin Hetrick, New Enterprise, Pennsylvania; James E. Hicks, La Canada, California; Marvin E. Hoffman, Miami Beach, Florida; James F. Hogan, New York City; Ed Howe, Coopers Mills, Maine; R. T. Huntington, New York City; George N. Hyatt, Wilmington, Delaware; L. C. Jackson, Dallas, Texas; W. G. C. Kimball, Woburn, Massachusetts; Joe Kindig, Jr., York, Pennsylvania; Wes Kindig, Lodi, Ohio; Harry C. Knode, Dallas, Texas; G. Robert Lawrence, Santa Ana, California; Gilbert J. Levy, Hialeah, Florida; B. R. Lewis, Vista, California; Ronald Lister, Flixton, Manchester, England; William M. Locke, Cincinnati, Ohio; Herschel C. Logan, Salina, Kansas; Duncan McConnell, Denver, Colorado; F. P. L. Mills, Old Deerfield, Massachusetts; Charles W. Moore, Schenevus, New York; C. Meade Patterson, Hyattsville, Maryland; Milton F. Perry, Independence, Missouri; Harmon L. Remmel, Fayetteville, Arkansas; Ray Riling, Philadelphia, Pennsylvania; James E. Serven, Santa Ana, California; N. E. Sharp, Allison Park, Runnemede, New Jersey; Samuel E. Smith, Markesan, Wisconsin; Richard K. Sprague, Salem, Massachusetts; Henry M. Stewart, Jr., Wynnewood, Pennsylvania; William T. Stroud, Roxborough, Pennsylvania; Peter Tillou, Buffalo, New York; C. H. Weiss, Arlington, Virginia; Frank Wheeler, Osborne, Kansas; Wes White, Freeville, New York; Lewis Winant, Island Heights, New Jersey; and Eldon G. Wolff, Milwaukee, Wisconsin.

Finally, the author thanks Carma R. Leigh, State Librarian; Allan R. Ottley, California Section Librarian; and other members of the staff of the California State Library, Sacramento. He also acknowledges the assistance of Donald C. Biggs, Director; and Manuel P. Servin, Editor, California Historical Society, San Francisco. These dedicated librarians and librarians all over the United States discovered long-lost records which constitute much of the original source material for arms history.

CHARLES EDWARD CHAPEL

Index